Barcode Back

MW01119546

1

COSTUMING THE
SHAKESPEAREAN STAGE

Studies in Performance and Early Modern Drama

General Editor's Preface

Helen Ostovich, McMaster University

Performance assumes a string of creative, analytical, and collaborative acts that, in defiance of theatrical ephemerality, live on through records, manuscripts, and printed books. The monographs and essay collections in this series offer original research which addresses theatre histories and performance histories in the context of the sixteenth and seventeenth century life. Of especial interest are studies in which women's activities are a central feature of discussion as financial or technical supporters (patrons, musicians, dancers, seamstresses, wigmakers, or 'gatherers'), if not authors or performers per se. Welcome too are critiques of early modern drama that not only take into account the production values of the plays, but also speculate on how intellectual advances or popular culture affect the theatre.

The series logo, selected by my colleague Mary V. Silcox, derives from Thomas Combe's duodecimo volume, *The Theater of Fine Devices* (London, 1592), Emblem VI, sig. B. The emblem of four masks has a verse which makes claims for the increasing complexity of early modern experience, a complexity that makes interpretation difficult. Hence the corresponding perhaps uneasy rise in sophistication:

> Masks will be more hereafter in request,
> And grow more deare than they did heretofore.

No longer simply signs of performance 'in play and jest', the mask has become the 'double face' worn 'in earnest' even by 'the best' of people, in order to manipulate or profit from the world around them. The books stamped with this design attempt to understand the complications of performance produced on stage and interpreted by the audience, whose experiences outside the theatre may reflect the emblem's argument:

> Most men do use some colour'd shift
> For to conceal their craftie drift.

Centuries after their first presentations, the possible performance choices and meanings they engender still stir the imaginations of actors, audiences, and readers of early plays. The products of scholarly creativity in this series, I hope, will also stir imaginations to new ways of thinking about performance.

Costuming the Shakespearean Stage

Visual Codes of Representation in Early Modern Theatre and Culture

ROBERT I. LUBLIN

University of Massachusetts-Boston, USA

ASHGATE

Published by
Ashgate Publishing Limited
Wey Court East
Union Road
Farnham
Surrey, GU9 7PT
England

Ashgate Publishing Company
Suite 420
101 Cherry Street
Burlington
VT 05401-4405
USA

www.ashgate.com

British Library Cataloguing in Publication Data
Lublin, Robert I.
  Costuming the Shakespearean stage: visual codes of representation in early modern theatre and culture. – (Studies in performance and early modern drama)
  1. Costume – Symbolic aspects – England – History – 16th century. 2. Costume – Symbolic aspects – England – History – 17th century. 3. Theater – England – History – 16th century. 4. Theater – England – History – 17th century.
  I. Title II. Series
  792'.026'0942'09031-dc22

Library of Congress Cataloging-in-Publication Data
Lublin, Robert I.
  Costuming the Shakespearean stage : visual codes of representation in early modern theatre and culture / by Robert I. Lublin.
    p. cm. — (Studies in performance and early modern drama)
  Includes bibliographical references and index.
  ISBN 978-0-7546-6225-9 (hardcover: alk. paper)
  1. Shakespeare, William, 1564–1616—Stage history—To 1625. 2. Shakespeare, William, 1564–1616—Stage history—England. 3. Theater—England—History—16th century. 4. Theater—England—History—17th century. 5. Costume—England--History—16th century. 6. Costume—England—History—17th century. I. Title.
  PR3095.L83 2011
  822.3'3—dc22

                                                                          2011021376

ISBN: 9780754662259 (hbk)
ISBN: 9781409436836 (ebk)

Printed and bound in Great Britain by the
MPG Books Group, UK

Contents

List of Figures   *vii*

Acknowledgements   *ix*

Introduction   1

1   Sex and Gender   9

2   Social Station   41

3   Foreigners   79

4   Religion   123

5   "An vnder black dubblett signifying a Spanish hart": Costumes and
    Politics in Middleton's *A Game at Chess*   163

Works Cited   *181*
Index   *193*

List of Figures

1.1   A Generalized Elizabethan Gentleman, drawn by Adam West.   11

1.2   Breeches, drawn by Adam West.   13

1.3   A Generalized Elizabethan Gentlewoman, drawn by
      Adam West.   16

1.4   Farthingales, drawn by Adam West.   18

2.1   Queen Elizabeth's 1597 Sumptuary Proclamation, abbreviated
      presentation.   46

2.2   Title page of Thomas Heywood, *The Four Prentices of London*
      (1632), STC 13322. By permission of the Beinecke Library,
      Yale University.   70

2.3   Title page of Christopher Marlowe, *Doctor Faustus* (1631),
      STC 17436. By permission of the Beinecke Library, Yale
      University.   76

3.1   Peacham drawing, by permission of the Marquess of Bath,
      Longleat House, Warminster, Wiltshire, Great Britain.   86

3.2   Title page of Thomas Coryate, *Coryats Crudities* (1611),
      STC 5808. By permission of the Huntington Library.   102

3.3   Title page of Thomas Kyd, *The Spanish Tragedy* (1623),
      STC 15093. By permission of the Huntington Library.   107

4.1   Generalized Catholic Priest and Bishop, drawn by Adam West.   130

4.2   Generalized English Priest and Bishop, drawn by Adam West.   131

4.3   Turkish Ruler by Amman in Phillip Lonicer, Chronicorum
      Turcicorum (1578), Vol. 1, leaf 21. By kind permission of the
      Watkinson Library at Trinity College, Hartford, Connecticut.   144

4.4   Tamburlaine in Richard Knolles, *The Generall Historie of the
      Turkes* (1603), STC 15051, p. 236. By permission of the
      Huntington Library.   153

5.1   Title page of Thomas Scott's, *Second Part of Vox Populi* (1624),
         STC 22103. By permission of the Folger Shakespeare Library.   167

5.2   Title page of Thomas Middleton, *A Game at Chess* Q1 (1625),
         STC 17882.2. By permission of the Folger Shakespeare
         Library.   168

Acknowledgements

My preparation to write this book began in the English Department at Albright College where my love of literature was nurtured and where the late, great Lynn Morrow sat me down and taught me how to write. My heavy debt to her is one I work to pay back every time I meet with my own students to help them with their writing. At Villanova University, Brown University, and the University of Texas at Austin, I was profoundly influenced by great teachers and scholars like Vincent Sherry, Phillip Pulsiano, John Emigh, and Oscar Brockett. Finally, at The Ohio State University, I was lucky enough to complete my Ph.D. under the guidance of Thomas Postlewait, the platonic ideal of a dissertation director.

Since coming to the University of Massachusetts Boston, I have been particularly fortunate. I have benefitted from wonderful, supportive colleagues in the Department of Performing Arts, especially John Conlon, Jon Mitchell, and David Patterson. I have also had the privilege to work with outstanding librarians like Bill Baer and Janet Stewart who have made me feel as though my research is their sole interest and responsibility, even though I know they make students and other professors feel the same way. Additionally, I have had the opportunity to present my scholarship before the Research Center for Urban Cultural History and receive constructive feedback from a group of distinguished scholars. I would particularly like to thank my mentor and friend Malcolm Smuts for responding thoughtfully and constructively to so much of my work as I developed it for publication and for giving me the kind of guidance and encouragement I would wish for all junior faculty.

From the first time I mentioned that I wished to undertake doctoral studies and become a professor as a sophomore in college, my ambitions have benefitted from the unflagging support of my family. This is a gift, and I attribute much of my success in completing my degree, in acquiring an academic position, in earning tenure, and ultimately in completing this book to the encouragement I have been so lucky to receive from those closest to me. To Mom, Dad, my brother A.J., and the rest of my family: thank you! I extend this appreciation also to my close friends Lee Bleyer, Brett Clifton, Bill Heller, Michael Jaros, and Karie Kirkpatrick who have served at various times as my sounding boards, my editors, my proofreaders, and my therapists. To my family, my teachers, my mentors, and my friends, I give my sincere thanks. You mean everything to me.

Two sections of this book have previously appeared in print. Thanks to the University of Delaware Press for permission to reprint the first half of chapter 4. Thanks also to *Theatre Survey* and Cambridge University Press for permission to reprint chapter 5.

Introduction

Now old desire doth in his death-bed lie,
And young affection gapes to be his heir;
That fair for which love groan'd for and would die,
With tender Juliet [match'd] is now not fair.
Now Romeo is belov'd and loves again,
Alike bewitched by the charm of looks;

Romeo and Juliet (2.0.1–6)[1]

In Shakespeare's *Romeo and Juliet*, the two eponymous lovers are spellbound when they first see each other, "Alike bewitched by the charm of looks." But what did Romeo and Juliet see when they looked upon one another on the early modern English stage? Predominantly, they saw each other's costume. This scene (act 1, scene 5) takes place at the house of the Capulets during a masque, and we can deduce from the lines of the play that the two young lovers were appropriately appareled for the event so that very little of their faces or bodies were visible behind the costumes they wore. We know that Romeo wore a mask, for Tybalt only recognizes him when he hears Romeo's voice: "This, by his voice, should be a Montague" (1.5.54). Juliet likely also appeared in a mask since the event called for it, particularly among those who were young and unmarried.[2] If both Romeo and Juliet wore masks, the charm of looks that bewitched them existed primarily in the clothes they wore. What, then, did the two characters wear in production?

To begin, we know that Romeo was dressed as a man and Juliet as a woman. Certainly this is stating the obvious; however since all of the actors on the Shakespearean stage were male, their characters' sex or gender resulted overwhelmingly from the clothes they wore. Juliet's feminine beauty differed from Romeo's masculine attractiveness only because the costumes they wore made it so. Next, their clothes presented Romeo and Juliet's social station as the eldest children of wealthy, prominent families. Early modern England was a highly stratified society that was well versed in the apparel that marked an individual's place in the hierarchy. Audiences would have noted the elite apparel in which Romeo and Juliet appeared and recognized that each was the other's social equal. The fact that they appeared at a masque does not change the likelihood that their clothes accurately spoke their social station. As Stephen Orgel explains:

---

[1]   For Shakespeare quotations throughout the book, I use the Riverside Shakespeare: William Shakespeare, *The Riverside Shakespeare*, ed. G. Blakemore Evans, 2nd ed., (Boston: Houghton Mifflin, 1997).

[2]   Capulet establishes the role of the mask for the young and unmarried when he says "I have seen the day / That I have worn a visor and could tell / A whispering tale in a fair lady's ear" (1.5.21–3).

appearing in a masque was not merely playing a part. It was, in a profound sense, precisely the opposite. . . . Masquers are not actors; a lady or gentleman participating in a masque remains a lady or gentleman, and is not released from the obligation of observing all the complex rules of behavior at court.[3]

One of the foremost rules governing one's social obligations required that one's apparel accurately depict one's place in society. Even costumed for a masque, Romeo and Juliet would have worn fabrics and accoutrements that clearly depicted their social station.

Audiences attending an early production of *Romeo and Juliet*, therefore, would have instantly recognized the social rank suggested by the costumes worn by the actors playing Romeo and Juliet. Moreover, the audience would have noticed how differently the two lovers were dressed from Count Paris, whose social superiority allowed him, indeed required him, to appear in sumptuous fabrics outside the purview of the Montagues and the Capulets. Consequently, when Romeo and Juliet first saw each other, the audience witnessed a pair of young, unmarried individuals of the same social station. They are ideal romantic partners, sartorially constructed according to the visual semiotics of the period to fall in love with one another and, if not for the hatred between their two families, enjoy a socially (and perhaps personally) propitious marriage. Costumes were crucial to the production of meaning on the Shakespearean stage and established the social topography on which the tragedy of *Romeo and Juliet* was figured in performance. To fail to consider the role that costume played in performances of Shakespeare's plays is to fail to do justice to how meaning was constructed in early modern performance.

This book seeks to make sense of the sartorial logic of the early modern English stage by addressing two related questions: what costumes were worn on the early modern English professional stage? and more importantly, what did those costumes mean to the London audiences that first saw them? Clothing and theatrical apparel carried specific meanings that were well understood by the playwrights, performers, and audiences of the time. As Stephen Greenblatt explains, "what can be said, thought, felt, in this culture seems deeply dependent on the clothes one wears—clothes that one is, in effect, *permitted* or *compelled* to wear, since there is little freedom in dress."[4] One's sex, social station, occupation, nationality, religion, and more could be established by the clothes one wore, which produced an individual as a member and constituent of the body politic. The complex ways that clothes signified in early modern England had profound consequences for the professional theatres. Before an actor uttered his first line of dialogue, the audience likely knew a great deal about his character by virtue of the clothes he wore. In performance, an actor could change from a man into a woman, an Englishman into a Spaniard, a Protestant into a Catholic, or a king into a pauper by altering his apparel before returning to the stage. And they often had

---

[3]   Stephen Orgel, *The Illusion of Power: Political Theater in the English Renaissance* (Berkeley: University of California Press, 1975), 38–9.

[4]   Stephen Greenblatt, "General Introduction," in *The Norton Shakespeare*, 2nd ed., Ed. Stephen Greenblatt, et al. (New York: WW Norton, 2008), 59.

to. The casts of Elizabethan and Jacobean plays frequently had far more roles than there were actors to play them.[5] The costume an actor wore visually established his identity to a high degree of specificity for an audience that was familiar with the visual codes of the period.

The importance of costumes was well understood at the time. Theatrical apparel typically represented the single largest financial investment made by playing companies, often costing more than scripts or even the playhouses themselves.[6] Companies made it their policy to accrue costume stocks that would support increased sumptuousness and greater variety in performance.[7] Studying the material practices surrounding the purchasing, translating, borrowing, and trading of costumes at the time, Ann Jones and Peter Stallybrass have gone so far as to argue that in early modern England, the theatre "was a new and spectacular development of the clothing industry."[8] Playing companies recognized that costumes were crucial to the practice of putting on plays and made the accumulation and maintenance of theatrical apparel a priority.

Theatrical apparel on the early modern English stage has been the subject of growing interest over the last thirty years. The modern study of the topic can be dated to the 1980s when scholars such as Lisa Jardine, Stephen Greenblatt, Laura Levine, Phyllis Rackin, Jean Howard, and Stephen Orgel combined feminist and New Historicist approaches to studying Renaissance theatre in an attempt to explain the English practice of having boys cross-dress to play the women's parts.[9] In these groundbreaking studies, costumes were typically of secondary importance as the

---

[5] Jean MacIntyre, *Costumes and Scripts in the Elizabethan Theatres* (Edmonton: The University of Alberta Press, 1992), 29–37.

[6] G. E. Bentley, *The Profession of Player in Shakespeare's Time, 1590–1642* (Princeton: Princeton University Press, 1984), 88; James H. Forse, *Art Imitates Business: Commercial and Political Influences in Elizabethan Theatre.* (Bowling Green, OH: Bowling Green State University Press, 1993), 15; Jean MacIntyre and Garrett P. J. Epp, "'Cloathes worth all the rest': Costumes and Properties," in *A New History of Early English Drama*, Ed. by John D. Cox and David Scott Kastan (New York: Columbia University Press, 1997), 284.

[7] MacIntyre, 319.

[8] Ann Rosalind Jones and Peter Stallybrass, *Renaissance Clothing and the Materials of Memory* (New York: Cambridge University Press, 2000), 176.

[9] Lisa Jardine, "Boy Actors, Female Roles, and Elizabethan Eroticism" in her book *Still Harping on Daughters* (Sussex: Harvester Press, 1983). Stephen Greenblatt, "Fiction and Friction," in Thomas C. Heller, Morton Sosna, and David E. Wellbery, eds., *Reconstructing Individualism: Autonomy, Individuality, and the Self in Western Thought* (Stanford: Stanford University Press, 1986), 30–52. Laura Levine, "Men in Women's Clothing: Anti-Theatricality and Effeminization from 1579 to 1642" *Criticism* 28.2 (1986): 121–43. Phyllis Rackin, "Androgyny, Mimesis, and the Marriage of the Boy Heroine on the English Renaissance Stage," *PMLA* 102 (1987): 29–41. Jean Howard, "Crossdressing, the Theatre, and Gender Struggle in Early Modern England," *Shakespeare Quarterly* 39.4 (1988): 418–40. Stephen Orgel, "Nobody's Perfect: Or Why Did the English Stage Take Boys for Women?" *South Atlantic Quarterly* 88.1 (1989): 7–29.

authors were more interested in the convention of cross-dressing than in the apparel that was actually worn by the boy actors to achieve it. Nevertheless, these works opened up the topic of theatrical apparel to widespread interest and demonstrated how crucial costumes could be to the creation of meaning in performance.

Since then, additional work has been devoted to the practice of cross-dressing, and the study of theatrical apparel has come to take on a life of its own. Peter Stallybrass deserves considerable credit for drawing attention to the importance of costumes and clothing in the period, editing volumes that explore early modern material culture and authoring and co-authoring a number of important studies on the topic.[10] Building on his work, scholars like Will Fisher and Amanda Bailey have taken the study of costume further and in new directions.[11] Fisher examines individual items, such as codpieces, handkerchiefs, and beards to understand the construction of gender in early modern England. Bailey addresses the ways that sumptuous apparel was deployed in production and society to challenge notions of authority. Where this book differs from the work that precedes it is in its attempt to step back from the trees to consider the forest. Rather than examine a single theatrical convention or article of apparel at length, I hope to make sense of the larger picture regarding costuming practices in early modern England. In order to accomplish this, I build upon the work that has come before and try to make various scholars speak to one another so as to develop a comprehensive sense of how theatrical apparel worked in production.

On the early modern English stage, the costumes were the characters. Looking at the fact that women were excluded from performance, Juliet Dusinberre makes an insightful observation about early modern English theatre:

> Were [women] there or not? Of course, physically they were not there. But to assert that is, in my view, to say nothing. Because none of the shadows on Shakespeare's stage are there. There are no kings, queens, murderers, monsters, fairies, politicians, wise counselors, or even fools. There are only actors. Why should it matter that they are not biologically female, any more than it should matter that they are not royal, Roman, Moors, Egyptian, or Italian?[12]

---

[10]   Peter Stallybrass, "Worn Worlds: Clothes and Identity on the Renaissance Stage," in *Subject and Object in Renaissance Culture*, ed. Margreta de Grazia, Maureen Quilligan, and Peter Stallybrass (New York: Cambridge University Press, 1996), 289–320. Peter Stallybrass, "Worn Worlds: Clothes, Mourning, and the Life of Things," in *Cultural Memory and the Construction of Identity*, ed. Dan Ben-Amas and Liliane Weissberg (Detroit: Wayne State University Press, 1999), 27–44. And most significantly, his book with Ann Jones, which has been cited already.

[11]   Will Fisher, *Materializing Gender in Early Modern English Literature and Culture* (New York: Cambridge University Press, 2006). *Amanda Bailey, Flaunting: Style and the Subversive Male Body in Renaissance England* (Toronto: University of Toronto Press, 2007).

[12]   Juliet Dusinberre, "Women and Boys Playing Shakespeare," in *A Feminist Companion to Shakespeare*, ed. Dympna Callaghan (Malden, MA: Blackwell, 2000), 251.

Dusinberre rightly concludes that the various identities that appeared on the Shakespearean stage "are figments of the actor's art."[13] It was not the actor's identity that figured principally in production, but the character's, which was primarily established by the clothes an actor wore for the part. We must suspend our notion of characters entering the early modern English theatres as ciphers to be filled with the playwright's words, and instead begin to consider how the plays of the period made use of characters whose identities were already firmly established by their costumes.[14] Theatrical apparel signified richly to an audience familiar with the various and overlapping visual codes that they engaged. Consequently, this book will proceed by establishing the various visual codes according to which theatrical apparel signified in performance. The first four chapters of this book examine specific visual codes and make sense of how meaning was materially produced through the use of costumes on stage. In the fifth chapter, I will consider how multiple visual codes figured in a single production.

Chapter 1 examines the visual codes of sex and gender to understand how notions of masculinity and femininity were constructed on stage. I begin by establishing the specific articles of apparel that an actor would have worn to assume the identity of a man or a woman and then consider how that information would have been received according to the diverse views on sex and gender that maintained at the time. I conclude that the stage relied upon and forwarded an essentialist view of sex. Many of the plays employ cross-dressing to upset notions of gender (e.g., *As You Like It*, *Epicoene*) but they ultimately reassert the idea that "male" and "female" are concrete and unambiguous categories by establishing the "rightness" of particular clothes for particular characters. Beyond its theoretical consideration of sex and gender in early modern England, an important part of this chapter is its concise presentation of the specific articles of clothing that were familiar to all who attended the theatre. Items such as breeches, doublets, swords, stomachers, farthingales, and cosmetics are frequently mentioned and employed in the plays. An introduction to these articles allows readers to imagine how a play might have appeared at the time and begin to consider how these items might have been seen by an audience accustomed to their wear.

Chapter 2 considers the visual codes of social station. On the early modern English stage, an individual's place in the social hierarchy would have been easily identifiable according to the strict rules delineated in the sumptuary decrees issued during the reign of Queen Elizabeth. Recent scholarship notes that these laws were often ignored in English society[15] (which accounts for the frequency with which they had to be reasserted), but the theatres proved to be the one place where the sumptuary laws regularly determined the clothes that people wore. Evidence in the drama demonstrates that specific apparel was understood to correspond to social

---

[13] Ibid.

[14] G. K. Hunter, "Flatcaps and Bluecoats: Visual Signals on the Elizabethan Stage," *Essays and Studies* 33 (1980): 27.

[15] Jones and Stallybrass, 188.

rank. The significance of this fact becomes clear when we note that the plays work to guarantee that characters wear the clothes appropriate to their station. *Macbeth* and *Richard III* exist visually as plays about men who dared dress outside their social rank and were destroyed for their presumption. Beyond delineating the social elite, apparel also established the status and occupation of commoners. For instance, Thomas Dekker's *The Shoemaker's Holiday* represents Simon Eyre's advancement to Lord Mayor through his changing of apparel from Shoemaker's apron to Alderman's black gown to Lord Mayor's scarlet. The play approves of the manner by which he achieves his advancement and, unlike Macbeth or Richard, Eyre is permitted to wear the clothes that reflect his social transformation.

Chapter 3 examines how non-English characters were presented on the early modern stage. Looking at the plays along with Peacham's drawing of *Titus Andronicus* and Henslowe's diary, I contend that the visual language of foreigners was often the language of English apparel. This argument challenges the recent suggestion that the companies commonly used foreign fashions in their productions.[16] Textual evidence from *Julius Caesar* demonstrates that Roman characters were costumed as English gentlemen. Furthermore, plays set in contemporary France, Spain, Denmark, and elsewhere costumed the great majority of their characters in English apparel. There are two significant exceptions to this rule. First, individuals of particular importance, kings and princes for instance, regularly appeared in "foreign" apparel. Second, in plays situated in England (such as city comedies), visitors commonly wore "foreign" clothing, frequently making the wearers targets for comic ridicule. I put quotation marks around the word "foreign" to note that the costumes worn on the English stage were not accurate depictions of foreign fashion but English notions of the apparel deemed appropriate to specific countries. Consequently, foreign costumes carried rich associations that were colored by foreign policy and national stereotypes.

Chapter 4 considers religion and establishes how Catholics, Protestants, Puritans, Jews, and Mahometans (Muslims) were visually presented on the English stage. The chapter divides into two parts with the first examining Christians and the second considering Jews and Mahometans. Looking at changes made in the Protestant *Book of Common Prayer*, I examine the very different apparel worn by Catholic and Protestant clergy at the time, and the religious associations carried by each. The move away from Catholic vestments during the reformation was anything but a simple sartorial choice. It visually demonstrated and asserted a transformation in the role of the clergy in English society. The drama of the sixteenth century registered this change by sometimes presenting the Vice characters appareled as Catholic priests, bishops, cardinals, and popes, and the Virtues dressed as English clergy. The association of Catholic apparel with iniquity remained strong all the way up to the closing of the playhouses in

---

[16]   Jean MacIntyre and Garrett P. J. Epp, "'Cloathes Worth All the Rest': Costumes and Properties." *A New History of Early English Drama*. Ed. by John D. Cox and David Scott Kastan (New York: Columbia University Press, 1997), 278.

1642. Puritan characters wore conspicuously humble apparel that mirrored their professed religiosity and made them easy targets of satire. The second half of the chapter deals with Mahometans and Jews. Such a study reveals that turbans served as a signifier of circumcision at the time and very likely were worn by Jewish characters as well as Mahometans. The appropriate weapon of the Turk was the scimitar, which suggested extreme cruelty even in the hands of a non-Mahometan. The Jew was most easily identified onstage not by a gabardine, but by his enormous nose, which bound him so closely to his profession as a usurer that plays with usurers of uncertain religion nearly always made reference to their oversized facial appendage. On the early modern stage, religion was not merely worn on one's heart, but also on one's body.

Chapter 5 considers a single production, Thomas Middleton's *A Game at Chess*, and serves as a model for how one can examine the costumes in a single work to explore the ways in which they intersect with various visual codes introduced earlier in the book. Through such a study, we learn that Middleton employed costumes as skillfully as he used dialogue to manifest the politics of his play. *A Game at Chess* engages and manipulates the visually based semiotics of the time to comment specifically and comically on the perfidy of Catholicism, the tyranny of Spain, and the immaturity of the Spanish King.

Central to this book is the simple argument that costumes mattered to the early modern English theatrical enterprise. Acting companies expended lavish amounts of money to purchase them; actors constructed their characters through the donning of them; action progressed through the changing of them; and audiences understood and appreciated theatrical productions by observing them. Ultimately, costumes contributed as much as dialogue to the staging of early modern theatre. If we wish to understand the drama of Shakespeare and his contemporaries, we must go beyond Greenblatt's desire to speak with the dead.[17] We must also attempt to see them. Furthermore, we must strive to see them as they saw themselves, referencing and cross-referencing evidence from the period to construct early modern bifocals that can move us closer to hearing and seeing the first performances of plays from the past.

---

[17] Stephen Greenblatt, *Shakespearean Negotiations: The Circulation of Social Energy in Renaissance England* (Berkeley: University of California Press, 1988), 1.

Chapter 1
Sex and Gender

dost thou think, though I am caparison'd like a man, I have a doublet and hose
in my disposition?

As You Like It (3.2.194–6)

Before an actor on the Shakespearean stage delivered his first words in performance,
the audience would have seen how he was dressed and understood whether the
character he was playing was male or female. This seems obvious, but it is also
significant and has far reaching consequences for how meaning was constructed
in performance and received by audiences in early modern England. Since all
of the actors in the public playhouses were male, the costume one wore served
to establish, not merely reflect, one's sex in performance.[1] I say "sex" instead of
"gender" (although it is anachronistic to draw a distinction between the two at this
point in history) to highlight the fact that there was no biological basis to appeal
to when all of the characters were played by male actors. Quite simply, as Stephen
Orgel has stated, "clothes make the woman, clothes make the man: the costume is
of the essence."[2] Since the biological sex of all of the actors was male, the essence
or root basis of a character's sex lay overwhelmingly in the manner in which
costumes were employed onstage.

To explore this phenomenon, this chapter will begin by presenting the basic
apparel that was common to early modern England and most frequently seen on
its stages. What becomes immediately apparent from such a survey is that clothing
from the period can only be presented logically by first dividing the articles
according to whether they belonged appropriately at the time to men or women.
The clothes themselves held gendered associations, ones they carried onto the
actors who wore them in performance. The second part of the chapter will explore
these associations and consider the consequences they had for the playwrights who
considered them when they wrote the plays, the actors who donned them when
they took part in productions, and the audiences that interpreted them when they
observed performances. What becomes apparent from such a study is that sartorial
choices served to construct notions of sex and gender every bit as vigorously for
the stage as did the spoken lines of any play.

---

[1]   Stephen Orgel has noted instances in which women performed in early modern
England, highlighting private performances, public singing, and Court Masques, but
acknowledges that for the commercial theatrical companies of Renaissance England, "the
stage was a male preserve." Stephen Orgel, *Impersonations: The Performance of Gender in
Shakespeare's England* (New York: Cambridge University Press, 1996), 10.

[2]   Ibid., 104.

Clothing Essentials

Whether or not Shakespeare's plays are for all time, they were originally written, as were those of his contemporaries, for a very particular time and place, specifically the professional stages of early modern London. The spatial and temporal specificity of the period's drama becomes particularly conspicuous when we look at the frequent references made to apparel, which nearly always mention contemporary items commonly worn in England. For modern readers to engage with the manner in which plays signified to their original audiences, it is crucial that we familiarize ourselves with the articles of clothing that were worn at the time.

Throughout the period from 1567 to 1642, there were a number of basic components of clothing for men and women that altered in style but remained staple items. The fundamental garments of the Elizabethan and Jacobean period were the same ones that had maintained for over a hundred years and would remain so until the latter half of the seventeenth century.[3] The list of garments that follows makes no attempt at comprehensiveness. There are innumerable additional articles of clothing and fashion trends that could be listed and described.[4] Here, I merely wish to establish a starting point from which we can consider the visually based semiotics according to which early modern audiences understood the apparel worn on English stages.

For men, the most commonly worn articles of apparel include the shirt, doublet, breeches, nether hose, jerkin, cape, robe or gown, ruff or band, hat, and footwear; for women, the chemise, dress or kirtle, farthingale, gown, ruff or band, headdress, and footwear. To clarify how this clothing actually appeared, Figure 1.1 presents a generalized Elizabethan gentleman. I urge readers to view this picture cautiously, for it suggests that the fine clothes depicted represent the norm at the time and threatens to occlude the enormous differences that marked people of different classes, a topic which will be pursued in Chapter 2. The picture is useful only for helping to familiarize readers with the particular articles of apparel. In much the same way that a wealthy man and a poor man in the twenty first century

---

[3]   Graham Reynolds, "Elizabethan and Jacobean: 1558–1625," in *Costume of the Western World* , ed. James Laver (New York: Harper and Brothers, 1951), 131.

[4]   For a more extensive consideration of individual articles of clothing, the different fabrics from which they could be made, and references made to them in early modern drama, one should look to M. Channing Linthicum's *Costume in the Drama of Shakespeare and his Contemporaries*. Although published in 1936, Linthicum's book remains a treasure trove of historical scholarship: M. Channing Linthicum, *Costume in the Drama of Shakespeare and His Contemporaries* (Oxford: Clarendon Press, 1936), For more specific fashion trends, particularly in court clothing, see C. Willett Cunnington and Phillis Cunnington's *Handbook of English Costume in the Seventeenth Century* (London: Faber and Faber, 1955). And, for a much more thorough discussion of the articles of apparel worn specifically by the upper class along with beautiful, full-color reproductions of paintings and woodcuts, see Aileen Ribeiro, *Fashion and Fiction: Dress in Art and Literature in Stuart England* (New Haven: Yale University Press, 2006).

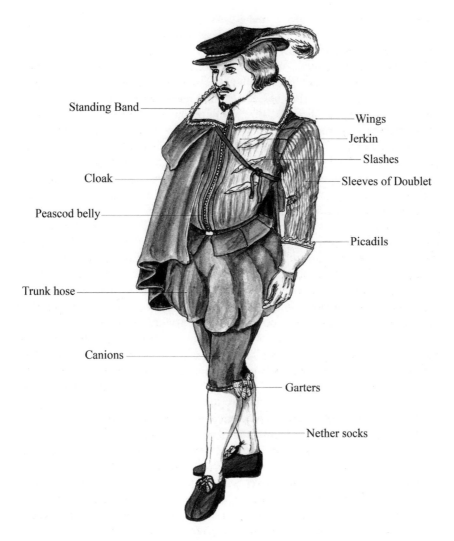

Standing Band

Wings

Jerkin

Slashes

Cloak

Sleeves of Doublet

Peascod belly

Picadils

Trunk hose

Canions

Garters

Nether socks

Fig. 1.1   A Generalized Elizabethan Gentleman, drawn by Adam West.

might both wear shirts, pants, shoes, and sport jackets yet look radically different, so was it possible for gentlemen and laborers in early modern England to wear the same basic articles of apparel yet present very different images.

The man's shirt was typically made of white linen and served primarily as an undergarment until roughly 1625, after which time the fashion changed and it was more commonly seen through the doublet. It was usually cut full and gathered into a round or square neckline, having long, raglan sleeves. Even before 1625, the fabric of the shirt might be seen through the doublet if there were *slashings* or *panes*, cuts made in the outer garment that allowed the undergarment to be seen. Among the wealthy, it was common to wear shirts that were embellished with drawn-work and embroidery.

The doublet was a thick, quilted upper garment of velvet, silk, satin, leather, or other material, which extended from the neck to below the waist and was buttoned up the center. Until 1580, the doublet was snug against the body, at which time the practice of having a *peascod* belly, a swelling lower abdomen, became popular. This fashion lasted until roughly 1610 when form-fitting doublets once again became the norm.[5] The sleeves of the doublet were sometimes detachable and would be connected by *points*, laces or ties which ended in small metal tips. Points were used to connect separate pieces of clothing at the time and required that a person receive assistance from others while dressing him or herself.

Breeches go by many names in the early modern period including: *trunk hose*, *canions*, *Venetians*, *galligaskins*, and *slops*. They constituted the upper part of the *hose* or *stocks* and served to cover the top part of the leg. The various terms for this article of clothing are used interchangeably in the drama of the period but distinguishable features for each can be identified. *Trunk hose* generally were well rounded and reached from the waist, where they were connected to the doublet by points, to the middle of the thigh, where they were connected to the *nether stocks*, which were much like stockings. *Canions* were close fitting extensions that were sometimes used to connect the trunk hose to the nether stocks; they typically reached from mid-thigh to the knee. *Panes* were often worn over the trunk hose and consisted of strips of fabric that reached from the waist to the bottom of the breeches. *Venetians* were breeches much like trunk hose but reached down below the knee. *Galligaskins* sloped gradually from a narrow waist to fullness at mid-thigh. *Slops* was a particularly slippery term that could refer to almost any breeches, but it could also refer to wide ones that were open at the knees. Breeches could follow the shape of the leg or be heavily padded with *bombast*, a stuffing made of almost any available fabric. The various terms defined here give some idea of the various fashions at the time, but we should be careful about assuming that we know how an actor's breeches looked simply because the lines of a play say that he is wearing a particular style since the terms were sometimes used interchangeably, even indiscriminately.

The nether stocks were worn like tights and showed off the leg of the wearer. They were held up with *garters*, lengths of cloth or silk that were tied around the leg, either above or below the knee. The brief fashion for cross-gartering, already outdated when Malvolio adopts it in *Twelfth Night*, consisted of wearing either garters both above the knee and below the knee or a single band rolled back on itself so that it would serve as a garter above the knee and below the knee and be crossed behind the leg.

The *jerkin* was a jacket-like garment that was worn over the doublet. In many of the paintings from the era, the jerkin is made of the same material and follows

---

5   Linthicum, 199.

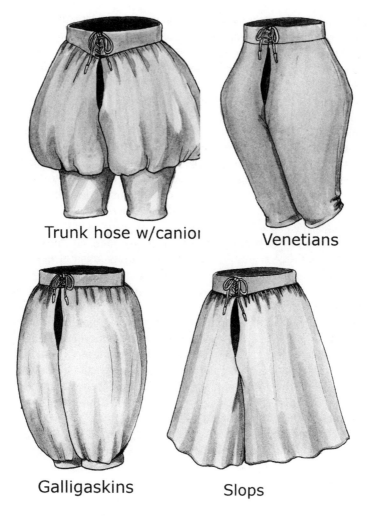

Trunk hose w/canioı

Venetians

Galligaskins

Slops

Fig. 1.2   Breeches, drawn by Adam West.

the same pattern as the doublet. As a result, it is sometimes difficult to tell if a jerkin is being worn. Jerkins frequently had short puffed sleeves or no sleeves. Most paintings of the era show the jerkin drawn in to the waist, but sometimes it had a *peplum* or *basque*, i.e., a skirted extension that covered part or all of the breeches.

English capes or cloaks were regularly half-length, extending from the shoulder to the middle of the body and are shown in most paintings to be slung over the left shoulder only. They often had fake sleeves attached. Capes or cloaks were apparently considered indispensable traveling gear for the gentility, for mention is made of men who are compared to tapsters for appearing without their cloaks.[6] Later in the sixteenth and into the seventeenth century, longer cloaks came into fashion in England.

Robes or gowns in early modern England reached to the ground and typically had large funnel-shaped or hanging sleeves. Before the middle of the sixteenth century, short gowns that reached to the hips were common and many depictions of Henry VIII show him wearing one. Pictorial evidence suggests that after 1550, the practice of wearing short gowns was replaced by the fashion of wearing a cloak. Full length gowns were the common attire of the professions: academicians, lawyers, judges, physicians, clergy. They were also commonly worn by older men and by members of the middle class on ceremonious occasions.[7]

The ruff was a popular fashion for most of the Elizabethan and Jacobean period. It appears merely as a small cambric, holland, lawn, or lace frill at the neck in illustrations prior to 1570. After that time, particularly as a consequence of the introduction of starch into England in 1564, the ruff expanded greatly. The starch held the ruff in a particular shape and kept it from bending.[8] In Ben Jonson's *The Alchemist* (1610), Subtle describes a man wearing a large ruff: "He looks in that deep ruff like a head in a platter" (4.1.24).[9] James Laver notes that the ruff, growing sometimes to a quarter of a yard in radius, was an article of clothing worn exclusively by gentlemen since it emphasized the fact that its wearer did not need to work.[10] The enormous ruffs that became more common towards the end of Elizabeth's reign may lead one to wonder how the wearer managed to eat. And yet, this article of clothing is so common in the portraits of nobles and gentry in the era that we must understand it to be common apparel of widely accepted taste.

---

[6]　Reynolds, 132.

[7]　Ibid., 132.

[8]　There were various kinds of starch, which had their own colors and textures. For a study of starch and the particular significance of yellow starch, see Ann Rosalind Jones and Peter Stallybrass, *Renaissance Clothing and the Materials of Memory* (New York: Cambridge University Press, 2000), chapter 3.

[9]　Ben Jonson, *The Alchemist*, in *Five Plays*, ed. by G. A. Wilkes (New York: Oxford Univerity Press, 1981).

[10]　James Laver, *The Concise History of Costume and Fashion* (New York: Harry N. Abrams, 1969), 91.

Instead of wearing a ruff (or even in addition to it), Englishmen sometimes wore collars, called *bands*. One could wear a falling band which folded down from the neck or a standing band that would stand out from the neck with the aid of starch. Matching ruffs or bands are often seen on sleeves in paintings from the period. By the 1630s, the band had largely replaced the ruff in English clothing.

Two types of hats were most popular in the Elizabethan and Jacobean period. The first, a bonnet, is low-crowned, made of soft material, and often decorated with a feather. The second is high-crowned, made of a stiff material, and built in sugar-loaf form.[11] Flat caps were also widely worn, primarily by citizens and apprentices. They were round, had a narrow brim, and were flat across the top. In *2 The Honest Whore*, Dekker explains how flat caps were understood at the time by stating that "Flat caps as proper are to Citty Gownes," as to "Kings their Crownes" (1.3.69–71).[12] In early modern England, hats were worn indoors as well as out. The doffing of one's hat was a sign of respect, and a courtier would typically only take off his hat and keep it in his hand in the presence of the king. Andrew Gurr has noted that this practice of demonstrating fealty with one's hat provides an explanation for why, in *Hamlet*, Osric keeps his hat off in the presence of Hamlet.[13]

Men's footwear in early modern England consisted of shoes and boots. Pictorial evidence shows that the shoes were square-toed in shape and did not begin to have heels until the end of the sixteenth century. They were made of a variety of fabrics, from silk and velvet to leather and plain cloth, and had soles of either leather or cork. Decorations included slashing, rosettes, or decorative stones. Boots were primarily used for riding until the last quarter of the sixteenth century when they began to receive more general use. Made of soft leather, they were of varying size and the tops are often shown turned down.

The undermost garment worn by women was the *chemise*, the equivalent of a man's shirt. However, the chemise often reached all the way down to the ankle. Typically made of white linen, it could have a rounded or square neckline, offering either covering for the neck or the possibility of décolletage. Although it served primarily as an undergarment, the chemise could sometimes be seen when it served to cover the neckline.

Most early modern Englishwomen's dresses or kirtles consisted of two parts, the *bodice* and the *skirt*, which were typically sewn together. The bodice was often quite rigid and tapered to a sharp point at or below the waistline. To maintain this shape, it was sometimes bolstered by busks or stays made of wood or whalebone, or even by iron bodies that were either a part of the garment or worn underneath it. Sometimes a V-shaped opening appeared in the front of the bodice which allowed a different fabric underneath, a *stomacher* or *placard*, to be seen. The stomacher

---

[11] Reynolds, 132.

[12] Thomas Dekker, *II The Honest Whore*, in *The Chief Elizabethan Dramatists*, ed. William Allan Neilson (Boston and New York: Houghton Mifflin, 1911), 425–55.

[13] Andrew Gurr, *The Shakespearean Stage*, 3rd ed. (New York: Cambridge University Press, 1992), 1–2.

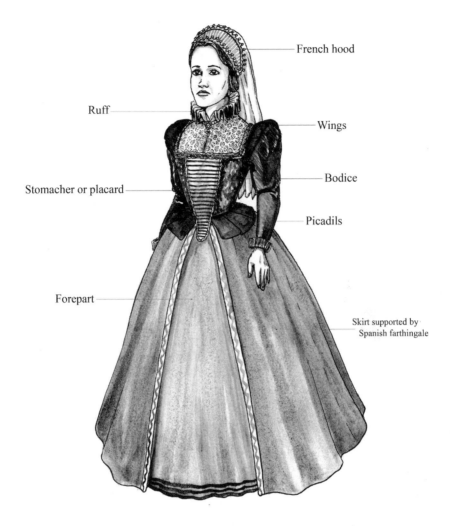

French hood

Ruff

Wings

Bodice

Stomacher or placard

Picadils

Forepart

Skirt supported by
Spanish farthingale

Fig. 1.3   A Generalized Elizabethan Gentlewoman, drawn by Adam West.

was a separate article of clothing from the bodice and was usually made of very stiff material. The sleeves were not a part of the bodice but were connected to it by points. They were close-fitting cylinders in the 1560s and grew to be puffed, slashed, leg-of-mutton sleeves in the 1580s.[14] By 1600, the sleeves had diminished in size but remained larger than the woman's arms. By the 1620s, the sleeves were once again close-fitting. Where the sleeves connected to the bodice, there were often decorative *wings* which hid the connecting links.

---

[14]   Reynolds, 134.

The skirt, covering the lower half of a woman and constituting the second part of the kirtle, was often bolstered by a *farthingale* and/or by *petticoats*, additional underskirts. Farthingales, stiff accessories consisting of hoops of padding, rushes, wood, wire, or whalebone which held out a woman's skirt, came in three varieties. The first ones worn in England were Spanish farthingales, which came into fashion and were common apparel before the first public theatres opened. Spanish farthingales were built like upside-down cones or bells; they were circular, being small at the waist and growing gradually to a wide circumference at the feet. With this farthingale, a woman's skirt would sometimes have an opening in the front in the shape of an upside-down V through which the fabric of a petticoat might be seen or a separate piece of fabric, a *forepart*, would be visible. The forepart was often made of cheap material around the back and of expensive fabric with highly wrought embroidery in that section where it would be seen through the skirt. The French farthingale came to dominate English fashion by the turn of the seventeenth century. It consisted of a padded roll that was worn around the waist, under the skirt, and resembled a life preserver. It was sometimes called a *bum roll*. The third type of farthingale was the *drum* farthingale which consisted of a hoop worn at the waist from which the skirt fell straight to the ground. This farthingale was commonly seen at court roughly from the 1560s to 1620.[15] A circle of soft pleats was often worn over the drum farthingale to cover the hoop and soften the perpendicular bend of the dress before it reached to the ground. Despite the widespread appeal of the farthingale, it was not worn by all women, even during its greatest popularity. By the 1620s, farthingales decreased in popularity in England, being replaced by full-gathered skirts which hung in soft folds.

The woman's gown was usually a loose piece of apparel that was open at the front and reached all the way down to the feet. Gowns were worn on top of all other garments except perhaps a cloak, although the gown would sometimes serve instead of a cloak to keep the wearer warm. Gowns might or might not have sleeves. A woman might also wear a *night-gown* which differs from the usual gown in being less elaborate, warmer, and less likely to be confined at the waist.[16] It is important to note that night-gowns at this time were not limited to the bedroom, but also would be worn outside as a common piece of apparel.

Ruffs and bands were fashionable among both women and men in early modern England, though women had more styles of neckwear available to them. For women, the ruff could be closed, presenting an unbroken circle around the neck, or it could be open at the front. The latter style is better suited to décolletage

---

[15] Linthicum, *Costume*, 181. Linthicum states that the style of the drum farthingale originated in Italy, 181. C. Willett Cunnington and Phillis Cunnington state that the style originated in France, *Handbook of English Costume in the Seventeenth Century* (London: Faber and Faber), 87. Neither presents convincing evidence to determine which origin is more likely.

[16] Linthicum, *Costume*, 182.

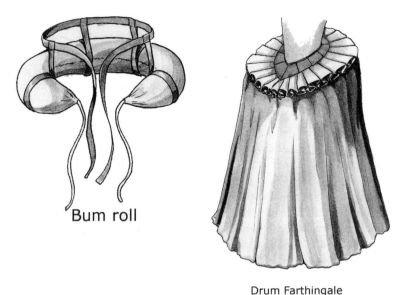

Bum roll

Drum Farthingale

Fig. 1.4   Farthingales, drawn by Adam West.

and was more frequently worn by unmarried women along with low-cut bodices.[17] The edges of the open ruff would rise from the sides of the décolletage and spread out like a fan behind the woman's head. With particularly large ruffs, women sometimes wore a frame, called a *supportasse*, to hold the garment in place and push up the rear. By 1610, the ruff was replaced in popularity by the standing band, a collar that reached straight out from the neck. Although ruffs became less popular in the seventeenth century, they were still widely worn until the 1630s when the fashion turned towards falling bands, collars that folded down, and the ruff largely disappeared from women's apparel in England. Women's falling bands were similar to men's, consisting of a wide collar at the neck that was usually starched, open at the front, and folded down against the bodice.

Women could choose among a number of overlapping fashionable choices of headdresses in early modern England. The articles most commonly seen in portraits of the era are the *coif* and the *French hood*. The coif was made of embroidered linen, lace, or other material and covered the back of the head. The French hood similarly covered the back of the head but was made of stiffened material, hanging down below the neckline in a veil on either side of the face. The hanging veil was sometimes drawn up and pinned to the crown of the French hood, or wired out to either side in a horn-shaped figure.[18] In the 1590s, fashionable women sometimes

[17]   Cunnington, *Handbook*, 99.
[18]   Reynolds, 134.

wore high hats similar to those worn by men at the time. This fashion did not last long, and afterwards women were frequently depicted wearing no headdress at all.

Women's hairstyles, like clothing, changed over time. Studying portraits from the era, Graham Reynolds concludes:

> With the advance of the 1570s and 1580s it was curled and wired out to either side in a horn-shaped figure, the width increasing step by step with the ruffs and puffed sleeves. After 1590 this horn-shaped coiffure gives way to one which rises vertically from the forehead, and by 1600 curls are superseded by hair brushed flat and shaped high over a pad. At this time and later, some ladies, perhaps mainly unmarried ones, adopted the delightfully romantic style of long hair falling loosely over their shoulders. The hair is bedecked with jewels, often wired into delicate cresting.[19]

It is important to note that Reynolds' evidence is limited to what can be seen in portraits. Naturally, this influences the conclusions he drew about the hairstyles that were popular at the time, particularly when we note that portraits were typically taken of wealthier women and may give less insight into the styles worn by less affluent women.

Women's shoes at the time were nearly identical to those worn by men. In portraits of the era, they are frequently hidden beneath the skirt or peek out from under it. These shoes were often decorated with ribbon ties, and after the 1590s, had roses made of ribbon or lengths of lace.

Taken together, a woman's articles of apparel likely would have provided a rather thorough illusion of a female character when worn by a boy in performance. The clothes of the period worked significantly to establish the shape of the wearer, not merely reflect it. A young male actor playing the part of a woman would look almost indistinguishable from an actual woman in the same clothes. The lower part of the body would have been obscured by a farthingale or the layers of a skirt. The upper body would have been shaped by the rigid bodice that provided the impression of breasts. On his head, the actor would have worn a wig and perhaps also a coif or French hood. In fact, the only part of the actor's body that would have been visibly his own was the very front of his face, from above his ruff to below his hair line. The rest would have been covered by clothing. And if the cross-dressing actor was prepubescent, as was typically the case, then his face would have been smooth and no stubble would have marred his ability to convincingly impersonate a woman.

Costume is of the Essence

The theatrical practice of cross-gender casting has drawn a great deal of attention in recent years from scholars attempting to explain why it was the custom in early modern England and how it was received by audiences at the time. The

---

[19] Ibid., 134.

most frequently asked question has turned out to be one of the most difficult to answer: why did the English stage take boys for women?[20] After all, there was no law prohibiting women from acting on the early modern English stage. A variety of explanations have been posited, but none of them has provided a clear and definitive answer. As Phyllis Rackin explains:

> Taking the moralists at their word, some scholars have explained it in terms of cultural taboos against women's public speech or anxieties about the powerful erotic allure of female players. Others have suggested that the players desired to exploit the even more powerful erotic allure of boys dressed in female clothes; but the reason why the English professional companies excluded women has never been satisfactorily explained.[21]

Despite the large body of work addressing the issue, determining why the English theatres used cross-dressed boys for women has proven elusive, and I will not address the issue here.

I will, however, consider how the practice of cross-gender casting was received at the time. Most of the scholars who have addressed the topic, even those who argue that there is no satisfactory explanation for why it took place, agree that we can in fact pursue a meaningful study of the impact that cross-gender casting had on playmaking at the time. And yet, this issue is almost as vexed as the earlier question. The reason lies in the relative paucity of documents from the period speaking to the experience that audience members had when they viewed boys playing the part of woman. Furthermore, the evidence that does exist is contradictory, lending itself to multiple, sometimes mutually exclusive conclusions.

A select grouping of extant documents from the period, for instance, supports the argument that the theatrical practice of cross-gender casting primarily served to provide homoerotic pleasure to audiences that lusted after the boy wearing women's apparel. John Rainoldes, an Oxford divine, states in *Th' Overthrow of Stage-Playes* (1599) that "The appareil of wemen is a great provocation of men to lust and leacherie . . . A womans garment beeing put on a man doeth vehemently touch and moue him with the remembrance and imagination of a woman; and the

---

[20] To address precisely this question and the difficulty of answering it definitively, Stephen Orgel wrote the essay "Nobody's Perfect: or, Why Did the English Stage Take Boys for Women?" *South Atlantic Quarterly* 88.1 (Winter 1989): 7–29. His book *Impersonations* represents his attempt to pursue the topic in further detail.

[21] Phyllis Rackin, "Shakespeare's Crossdressing Comedies," in *A Companion to Shakespeare's Works: The Comedies*, eds. Richard Dutton and Jean E. Howard (Malden, MA: Blackwell, 2003), 115. For those interested in pursuing the issue, I recommend Jean E. Howard's "Crossdressing, The Theatre, and Gender Struggle in Early Modern England," *Shakespeare Quarterly* 39.4 (1988): 418–40; Orgel's *Impersonations*; and Michael Shapiro's *Gender in Play on the Shakespearean Stage: Boy Heroines & Female Pages* (Ann Arbor: University of Michigan Press, 1996), particularly the introduction. These excellent studies will direct interested readers to the larger body of research on the subject.

imagination of a thing desireable doth stirr up the desire."[22] The thrust of Rainolde's argument, Lisa Jardine explains, is that "male prostitution and perverted sexual activity is the inevitable accompaniment of female impersonation."[23] William Prynne spelled out this fear clearly in *Histrio-Mastix* (1633):

> Players and Play-haunters in their secret conclaves play the Sodomites: together with some moderne examples of such, who have been desperately enamored with Players Boyes thus clad in womans apparell, so fare as to solicite them by words, by Letters, even actually to abuse them.[24]

Cross-dressed boys, Prynne argues, inspire lust in audience members who cannot help but pursue them for sexual satisfaction.

Jardine recognizes, however, that there is a "hysterical edge" to these statements. The extreme positions that Rainoldes, Prynne, and other antitheatrical writers espouse suggest that their opinions fall well outside the norm for theatre audiences at the time. As Thomas Postlewait rightly warns, "unless we can demonstrate that audiences saw the theatre through the eyes and mind of the tract writers, we should be careful about how we use the tracts to support our ideas about an antitheatrical society. Most pamphlets had a limited distribution, so they probably did not carry much weight with theatre audiences, many of whom were not literate."[25] But Ben Jonson provides support to the argument that the boys who played women's parts were the objects of homosexual desire. In *Poetaster* (1601), a father worries that his son's decision to write for the theatre will lead to sex with men: "What shall I have my sonne a stager now? an enghle for players?" (1.2.15–16).[26] Middleton similarly suggests the sexual desirability and availability of boy players in *Father Hubburd's Tales* (1604), in which a young gentleman is encouraged "to call in at the Blackfriars where he should see a nest of boys able to ravish a man." (559–61).[27] Coming from individuals who worked within the theatrical enterprise, Jonson's and Middleton's statements lend credibility to Rainoldes' and Prynne's conclusion that using cross-dressed boys to play the part of women incited homoerotic desire in their audiences.

---

[22]   J. Rainoldes, *Th' Overthrow of Stage-playes* (Middleburgh, 1599), 97.

[23]   Lisa Jardine, "Boy Actors, Female Roles, and Elizabethan Eroticism," in *Staging the Renaissance: Reinterpretations of Elizabethan and Jacobean Drama*, eds. David Scott Kastan and Peter Stallybrass (New York: Routledge, 1991), 57.

[24]   William Prynne, *Histrio-Mastix* (London, 1633), 211–12.

[25]   Thomas Postlewait, "Theatricality and Antitheatricality in Renaissance London" in *Theatricality*, eds. Tracy C. Davis and Thomas Postlewait (New York: Cambridge University Press, 2003), 98.

[26]   Ben Jonson, *The Complete Plays of Ben Jonson*, ed. by G. A. Wilkes, Vol. 2 (Oxford: Clarendon Press, 1981).

[27]   Adrian Weiss, *Father Hubburd's Tale* in Gary Taylor and John Lavagnino eds., *Thomas Middleton: The Collected Works* (New York and Oxford: Oxford University Press, 2007), 149–82.

Frustratingly, the diametrical position can also be argued. In Lady Mary Wroth's prose romance *The Countess of Montgomery's Urania* (1621), the experience of watching a boy play a woman's part is presented merely as one of appreciating dramatic action. In this configuration, the practice of cross-gender casting is divorced entirely from sexual desire:

> there he [her first lover] saw her with all passionate ardency, seeke, and sue for the strangers love; yet he [the stranger] unmoveable, was no further wrought, then if he had seene a delicate play-boy acte a loving womans part, and knowing him a boy, lik'd onely his action.[28]

As it is figured here, the boy playing a woman's role is protected from inciting lust precisely by the convention of cross-gender casting. Precluding women from performance serves, therefore, to safeguard the stage from sexual desire. Thomas Nashe supports this notion of cross-gender casting and the morality of the English stage in *Pierce Penilesse his Supplication of the Divell* (1592): "Our Players are not as the players beyond Sea, a sort of squirting baudie Comedians, that haue whores and common Curtizens to playe womens partes, and forbeare no immodest speech, or vnchast action that may procure laughter."[29] Nashe suggests that the threat of sexualizing the English stage is quelled by restricting women from performance. Not only homoerotic lust, but heterosexual desire as well are contained by having the women's parts played by boys.

Thomas Heywood specifically targets and counters the arguments of antitheatrical writers when he states that the custom of cross-gender casting was a moral one with a respectable tradition in his *An Apology for Actors* (1612):

> To see our youth attired in the habit of women. [W]ho knows not what their intents be? Who cannot distinguish them by their names, assuredly knowing that they are but to represent such a lady, at such a tyme appointed? Do not the universities, the fountains, and well springs of all good arts, learning and documents, admit the like in their colleges? [A]nd they (I assure myself) are not ignorant of their use. In the time of my residence at Cambridge, I have seen tragedyes, comedyes, historyes, pastorals and shows publickly acted, in which the graduates of good place and reputation have bene specially parted.[30]

The dressing of boys in women's clothing, Heywood argues, serves only to represent women. Far from inspiring inappropriate desire, the practice of cross-gender casting is an ethical exercise that derives from the venerable practices of the universities.

Ultimately, one can examine the extant documents of the early modern English stage and reasonably conclude both that the practice of cross-gender casting

---

28   Lady Mary Wroth, *The Countesse of Mountgomeries Urania* (London, 1621), 60.

29   E. K. Chambers, *The Elizabethan Stage*, 4 vols. (Oxford: Clarendon Press, 1923), 4.239.

30   Ibid, 1:252.

encouraged homoerotic lust for the boys who wore women's clothing onstage and, at the same time, that the custom was a highly moral practice that focused audience attention upon the action of the play to the exclusion of sexual desire for the actors. I want to suggest that both conclusions are reasonable possibilities for those who attended the theatre at the time. As Michael Shapiro explains, we cannot assume "a homogenous collective response by audiences to play-boys, for in every theater audience there is a range of sophistication, alertness, and theatergoing experience, plus differences in gender, class, and other variables."[31] The possibility that boys served merely to incite homoerotic desire among audiences is immediately challenged by the fact that women attended plays in significant numbers at the time. Writers at the time simply made no mention of the heterosexual desire women might have had for the men, let alone the cross-dressed boys, performing onstage. The available evidence from the period clearly does not represent the great variety of reactions people had to the practice of cross-gender casting. It might, however, fairly represent the extreme poles on a continuum between which the experiences of many playgoers can be identified. For some, cross-dressing by male actors was a scandalous source of homoerotic attraction, while for others it was the logical, moral alternative to the practice of having women perform onstage, and for many more, an experience that fell somewhere in the middle.[32] It makes sense that there would be scant written responses to the practice of cross-gender casting from those who were neither shocked by the practice of having boys play the women's parts nor felt the need to defend it.

The simple longevity of the practice supports the likelihood that most theatre goers accepted the convention. From the opening of the first public playhouses in 1567 to their closing in 1642, the custom of having boys play the women's parts continued unabated and essentially unchanged. Kathleen McLuskie is right to conclude that, on some level, boy actors playing women must have simply been accepted by the great majority of theatre goers as a convention.[33] Otherwise, audiences would have been unable to engage the dramatic narratives that are premised on heterosexual love and the differences distinguishing men from women.[34] Despite the range of responses some individuals might have had to the convention, we can chart meaningfully the ways that the convention itself was employed at the time. Since women were consistently and completely divorced from the practice of staging plays on the English professional stage at this time, we can examine the means whereby notions of sex and gender were constructed, engaged, and negotiated in performance. Costuming choices and changes constitute the primary means by which this was done.

---

[31] Shapiro, 41.

[32] Howard, 419.

[33] Kathleen McLuskie, "The Act, the Role, and the Actor: Boy Actresses on the Elizabethan Stage," *New Theatre Quarterly* 3 (1987): 121.

[34] Howard, 435.

The articles of apparel that an actor wore in performance did more than reveal his character's sex. They materially constructed the wearer's femininity or masculinity according to the gendered assumptions that maintained at the time. A doublet and hose, such as Rosalind mentions in the quote that begins this chapter were understood to be male before they were put on. Likewise, a woman's dress was figured as female. Each item listed in the earlier part of this chapter dictated to the knowing audience a range of actions that the wearer was able to pursue as well as those actions the wearer ought to pursue. Conversely, costumes also established those actions the wearer was unable to pursue and ought not to pursue. And yet, if we are to consider the articles of apparel that were worn on the early modern stage to construct the wearer's masculinity or femininity, we need to expand the range of items that we will consider. Beyond doublets and breeches, bodices and farthingales, we must also consider such items as a character's beard, hair, codpiece, sword, handkerchief, make-up, and more. In early modern English society, these items were integral to a subject's sense of identity or self and at the same time detachable or auxiliary.[35] For the professional theatres, they were costume pieces, put on by an actor in the process of materially constructing or manipulating his character in a production.

When Richard Burbage assumed the role of Hamlet, for example, he put on the clothes that spoke his character's masculinity. From Ophelia's lines (2.1.76–7), we know that these included a shirt, a doublet, a hat, breeches, and nether stocks. Equally important to his character and mentioned at other points in the play are Hamlet's beard and sword. Taken together, these items established the male sex of the wearer and also suggested the masculine characterization that was expected of the person for whom these articles of clothing were appropriate apparel. One of the key traits of masculinity was courage, for men were expected to exercise their agency in the English patriarchal society. It follows that when Hamlet questions his bravery, he does so by referencing his beard, a material representation of his masculinity: "Am I a coward? / Who calls me villain, breaks my pate across, / Plucks off my beard and blows it in my face" (2.2.571–3). In failing to act, Hamlet feels he is failing to live up to the expectations of masculinity represented physically by his facial hair. He explains "This is most brave, / That I, the son of a dear [father] murthered, / Prompted to my revenge by heaven and hell, / Must like a whore unpack my heart with words" (2.2.582–5). Empty words and a beardless face are appropriate to women who ought not act on their own behalf and for whom cowardice was believed to be an appropriate behavior. As Helena proudly and un-ironically states in *A Midsummer Night's Dream*, "I am a right maid for my cowardice" (3.2.302). When Hamlet similarly fails to act, he questions his courage and, by extension, his own masculinity. He describes the threat to his masculinity as the forced removal of his facial hair, essentially equating it to castration.

---

[35]   Will Fisher, Materializing Gender in Early Modern English Literature and Culture (New York: Cambridge University Press, 2006), 26.

When Hamlet feels his courage questioned as the plucking of his beard, he invokes a longstanding tradition in the theatre and in English society of equating courage with masculinity and masculinity with facial hair. According to this tradition, manhood was materially achieved and recognized by the growth of a beard. In *As You Like It*, Jaques marks the difference between boyhood and manhood in precisely these terms, contrasting the "schoolboy" with a "shining morning face" to the "soldier" who is "bearded like the pard" (2.7.144–9). Building on the differences between childhood and adulthood, Will Fisher argues that men and boys were quite literally two distinct genders.[36] Accordingly, a study of the material construction of gender on the early modern stage should include a consideration of men, women, and boys. Men were differentiated from boys and women largely on the basis of their ability to grow beards, their ability to fight, and their ability to procreate with women, all three of which were visually suggested by facial hair.[37]

Beatrice in *Much Ado About Nothing* states that it is the beard that marks the difference between men and boys and goes one step further to suggest that the boy more closely resembles a woman for the absence of facial hair: "What should I do with [a husband who hath no beard]? dress him in my apparel and make him my waiting-gentle-woman? He that hath a beard is more than a youth, and he that hath no beard is less than a man" (2.1.34–6). Facial hair was so tightly connected to the visual presentation of masculinity at the time that nearly all of the portraits of men from sixteenth- and seventeenth-century England portray the sitter wearing a beard.[38]

The beard's ability to materially establish masculinity made artificial facial hair indispensible to boy companies that had to use costume items to construct both their adult male and female characters. Fisher has noted numerous instances in which boy companies and universities rented beards for their productions. More surprisingly, he has found that facial hair is mentioned in fully half of the extant boys' company texts. In most of these cases, the comments required that characters be played with facial hair, which would have been provided for by the use of fake beards. These costume items were un-ironically employed for the creation of masculine identity and were not limited to comedy.[39] In both boy troupes and adult companies, the beard served to visually and materially establish the masculine, adult character of the actor who wore one.

When the beard was absent from male characters who otherwise were adults, it warranted mention. When he was only sixteen, Shakespeare's Coriolanus had no beard and yet demonstrated considerable martial prowess in apparent contradiction of the rule that beards were equated with masculine courage. In this instance, however, the text makes it clear that Coriolanus is an exception that proves the

---

[36] Fisher, 87.
[37] Ibid., 106.
[38] Ibid., 94.
[39] Ibid., 83–7.

rule. Cominus says "At sixteen years . . . with his Amazonian [chin] he drove / The bristled lips before him" (2.2.87–92). So masculine was Coriolanus that he surpassed the feats of other men before he had grown a beard. Earlier in the same speech, Cominus reifies the connection between masculinity and courage, stating that "Valor is the chiefest virtue, and / Most dignifies the haver" (2.2.84–5). The suggestion is that Coriolanus was more valorous than other men before he had a beard and even greater when he finally grew one. The masculine significance of the beard also explains why, in Marlowe's *Edward II* (1592–3), the king is washed and shaved before his death. The shaving of the beard suggests the act of castration so that the king is unmanned even as he is dethroned.

The masculine, martial prowess suggested by the beard was similarly embodied in the sword. Swords carried significant social currency that will be considered in the next chapter, but they must also be considered for the fact that were deemed to be exclusively male accoutrements and imparted notions of masculinity and courage to the individuals who wore them. As Phyllis Rackin has noted, the ability to fight, and specifically swordsmanship, were quintessentially male activities in early modern England, and were depicted onstage through the wearing of swords.[40] This explains why Viola in *Twelfth Night* wears a sword when she plays the part of Cessario, but she cannot fight with it. She tries to convince others that she is a proper gentleman, but the feminine clothing that is appropriate to her character specifically excludes the sword. It follows that her brother Sebastian looks identical to his cross-dressed sister, but distinguishes his masculinity by his ability to draw the sword that is the appropriate complement to his male sex. The gendered significance of the sword in this instance also serves to further the plot as the play moves toward the point where Viola will be able to take up her woman's weeds, which accurately represent her identity. Sebastian, it must be noted, lacks facial hair, potentially introducing a contradiction regarding the visual codes of sex since he clearly fights with the courage and skill of a man while lacking the beard that typically attends mature masculinity. I take this to suggest that he is a young man who is just emerging from adolescence and ready to assume adult responsibilities. In *As You Like It*, Jaques lists the age of the lover in between that of the fair faced school boy and the bearded soldier. It follows that Sebastian is a lover who transitions from boyhood to manhood during the course of the play, and his beard will shortly follow suit.

Like the beard and the sword, the codpiece also materially asserted masculinity in early modern drama, but with a comic twist. The codpiece had fallen out of fashion by the end of the sixteenth century and was rarely worn in English society.[41] And yet, plays from the period still employed it to establish and comment upon the wearer's masculinity. In the anonymously written *Wiley Beguiled* (1606), when William Cricket lists his masculine features, he notes that he has "a fine beard,

---

[40]   Rackin, "Shakespeare's Crossdressing Comedies," 124.

[41]   Fisher, 79. Fisher devotes a chapter of his book to examining the historical and social significance of the codpiece.

[a] comely corps, And a Carowsing Codpeece."[42] Cricket identifies the codpiece and the beard along with his handsome body as jointly constituting his masculine identity.

However, the codpiece did not typically assert the masculinity of the wearer in a straightforward manner. Rather, it most commonly served to comically question and consequently undermine the masculinity of the wearer. Since the item was no longer worn by the men who attended the theatre, codpieces appeared on characters whose masculinity ought to be doubted. Thus, when William Cricket announces his "Carowsing Codpeece," he does more to undercut his masculinity than assert it. It follows that in *The Two Gentlemen of Verona* (1594), Lucetta insists that Julia wear a codpiece along with her breeches if she is to impersonate a man, for "A round hose, madam, now's not worth a pin, / Unless you have a codpiece to stick pins on" (2.7.55–6). As a woman, Julia needs to embrace all signs of masculinity if she is to appear as a man. Thus, codpieces were clearly deemed masculine apparel, but in their comic deployment served as signs of emasculation. Thus, as the codpiece grew less common in English society, it took on a different role for the stage.

In addition to suggesting that Julia wear a codpiece if she is to play the part of a man, Lucetta also insists that she cut her hair. Indeed, this is Lucetta's first piece of advice:

> LUCETTA: But in what habit will you go along?
> JULIA: Not like a woman, for I would prevent
> The loose encounters of lascivious men:
> Gentle Lucetta, fit me with such weeds
> As may beseem some well-reputed page.
> LUCETTA: Why then your ladyship must cut your hair. (2.7.39–44)

Just as breeches, beards, swords, and codpieces materially constituted masculinity on the early modern English stage, so did long hair serve to assert the wearer's femininity. Noting the extraordinary number of works that address the topic, Fisher has found that there was a well-developed discourse on hair in England during the seventeenth century. This body of work almost uniformly agrees that hair is tightly connected to one's sex with short hair properly belonging to men and long hair to women.[43] Beyond fashion choices, the way that one wore one's hair in English society and particularly on the stage served to establish visually the wearer's sex.

When an actor put on a wig in the act of constructing the female gender of the character he played, he engaged the feminine associations that the article invoked. Long hair marked female inferiority to men and visually suggested the ideal of feminine submissiveness. The anonymously written *Hic Mulier* (1620) states "The long hair of a woman is the ornament of her sex, and bashful shamefastness

---

[42]   Quoted from Fisher, 64.
[43]   Fisher, 130–31.

her chief honor."[44] Anatomists from the period often noted that just as men have beards, so do women have long hair, making conspicuous the ways that sex was visually understood at the time.[45] Just as plays employed the connection between one's facial hair and one's masculinity so did other plays take advantage of the associations carried by long hair to comment upon the characters that wore it. It follows that the first thing a female character had to do when she sought to cross-dress as a boy was hide her long hair. And yet, a female character could not actually cut her hair, for doing so threatened her ability to return back to being a woman. In *Two Gentlemen*, Julia decides that instead of cutting her hair, she will "knit it up in silken strings, / With twenty odd-conceited true-love knots: / to be fantastic may become a youth" (2.7.45–7). In other plays, female characters most likely hid their hair under their hats. Since sex was materially constructed by one's hair style, an actor playing a cross-dressed female character could revert back to the female sex by revealing long hair.

David Mann has recently argued that the female gender was also sometimes established on stage through the wearing of prosthetic breasts. Citing numerous instances in which female breasts are exposed in early modern plays, he concludes that they were an important costume piece at the time. About the prosthetic breasts, Mann states "female torsos were presumably moulded in papier maché or leather, their edges concealed by heavy necklaces and puffed sleeves. Without the aid of modern materials, such simulations are unlikely to have been of a very high level of realism."[46] I am not entirely convinced. Looking at contemporary portraits, Stephen Orgel has noted that the Elizabethan ideal of aristocratic womanhood, was "what we would call boyish and they called womanly: slim-hipped and flat-chested."[47] Boys looked the part when they wore women's clothes, and with some careful staging, prosthetic breasts would not have been necessary to present most of the scenes that call for the exposing of the breast. And yet, the evidence is by no means certain on either side.

Far more evidence exists to support the likelihood that the visual presentation of femininity required that actors playing women's parts wear make-up. Facial powder and paint was widely worn in English society and throughout western Europe by the time the first public theatres opened in London and would have been

---

[44]　*Hic Mulier; or, The Man Woman in Half Humankind: Contexts and Texts of the Controversy about Women in England, 1540–1640*, eds. Katherine Usher Henderson and Barbara F. McManus (Urbana and Chicago: University of Illinois Press, 1985), 270.

[45]　Fisher, 133.

[46]　The primary point of Mann's observation is to counter Peter Stallybrass's argument that the practice of having boys play women's parts inspired homoerotic desire for the male body underneath the woman's clothing, what Mann calls paedophilic voyeurism. I do not wish to enter their debate regarding the reception of the convention of cross-dressing, for I am primarily interested in exploring the convention itself. David Mann, *Shakespeare's Women: Performance and Conception* (New York: Cambridge University Press, 2008), 102–9.

[47]　Orgel, *Impersonations*, 70.

expected among aristocratic women.[48] M. S. Balsam and Edward Sagarin have explored the history of cosmetic practices, and note that:

> The Elizabethan woman used cosmetics of all kinds without restraint. Face powder consisted chiefly of white lead, occasionally mixed with sublimate of mercury and ground orris. Rouge was red ocher, vermillion, or cochineal; extracts of sandal or brazilwood were considered very new and smart. A typical "tooth whitener" contained powdered brick, cuttle bone, red and white coral, egg shells, alum, mastic, sandarac, pumice, and myrrh. Annoying pimples were to be covered for an hour with powdered sulfur and turpentine and then anointed with fresh butter.[49] (3: 73)

The widespread use of cosmetics points to the belief at the time that fair skin was the ideal of feminine beauty. Considering the importance of make-up to both English society and its public theatres, Dympna Callaghan has argued that whiteface was the primary way of signifying femininity onstage.[50]

And yet, while make-up was deemed indispensable to women at the time, it simultaneously served as a signifier of deceit and sinfulness. When cosmetics or "painting" are mentioned in plays throughout the period, they nearly always serve to suggest immorality in the wearer who seeks to alter the natural visage that God has given. Thus, Hamlet is able to assail Ophelia's and, by extension, all women's virtue by stating "I have heard of your paintings, well enough. God hath given you one face, and you make yourselves another" (3.1.141–2). Similarly, in *A Midsummer Night's Dream*, Hermia insults Helena by calling her a "painted maypole" (3.2.296). The suggestion is that a proper woman's skin is naturally white and her morality equally pure. Any blemish serves to distance a woman from the visual and consonant moral ideal.[51] In this configuration, one's effort to hide imperfection serves as deceitfulness, a conscious attempt to conceal one's true nature. The plays of the period most frequently forwarded the sexual consequences of this deceitfulness, proffering the general argument that cosmetics serve to cover up the signs of venereal diseases and that red and white paint serve as brands or signs of sin and lust.[52] In *Hamlet*, Claudius makes this connection clear: "The harlot's cheek, beautied with plast'ring art" (3.1.50).

---

[48]   Shirley Nelson Garner, "'Let Her Paint an Inch Thick': Painted Ladies in Renaissance Drama and Society," *Renaissance Drama* 20 (1989): 131.

[49]   M. S. Balsam and Edward Sagarin, *Cosmetics, Science, and Technology*, Vol. 3 (New York: Wiley-Interscience, 1974), 73.

[50]   Dympna Callaghan, *Shakespeare without Women: Representing Gender and Race on the Renaissance Stage* (London and New York: Routledge, 2000), 84.

[51]   T. W. Craik has observed that in the Tudor Interlude, spots "always signify moral corruption," *The Tudor Interlude: Stage, Costume and Acting* (Leicester: Leicester University Press, 1967), 72.

[52]   Annette Drew-Bear, "Face-Painting in Renaissance Tragedy," *Renaissance Drama* 12 (1981): 76.

The insidious connotations of make-up presented women of the time with a conundrum. If a woman failed to live up to the ideal of beauty, she would have been marked by her natural, visible flaws as immoral, and if she attempted to hide those flaws with cosmetics, she would have been marked as immoral by her painting. It was almost impossible for a woman's visual presentation to suggest anything but immorality. Even the most beautiful woman would eventually exhibit the effects of time and be forced to choose whether to reveal her sinfulness through her signs of aging or through her efforts to hide it. What makes the matter worse is that the dangerous ingredients used in make-up were harmful to the skin and encouraged the use of additional make-up to cover new blotches.

In performance, boys playing women's parts regularly employed make-up. They could wear a modest amount to suggest the ideal of beauty or much more if they were undertaking a role that called for it, i.e., a woman whose immorality informed her character. Jonson's *Epicoene* notes the excessive use of cosmetics among a group of women calling themselves the Collegiates, whose visual presentation provides an appropriate cognate to their coarse sexuality and promiscuity.[53] The leader of these women, Lady Haughty, is described in terms that demonstrate the popular view of face painting. Clerimont says "A pox of her autumnal face, her pieced beauty! There's no man can be admitted till she be ready nowadays, till she has painted and perfumed and washed and scoured" (1.1.81–3).[54] It is unclear whether Lady Haughty or the other Collegiates were immoral as girls, but as older women who require make-up to cover the effects of aging, their imperfect visual presentation literally sets the stage for their questionable morality, making them ripe objects of comic derision. Their desperate efforts to cover their flaws serve to bring those flaws to the fore and render the Collegiates ridiculous and worthy of an audience's scorn. By the end of the play, they are suitably humiliated.

The sinfulness suggested through the use of make-up made cosmetics potent signifiers in tragedy, and numerous plays used painting as shorthand for "whore" or "pride-filled woman."[55] Barnabe Barnes's *The Devil's Charter* (1607) makes particularly effective use of the popular associations that surrounded cosmetics. Lucretia earns a severe demise for licentiousness, incest, and murdering her husband. It is fitting, then, that she dies at her cosmetics table, applying poisoned make-up that burns her flesh. The method of death provides the agony Lucretia's actions warrant and time for her to reflect on her affair with Sforza before she finally expires. Unsurprisingly, she does so using terms specific to cosmetics: "What, haue I caught you Sforza, / Who painted my faire face with these foule spots, / You see them in my soule deformed blots" (ln. 2106–8).[56] The painted exterior mirrors the tainted interior, creating a potent visual signifier that was specifically feminine.

---

[53]   Garner, 136.

[54]   Ben Jonson, *Epicoene or The Silent Woman*, ed. R. V. Holdsworth (New York: W W Norton, 1990).

[55]   Garner, 135.

[56]   Barnabe Barnes, *The Devil's Charter*, ed. Ronald Brunless MacKerrow (Louvain: Uystpruyst ,1904).

Whether with make-up or prosthetic beards, farthingales or breeches, actors carried notions of femininity and masculinity onto the stage in the costumes they wore. A character's sex would have been primarily defined by these costume choices, and his or her dialogue would have been understood according to how it corroborated or clashed with the gendered expectations established by the clothes in which he or she appeared. A character that appeared in all the accoutrements of masculinity, including a doublet, breeches, a beard, and carrying a sword would instill in the audience expectations of masculinity and courage. Such is the case in *Twelfth Night*, in which Sir Andrew Aguecheek wears the clothes that bespeak manliness. When he then falls short on all fronts, he proves an appropriate butt of comedy. The play suggests that the clothes he wears are actually a costume; his proper apparel would not present such brazen masculinity.[57] On the other hand, in *Much Ado About Nothing*, the young Claudio proves to be particularly brave by demonstrating martial prowess before he is old enough to grow a beard, a visual signifier of masculine bravery. The messenger states that Claudio "hath borne himself beyond the promise of his age, doing in the figure of a lamb the feats of a lion" (1.1.12–15). Benedick later notes how Claudio's youthfulness appears onstage by calling him "my Lord Lack-beard" (5.1.192). As with Coriolanus, Claudio proves to be particularly courageous by demonstrating traits of masculinity even before he has achieved the signs of those characteristics. We can assume that with the growth of a beard, Claudio will achieve even greater honors.

Every play performed in the early modern English theatre made use of the visual codes of sex for the establishment of meaning in performance. The familiarity of these gendered semiotics allowed playwrights to employ them in complex, nuanced ways. Characters were not understood merely according to whether they wore a beard or not, whether they wore cosmetics or not. Instead, it was possible for them to wear different varieties and shapes of beards and different quantities of make-up. A character did not achieve a masculine or feminine identity by simply filling in a checklist of visual codes. Rather, as Will Fisher has suggested, it was more like weights on a scale. Different costume elements "mattered" to different degrees at various times in various plays, allowing costume elements to have an infinite variety of ways they could be employed to comment on the role that sex played in performance.[58]

The complex manner in which sex was materially and visually constructed onstage has consequences for how we consider the practice of cross-dressing in the plays. In many discussions of transvestite sub-plots, the practice has been considered in fairly broad strokes, as though all uses of cross-dressing employed the same apparel to take on the persona of the opposite sex. For such studies, the question is merely: what happens when a character puts on the apparel of the opposite sex? Instead, we would do well to note how a character's masculinity

---

[57] Aguecheek is also abused for the fact that he does not deserve his knighthood, an issue considered in Chapter 2.

[58] Fisher, 111.

or femininity is constructed in the clothes that visually produce his or her sex and then see how that information is manipulated or played with when another set of apparel is donned. As Michael Shapiro has rightly noted, the practice of cross-dressing presented a layering of gender identity, allowing for "skillful and precise oscillations between them."[59] The costumes actors wore offered nuanced notions of sex and gender that went beyond simply establishing whether the wearer was male or female.

A close analysis of the apparel worn on stage can sometimes be difficult since the play texts and limited extant documentation often do not provide enough information to determine what the characters wore. When the costumes can be established, however, they have the potential to provide insight into how early productions of a play visually produced and manipulated meaning in performance. In *As You Like It*, for instance, it is not fait accompli that Rosalind will assume the role of a man when she prepares to flee to the woods with Celia. Instead, the two women discuss the choices that are available to them, seeking primarily to invent disguises that will keep them safe on their travels, for "Beauty provoketh thieves sooner than gold." Celia first suggests that they adopt "poor and mean attire, / And with a kind of umber smirch my face." Rosalind considers the disguise and encourages Celia to adopt it, but chooses a different one for herself:

> Were it not better,
> Because that I am more than common tall,
> That I did suit me all points like a man?
> A gallant curtle-axe upon my thigh,
> A boar-spear in my hand (1.3.114–19).

This negotiation between Celia and Rosalind does more than simply inform us that Rosalind will dress as a man. It encourages the audience to consider how the costumes they don will influence the ways that others interact with them in the future. Moreover, their discussion informs us that Rosalind will not merely take on a male disguise. Instead, she will suit herself to "all points like a man."

Rosalind does not assume the role of a page, whose youthfulness would render her femininity less conspicuous. Instead, she attempts to embrace fully the masculine ideal that maintained at the time. Sir Thomas Elyot defined masculinity and femininity in terms that maintained throughout the period:

> A man in his natural perfection is fierce, hardy, strong in opinion, covetous of glory, desirous of knowledge, appetiting by generation to bring forth his semblable. The good nature of a woman is to be mild, timorous, tractable, benign, of sure remembrance, and shamefast.[60]

In her choice of apparel, Rosalind attempts to embrace Elyot's definition of an ideal man. Two items Rosalind specifically mentions are a "gallant curtle-axe" and a "boar-spear." These items resonated with early modern audiences,

---

[59] Shapiro, 7.

[60] From Elyot's *The Boke named the Governour*, quoted in Orgel, 107.

the curtle-axe especially. In Marlowe's *Tamburlaine* (c. 1587–8), the eponymous warrior prepares to conquer the world by removing his shepherd's apparel and donning "This complete armour and this curtle-axe," for they "Are adjuncts more beseeming Tamburlaine" (1.2.42–43).[61] In Shakespeare's comedy, then, Rosalind does more than cross-dress as a man. She assumes the apparel appropriate to a valiant warrior, her diametrical opposite.

Much of the comedy inherent to Rosalind's character on the early modern stage derived from the ways in which the actor sought to pursue Elyot's notion of ideal femininity when he appeared as a beautiful noblewoman and then layered that characterization with Elyot's notion of ideal masculinity by cross-dressing in men's attire. When he then attempted, from beneath the clothes that suggested martial bravery to assume the character of Rosalind for Orlando, the potential for comedy multiplied. It then had the opportunity to hit a new peak when that mighty warrior, armed with Tambrulaine's weapon of choice, swooned at the mere sight of blood (4.3.155–64).[62] What we have is more than a general layering of femininity on masculinity on femininity. Such generality would eventually become boring as different plays employed cross-dressing to more or less the same result. Instead, we have a layering of specific identities, forwarded in the chosen articles of clothing, requiring that the actor underneath demonstrate considerable skill as he present each identity clearly and switch back and forth between them. The young actors who undertook this challenge were likely up to the task. As Shapiro has noted, female roles were typically played by recognized specialists in female impersonation.[63] Moreover, available evidence suggests that the "boys" who typically played the lead female roles were between the ages of fifteen and eighteen and thus had several years of experience playing lesser roles to draw upon.[64] The layering of complex, specific identities allowed for each play that employed cross-dressing to accomplish it in new and exciting ways.

The great variety of ways in which various female and male identities could be layered provides a compelling explanation for the popularity of cross-dressing sub-plots in early modern English theatre. Shapiro has counted eighty-one plays by nearly forty dramatists throughout the period that employ the practice.[65] These works demonstrate remarkable creativity in their uses of cross-dressing. It is important to note, however, that in all of these works, the sex prescribed by the clothing that denotes a character's essence remains stable. In *As You Like It*, Rosalind puts on the apparel of a mighty warrior, but cannot escape the fact that at

---

[61] Christopher Marlowe, *The Complete Plays*, ed. J. B. Steane (London: Penguin, 1986).

[62] Much has been written on the practice of cross-dressing in *As You Like It*. I recommend interested readers begin by looking at Shapiro, chapter 6, and Rackin's "Shakespeare's Crossdressing Comedies."

[63] Shapiro, 33.

[64] Mann, 58.

[65] Shapiro, 9.

her core, she is a woman, defined by the decidedly and distinctively feminine attire in which she first appears. The mild, timorous nature appropriate to that clothing makes her swoon at the sight of blood. In *Twelfth Night*, Viola and Sebastian are indistinguishable from one another when dressed in the same apparel, yet they have significant differences defined by the clothing appropriate to each sibling. One difference, which has already been discussed, is the ability to fight. Another is the ability to procreate. Since all of the actors were male, there was no biological reality to appeal to; costume served to establish a character's female sex and ability to have children. Based on this fact, a character's appropriate apparel also established whom he or she could ultimately marry.

In many plays, cross-dressed women assume the apparel of younger men. This makes sense for it allows women to disguise themselves yet eschew false beards and circumvent the expectations of adult masculinity. In Thomas Heywood's *The Four Prentices of London* (1592), Bella Franca (daughter to the King of France) dresses as a page to follow, serve, and be close to the English man with whom she falls in love. In *The Merchant of Venice*, Jessica similarly dresses as a page to effect her elopement with Lorenzo. In *Cymbeline*, Imogen dresses as a boy. The examples go on. On the other hand, it was less important for male characters cross-dressing as women to choose their roles so carefully, for the actions of men were not proscribed as were those of women.[66]

Regardless of costume changes or the layering of identity, a character's sex continued to be primarily established by the specific apparel that defined his or her core identity. Cross-dressing plots worked with this aspect of early modern drama by moving toward the point where characters would remove their disguises and resume their appropriate apparel. As Stephen Greenblatt notes with regard to Shakespearean cross-dressing:

> The "masculine usurp'd attire" that is donned by Viola, Rosalind, Portia, Jessica, and other Shakespeare heroines alters what they can say and do, reveals important aspects of their character, and changes their destiny, but it is, all the same, not theirs and not all of who they are. They have, the plays insist, natures that are neither transformed nor altogether concealed by their dress.[67]

The difference between borrowed apparel and the clothes that constitute one's true nature proves to be the primary conceit in Jonson's *Epicoene* (1609), which advanced the practice of cross-dressing by not letting the audience in on the secret that a female character is actually a boy in disguise until late in the play. Morose is tricked by his nephew into marrying Epicoene, a woman believed to be silent and demure. When she proves to be overwhelmingly loud and domineering, Morose promises his nephew, Dauphin, that he will bequeath to him his inheritance if only he will help Morose divorce his new wife. In the final act of the play, Dauphin

---

[66]   David Cressy, "Gender Trouble and Cross-Dressing in Early Modern England," *Journal of British Studies* 35 (1996): 453.

[67]   Stephen Greenblatt, "General Introduction," in *The Norton Shakespeare*, 2nd ed., ed. Stephen Greenblatt, et al. (New York: WW Norton, 2008), 61.

accomplishes this by removing Epicoene's dress and revealing the male clothing of the boy underneath. The masculine apparel that lies under the female disguise constitutes Epicoene's true sex, and the marriage is dissolved, for men could not legally be married to men.

And so we return to where we started: costume is of the essence. Epicoene is actually male because the apparel appropriate to his character is masculine according to the conventions of the early modern English theatre. The fact that he appears in female clothing for most of the play and is only revealed to be male in the final act serves merely as a function of cross-dressing on the professional stage. In this way, cross-dressing in early modern drama works according to an essentialist notion of sex and counter to the one-sex model forwarded in Galenic conceptions of the body. According to the one-sex model, differences between men and women were understood to be merely a matter of degree with women existing as imperfect men.[68] According to this model, which appeared in some of the medical texts of the period and has been forwarded by a number of leading early modern critics, it was possible for a woman to transform into a man if she overexerted herself and possible for a man to revert into a woman if he proved too feminine.[69] The widespread acceptance of the one-sex model in early modern England has been hotly contested in recent years, and the matter remains open.[70] We cannot know to what degree audiences accepted the Galenic notion of sex, but the plays forward the firm sense that men and women have essential natures that are defined overwhelmingly by the clothes that are appropriate to each on stage. In no extant play from the period does an effeminate man run the risk of transforming into a woman or an especially masculine woman of evolving into a man. Rather, in those instances when a character dresses inappropriately or acts contrary to his or her sex as it is defined by the character's appropriate apparel, the play works to correct the situation.

An extreme instance of such a correction can be found in *Love's Cure, or the Martial Maid* (c. 1606–10), written primarily by John Ford. Lucio is the son of a nobleman, and yet to protect him from the vengeance of a family enemy, he has been raised as a woman and dressed accordingly. His sister, Clara, the martial maid of the title, has for related reasons been raised and dressed as a man. At the start of the play the political waters have shifted, and each becomes free to assume the clothing and customs of his and her sex. However, both characters like the gender roles and clothing in which they have been reared and are unwilling to change.

---

[68] Thomas Laquer, *Making Sex: Body and Gender from the Greeks to Freud* (Cambridge: Harvard University Press, 1990), 63–113.

[69] Janet Adelman provides a survey of the critics and major works of scholarship that forward this notion of sex in Alison Findlay, "Gendering the Stage," in *A Companion to Renaissance Drama*, ed. Arthur F. Kinney (Malden, MA: 2002), 43–4.

[70] Janet Adelman compellingly argues that the one-sex model did not hold much sway in medical texts at the time. Michael Shapiro similarly states that "the prevailing view of Shakespeare's contemporaries were essentialist with regard to gender identity" (40).

Clara continues to be bold and quick to fight, while Lucio remains timorous and attends to cooking and the mending of clothes. When their parents force them to put on clothes appropriate to their sex, they resist the unfamiliar attire. Donning masculine apparel for the first time, Lucio states

> this scurvy sword
> So galls my thigh: I would 't wer burnt: pish, looke,
> This cloak will ne'r keep on: these Boots too hide-bound,
> Make me walk stiff, as if my legs were frozen,
> And my Spurs gingle, like a Morris-dancer:
> Lord, how my head akes with this roguish Hat;
> This masculine attire is most uneasie,
> I am bound up in it: I had rather walk
> In folio, again, loose, like a woman. (2.2.12–20)[71]

Clara's reaction to feminine attire is similar:

> These clothes will never fadge with me: A pox o' this filthy fardingale, this hip hape! Brother, why are women's haunches only limited, confin'd, hoop'd in as it were, with these same scurvy vardingales? (77–9)

The discomfort both characters feel when they attempt to act and dress "properly" seems to suggest that nurture may overcome nature and offers a striking statement in support of the fluidity of gender roles.[72] Much of the rest of the play, however, works toward the point when they will accept the validity of their sex. The difficulty the two have in fitting their apparel and manners to their essential natures serves as a source of comedy as various strategies are brought to bear against them. Ultimately, the two fall in love with partners of the opposite sex and accept the clothes and demeanors appropriate to their true natures so that they may marry. The play fittingly concludes when the gendered expectations of the stage were met. Peter Berek explains, "as in Shakespeare, . . . reestablishing right gender is associated with stabilizing a disordered society."[73] Crediting the power of love, the play subsumes the challenging possibilities of gender fluidity within the conventions of comedy and the theatre.

The rule of the stage was that one's natural apparel asserted the wearer's sex according to the visual codes that maintained at the time. And yet, there are instances in which the clothing appropriate to a character's sex included elements belonging to both men and women. One notable instance can be found in *Macbeth*,

---

[71]   Francis Beaumont and John Fletcher, *Loves Cure, or, The Martial Maid*, in *The Works of Francis Beaumont and John Fletcher*, Vol. 7, ed. A. R. Waller (Cambridge: Cambridge University Press, 1909).

[72]   Jean MacIntyre, *Costumes and Scripts in the Elizabethan Theatres* (Alberta: The University of Alberta Press, 1992), 310.

[73]   Peter Berek, "Cross-Dressing, Gender, and Absolutism in the Beaumont and Fletcher Plays," *SEL* 44.2 (2004): 367.

in which the weird sisters exhibit traits of both masculinity and femininity. Banquo says: "You should be women, / And yet your beards forbid me to interpret / That you are so" (1.3.45–7). The overlapping of both masculine and feminine signifiers works to establish the deviancy or monstrousness of the characters that exhibit them. As Phyllis Rackin has stated, during the high Renaissance, sexual ambiguity came to be understood primarily in terms of the hermaphrodite, "a medical monstrosity or social misfit, an image of perversion or abnormality."[74] Instances of androgyny, therefore, did not threaten to break down essentialist notions of sex on the stage. Instead, they stood out as exceptions that proved the rule.[75]

One particularly exciting exception is the title character in *The Roaring Girl* (1611) by Thomas Middleton and Thomas Dekker. Moll Cutpurse is a woman yet regularly wears both feminine and masculine attire, carries a sword, and proves courageous and capable in a fight. She stands out in early modern drama for the fact that she does not use male apparel as a disguise.[76] Rather, as Jean Howard explains, Moll "adopts male dress deliberately and publicly; and she uses it to signal her freedom from the traditional positions assigned a woman in her culture."[77] Moll proves to be truly androgynous: the apparel of both sexes signify her true nature. Moreover, the play revels in Moll's sartorial androgyny, devoting considerable attention to the clothes she wears. When she first enters, the text notes that Moll wears "a frieze jerkin and a black safeguard," establishing her character according to the visual codes of both masculinity and femininity (a safeguard is an outer skirt or petticoat). Later, a tailor approaches to discuss the clothes that she has ordered, specifically a new pair of breeches. When Sir Alexander fears that his son wishes to marry Moll, he states "I have brought up my son to marry a Dutch slop and a French doublet: a codpiece daughter" (2.2.91–3).[78] The visual semiotics that worked as stable codes delineating masculinity from femininity in other plays are purposefully crossed here.

But Moll does not merely bend the rules governing apparel on the early modern stage. She breaks them entirely. Indeed, she breaks them so thoroughly that she is defined by her deviancy. Before she appears on stage, Moll is described as the exception to the rules governing the visual presentation of masculinity and femininity.

---

[74]   Phyllis Rackin, "Androgyny, Mimesis, and the Marriage of the Boy Heroine on the English Renaissance Stage," *PMLA* 102.1 (1987): 29.

[75]   In *The Winter's Tale*, when Leontes finds himself incapable of controlling Paulina, he calls her a "mankind witch" in an attempt to link her assertiveness with hermaphroditic monstrosity.

[76]   Mary Beth Rose, "Women in Men's Clothing: Apparel and Social Stability in *The Roaring Girl*," *ELR*, 14.3 (1984): 367–91.

[77]   Howard, 436.

[78]   Thomas Middleton and Thomas Dekker, *The Roaring Girl*, ed. Paul Mulholland (Manchester: Manchester University Press, 1987).

> It is a thing
> One knows not how to name: her birth began
> Ere she was all made. 'Tis woman more than man,
> Man more than woman, and—which to none can hap—
> The sun gives her two shadows to one shape; (1.2.128–32)

Again and again, throughout the play, Moll presents herself or is presented by others as deviant for the ways that she exhibits traits of both sexes. In this manner, Moll serves to more firmly establish the normalcy of the visual codes from which she breaks. All of the other characters in the play cling firmly to the visual codes governing sex that maintained in early modern drama. Only Moll presents an exception, and in doing so, she not only fails to change the rules, but actually strengthens them. Importantly, Moll never threatens to undo the heterosexual ideal that is endemic to the division of apparel into masculine and feminine categories. Although desired by men, Moll has no sexual interest in them (or women) and refuses ever to marry stating "I have no humour to marry. I love to lie o' both sides o'th' bed myself" (2.2.36–7). Instead, she works from her particular position to encourage the heterosexual ideal for others, helping the young lovers Sebastian and Mary to overcome the objections of his father and marry. Middleton and Dekker make Moll an exception to society's rules concerning women's behavior and dress but not a fundamental threat to the sex-gender system or the visual codes of the stage.[79]

A potentially more troubling exception to the visual codes of the stage can be found in the epilogue to *As You Like It*. Here, the character playing Rosalind openly embraces gender ambiguity by highlighting the fact that she is, in fact, a male actor in disguise. The speech begins with Rosalind firmly in character, stating "It is not the fashion to see the lady the epilogue." Soon, however, she deconstructs the stability of her feminine identity:

> If I were a woman I would kiss as many of you as had beards that pleas'd me, complexions that lik'd me, and breaths that I defied not; and I am sure, as many as have good beards, or good faces, or sweet breaths, will for my kind offer, when I make curtsy, bid me farewell. (18–23)

With this proclamation, the female Rosalind, who has cross-dressed as a man and then played the part of a woman, reveals that she has another layer underneath, one that is not defined by the apparel she wears but by the male sex of the actor. He then curtseys, offering a feminine close to the production, and the gender of the speaker is rendered completely indeterminate.

Phyllis Rackin has argued that this moment of gender indeterminacy appears in other plays that employ the practice of cross-dressing. In *Shakespeare and Women*, she directly connects it with the scene in *The Two Gentlemen of Verona* in which Julia, disguised as the boy Sebastian, is asked whether (s)he knows Julia. The

---

79   Howard 438.

cross-dressed Julia responds that "he" knows her "[a]lmost as well as I do know myself" (4.4.143). Sebastian then goes on to state that they are so close in height that he was able to wear her gown in a pageant when he played "the woman's part," a claim that Rackin says "might have reminded Shakespeare's original audience that the same boy actor who was now dressed as the boy Sebastian had earlier taken on the 'woman's part' of Julia by wearing her gown."[80] So far, I agree. However, Rackin goes further to state:

> The same combination of layered, cross-gendered impersonation and solicitation of the playgoers' admiration reappears in the Epilogue to *As You Like It*, where the indeterminate gender identity of the cross-dressed heroine is again featured in an advertisement for the players' craft.[81]

However, it is not the "same combination." In *Two Gentlemen*, the craft of the actor is certainly suggested in the lines, but the gender identity of the cross-dressed heroine is not rendered indeterminate. Underneath multiple, discreet layers of identity, the essence of Julia's character is female, defined by the clothes that allow her to reunite romantically with Proteus at the end of the play. Contrarily, in *As You Like It*, it would be impossible for the play to continue beyond the epilogue. Rosalind's female sex has been deconstructed and thrown into question. As a result, all of the relationships predicated upon her being a woman are similarly thrown into doubt. But *As You Like It* is not ruined by Rosalind's proclamation, for it comes after the drama has concluded. It is crucial that Rosalind's proclamation comes in the epilogue. There, it can reveal the actor's body beneath the character's apparel without undermining the integrity of the play to which it is appended. There, it can highlight the male actor's craft without disrupting the visual codes that established the sex of the character in performance. For the rest of the play, as with the rest of early modern English drama, the costumes, not the bodies underneath, were of the essence.

---

[80] Phyllis Rackin, "Shakespeare's Crossdressing Comedies," in *A Companion to Shakespeaere's Works: The Comedies*, eds. Richard Dutton and Jean E. Howard (Malden, MA: Blackwell, 2003), 117–18.

[81] Ibid., 81.

Chapter 2
Social Station

> Runne persently to the Mercers, buy me seuen ells
> of horse flesh colour'd taffata, nine yards of yellow
> sattin, and eight yerds of orenge tawney veluet; then
> runne to the Tailers, the Haberdashers, the Sempsters,
> the Cutlers, the Perfumers, and to all trades whatsoe'r
> that belong to the making vp of a Gentleman.
>
> J. Cooke, *Grene's Tu Quoque* (Sig. D3)[1]

Along with establishing a character's gender, the most immediate and important function costume served on the Shakespearean stage was to assert the wearer's social status in the highly stratified dramatic world of the performance. Historian Keith Wrightson notes that early modern England's predilection to understand itself in terms of social hierarchy is of the first significance, for "it bears witness to the fact that the most fundamental structural characteristic of English society was its high degree of stratification, its distinctive and all-pervasive system of social inequality."[2] As social historians have noted, however, issues of "class," "estates," "degrees," "ranks," and "sorts" were in a state of transition in England at the end of the sixteenth and beginning of the seventeenth centuries.[3] During the previous, medieval period, writers tended to divide the people of England into three "estates": laborers, lords, and priests. Each was defined by its function in the commonwealth. The laborers worked to provide for the land; the lords fought to protect it; and the priests prayed for the salvation of everyone's souls.[4] As we enter the period when the first public theatres opened, however, England was on a slow path toward becoming a class-based system that was only finally complete at the end of the eighteenth century.[5]

The appellation "early modern" highlights this transition from a pre-modern sense of social categories and complicates the ways in which we discuss the issue of one's place in the body politic. Wrightson explains, "in the historical shift from the language of 'estates' to that of 'classes,' then, we have more than a change in the conventional terminology of social description and analysis. We have a

---

[1]   J. Cooke, *Grene's Tu Quoque*, ed. Alan J. Berman (New York: Garland, 1984).

[2]   Keith Wrightson, *English Society, 1580–1680* (New Brunswick, NJ: Rutgers University Press, 1982), 17.

[3]   See Lee Beier, "Social Discourse and the Changing Economy," in *A Companion to Renaissance Drama*, ed. Arthur F. Kinney (Malden, MA: Blackwell, 2002), 50–67.

[4]   Ruth Mohl, *The Three Estates in Medieval and Renaissance Literature* (New York: Columbia University Press, 1933).

[5]   Keith Wrightson, "Estates, Degrees, and Sorts," *History Today* 37.1 (1987): 17.

revolution in the very way in which people conceived of their social world, a conceptual transformation of vital significance in the making of 'modern' society."[6] A discussion of medieval drama would benefit from a consideration of the tripartite division of society that maintained at the time. Similarly, examinations of eighteenth and nineteenth century drama should consider the ways in which class had become crucial to how the English understood themselves. Both approaches, however, are anachronistic to a study of the Shakespearean stage.

The increasing wealth of tradesmen, the English Reformation, and the changing role of the elite nobility upended the older "estates." Instead, for the period reaching from 1567 to 1642, English writing on the topic of social stratification was dominated by a discussion of "degrees." The English no longer divided society based on people's function, opting instead for a system in which they were ranked hierarchically based on social station. With this change, the number of parts into which society was divided increased. For instance, in 1577 William Harrison partitioned the people of England broadly into four "sorts": gentlemen, citizens or burgesses, yeomen, and artificers or laborers.[7] He then further divided each category, establishing who was higher or lower and asserting the notion that identity arises from one's vertically defined allegiances.[8] Gentlemen, for instance, are divided into the "greater sort" (kings, princes, dukes, marquises, earls, viscounts, and barons) and the rest (among whom Harrison lists knights, squires, and "last of all they that are simplie called gentlemen").[9] The critical importance of social stratification to England's sense of itself appears widely in the drama of the period and is set forth nowhere more clearly than in Shakespeare's *Troilus and Cressida*:

> O, when degree is shak'd,
> Which is the ladder of all high designs,
> Then enterprise is sick. How could communities,
> Degrees in schools, and brotherhoods in cities,
> Peaceful commerce from dividable shores,
> The primogenity and due of birth,
> Prerogative of age, crowns, sceptres, laurels,
> But by degree stand in authentic place?
> Take but degree away, untune that string,
> And hark what discord follows. (1.3.101–10)

---

    6   Ibid.

    7   William Harrison, *Harrison's Description of England in Shakespeare's Youth*, ed. Frederick J. Furnivall (London: N. Trübner & Co., 1877), 105.

    8   Jean E. Howard, "Shakespeare, Geography, and the Work of Genre on the Early Modern Stage," *MLQ: Modern Language Quarterly* 64.3 (2003): 308.

    9   Harrison, 106.

The monologue continues on for some time in further support of preserving the integrity of a hierarchical society, making conspicuous the social system that existed both onstage and off.[10]

The centrality of social stratification to England's sense of itself was reflected and reified in the visual culture of the period, particularly in one's choice of apparel. English society broadly maintained that one's clothes ought to accurately reflect one's rank.[11] As Amanda Bailey has noted, status was materially represented and constituted at the time, and apparel was one of the preeminent forms by which individuals experienced and expressed their sense of social value.[12] A duke should be visually distinguishable from a knight, and both should look markedly different from someone who labors for a living. Numerous and diverse forces in England worked to guarantee that citizens dressed in apparel appropriate to their stations: Queen Elizabeth passed numerous sumptuary laws, preachers made excess of apparel the subject of their sermons, and writers frequently excoriated the practice of wearing sumptuous clothing. Of course, many refused to confine themselves to the apparel deemed appropriate to their social station. The frequent royal proclamations passed during Queen Elizabeth's reign (1559, 1562, 1566, 1571, 1574, 1580, 1588, and 1597) justify their own passing by "consydering to what extremityes a great nombre of her subjects are growne by excesse in apparel, both contrary to the lawes of the realm and to the disorder and confusion of the degrees of all states" (issued in 1566).[13] Reviewing the evidence, Ann Jones and Peter Stallybrass conclude that sumptuary laws in England were more honored in the breach than the observance.[14]

The theatres proved to be the one place where the sumptuary laws largely succeeded in determining the apparel that people wore. There, it was essential that the clothes worn by an actor clearly represent his character's social standing.[15] As G. K. Hunter has observed, the early modern stage engaged individuals first and foremost as expressions of their social rank. The *dramatis personae* for plays from the period demonstrates the predilection of the drama to consider people

---

[10]   I do not mean to suggest that the hierarchy was static, unchanging, and unchallenged but merely that it was broadly accepted as a natural part of a well-ordered society. It is worth noting that this monologue is delivered as a plea to restore order.

[11]   R. Malcolm Smuts, "Art and the material culture of majesty in early Stuart England," in *The Stuart Court and Europe: Essays in Politics and Political Culture*, ed. R. Malcolm Smuts (New York: Cambridge University Press, 1996), 91.

[12]   Amanda Bailey, "'Monstrous Manner': Style and the Early Modern Theater," *Criticism* 43.3 (2001): 249.

[13]   Qtd. in Frances Elizabeth Baldwin, *Sumptuary Legislation and Personal Regulation in England* (Baltimore: The Johns Hopkins University Press, 1926), 222.

[14]   Ann Rosalind Jones and Peter Stallybrass, *Renaissance Clothing and the Materials of Memory* (New York: Cambridge University Press, 2000), 188.

[15]   Jean MacIntyre and Garrett P. J. Epp, "'Cloathes Worth All the Rest': Costumes and Properties," in *A New History of Early English Drama*, eds. John D. Cox and David Scott Kastan (New York: Columbia University Press, 1997), 270.

by social status first, moving from King to peasant, and with the women listed separately. Accordingly, plays are populated primarily not by named individuals, but by kings, queens, dukes, counselors, shepherds, citizens, etc.[16] The sumptuary laws, as a consequence of the broad (if ineffectual) attempts to enforce them, constituted a widely understood visual code denoting the social station of the characters appearing on the early modern stage. We can be sure characters dressed according to their degree by looking at the dumb shows that frequently appeared in plays. These performances required that audiences be able to identify on sight such varied characters as King, Queen, Pope, Monk, Doctor of Physic, Nurse, Ambassador, Councilor, Roman Senator, Herald, Nymph, Irishman, and more.[17] Without recourse to dialogue, the characters established their identity onstage immediately and almost entirely from the apparel they wore. For speaking characters, therefore, dialogue did not serve to constitute otherwise blank identities, but rather to modify the identities posited by their social station as it had been established by their apparel and understood by virtue of the sumptuary legislation of the period.

Mention of the sumptuary laws appears in an interlude from the period. In *Godly Queene Hester* (printed in 1561), the character Pride appears poorly arrayed, complaining that Aman has bought up all the good cloth, leaving none for others to buy. Pride further notes that if Aman catches anyone wearing fine clothes, he has them punished for violating the statute of apparel:

> I tell you at a worde, Aman that newe lorde,
> Hathe bought vp all goood clothe,
> And hath as many gownes, as would serue ten townes
> Be ye neuer so lothe:
> And any manne in the towne, doe by him a good gowne,
> He is verye wrothe.
> And wyll hym strayte tell, the statute of apparell,
> Shall teache hym good:
> wherefore by thys daye, I dare not goe gaye.[18]

The sumptuary laws may not have succeeded in controlling what was worn in English society, but they provided a stable referent for the theatres. Accordingly, the costume that an actor wore on stage served to visually establish his character's place in the body politic before an audience that was highly attuned to the specific fabrics and articles of apparel appropriate to particular social stations.

---

[16] G. K. Hunter, "Flatcaps and Bluecoats: Visual Signals on the Elizabethan Stage," *Essays and Studies* 33 (1980): 25–7.

[17] Ibid., 28. Hunter includes a longer list and mentions the plays in which these unspeaking characters appear.

[18] *A New Enterlude of Godly Queene Hester: Edited from the Quarto of 1561*, ed. W. W. Greg. (London: David Nutt, 1904), 16.

The sumptuary laws remained stable referents for the theatres even after they were repealed by parliament in 1604. This results from the fact that parliament's actions had little to do with the widely held belief that one's apparel should accurately reflect one's social station, and much more to do with the political conflict that existed between parliament and the pre-interregnum Stuart monarchs, James I and Charles I. Both kings sought to regulate dress by royal proclamation and both were unsuccessful due to parliament's refusal to encourage the absolutist policy whereby control over clothing would be located entirely in the hands of the monarch (per the workings of royal proclamations).[19] At the late date of 1620, the anonymous author of *Hic Mulier* could still call upon "the powerful statute of apparel [to] lift up his battle-ax and crush the offenders in pieces, so everyone may be known by the true badge of their blood or fortune."[20] Thus, despite the fact that some people did not adhere to the sumptuary laws before 1604 and nobody was legally required to afterwards, English men and women shared a well defined, widely understood set of rules governing apparel.

For the professional stages throughout the early modern period, the sumptuary laws provide the clearest picture of the apparel deemed appropriate to the most socially elite members of society. Queen Elizabeth passed her final sumptuary legislation in 1597. Like those before it, this law specifies the fabrics and apparel that would have visually asserted the social class of the one who wore it.

Evidence from the plays of the period makes it clear that the most elite characters on stage regularly appeared in apparel that would have immediately established their social station. The most obvious instance of this, and one we must consider before we go further into exploring the particulars of the sumptuary laws, is the wearing of crowns. Walking onto the stage, a monarch's social superiority would have been (and continues to be) clear on sight by virtue of his or her crown. However, not all crowns are created equally. Henslowe's diary includes in its inventories listings for three imperial crowns, one plain crown, one ghost crown, and one crown with a sun.[21] The differences between these crowns are significant and would have been noted by early modern viewers, particularly the differences between the imperial crown and the plain crown.

The plain or royal crown was open at the top, with the points aimed upward. It was the crown most frequently worn by the kings of England up to the first half of the reign of Henry VIII. As a part of his separation from the Catholic Church, Henry VIII asserted that England was not merely a kingdom but an empire over which the monarch wields imperial authority. Parliament's 1533 act of Appeals states: "Where by divers sundry old authentic histories and chronicles, it is manifestly declared and expressed that this realm of England is an empire,

---

[19] Reed Benhamou, "The Restraint of Excessive Apparel: England 1337–1604," *Dress* 15 (1989): 32 and Baldwin, 258–60, 263.

[20] *Hic Mulier: or, the Man-Woman* (London, 1620), sig. C1v.

[21] R. A. Foakes, ed., *Henslowe's Diary*, 2nd ed. (New York: Cambridge University Press, 2002), 320–21.

Men's Apparel

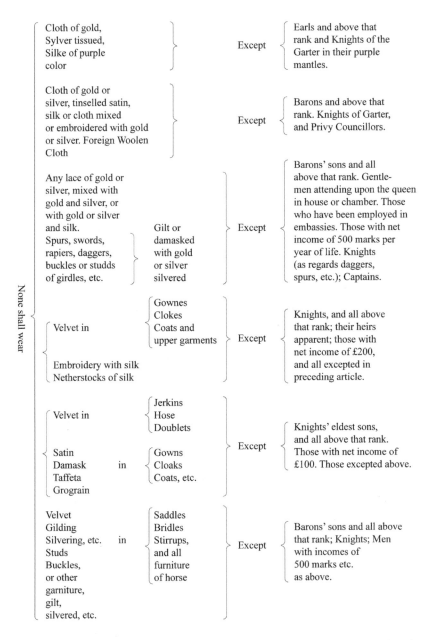

None shall wear

Cloth of gold, Sylver tissued, Silke of purple color		Except	Earls and above that rank and Knights of the Garter in their purple mantles.
Cloth of gold or silver, tinselled satin, silk or cloth mixed or embroidered with gold or silver. Foreign Woolen Cloth		Except	Barons and above that rank. Knights of Garter, and Privy Councillors.
Any lace of gold or silver, mixed with gold and silver, or with gold or silver and silk. Spurs, swords, rapiers, daggers, buckles or studds of girdles, etc.	Gilt or damasked with gold or silver silvered	Except	Barons' sons and all above that rank. Gentlemen attending upon the queen in house or chamber. Those who have been employed in embassies. Those with net income of 500 marks per year of life. Knights (as regards daggers, spurs, etc.); Captains.
Velvet in ... Embroidery with silk Netherstocks of silk	Gownes Clokes Coats and upper garments	Except	Knights, and all above that rank; their heirs apparent; those with net income of £200, and all excepted in preceding article.
Velvet in ... Satin Damask in Taffeta Grograin	Jerkins Hose Doublets ... Gowns Cloaks Coats, etc.	Except	Knights' eldest sons, and all above that rank. Those with net income of £100. Those excepted above.
Velvet Gilding Silvering, etc. in Studs Buckles, or other garniture, gilt, silvered, etc.	Saddles Bridles Stirrups, and all furniture of horse	Except	Barons' sons and all above that rank; Knights; Men with incomes of 500 marks etc. as above.

Fig. 2.1   Queen Elizabeth's 1597 Sumptuary Proclamation, abbreviated presentation.

Women's Apparel

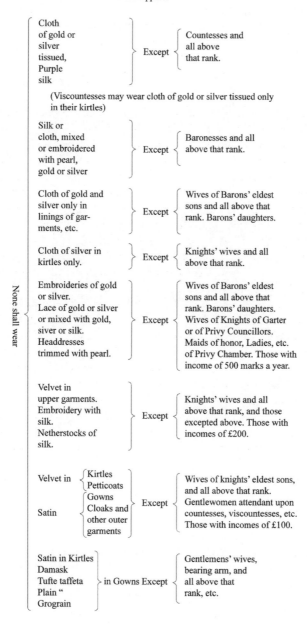

None shall wear

Cloth of gold or silver tissued, Purple silk — Except — Countesses and all above that rank.

(Viscountesses may wear cloth of gold or silver tissued only in their kirtles)

Silk or cloth, mixed or embroidered with pearl, gold or silver — Except — Baronesses and all above that rank.

Cloth of gold and silver only in linings of garments, etc. — Except — Wives of Barons' eldest sons and all above that rank. Barons' daughters.

Cloth of silver in kirtles only. — Except — Knights' wives and all above that rank.

Embroideries of gold or silver. Lace of gold or silver or mixed with gold, siver or silk. Headdresses trimmed with pearl. — Except — Wives of Barons' eldest sons and all above that rank. Barons' daughters. Wives of Knights of Garter or of Privy Councillors. Maids of honor, Ladies, etc. of Privy Chamber. Those with income of 500 marks a year.

Velvet in upper garments. Embroidery with silk. Netherstocks of silk. — Except — Knights' wives and all above that rank, and those excepted above. Those with incomes of £200.

Velvet in { Kirtles Petticoats } Satin { Gowns Cloaks and other outer garments } — Except — Wives of knights' eldest sons, and all above that rank. Gentlewomen attendant upon countesses, viscountesses, etc. Those with incomes of £100.

Satin in Kirtles Damask Tufte taffeta Plain " Grograin — in Gowns Except — Gentlemens' wives, bearing arm, and all above that rank, etc.

Fig. 2.1 (*continued*)

and so hath been accepted in the world, governed by one supreme head and king, having the dignity and royal estate of the imperial crown of the same." With this change in designation, Parliament claimed for England national immunity to Rome's sovereignty as well as imperial status for Henry VIII, which allowed for no superior on earth.[22] Unlike a royal crown, an imperial crown's points meet at the top, forming a dome. By donning such a crown, Henry VIII visually reified the political and religious supremacy that he sought to establish with his policies. Henry's new status was further secured by Parliament in 1534 when it passed the Act of Supremacy, which stated that the king of England was "the only Supreme Head in earth of the Church of England called Anglicana Ecclesia, and shall have and enjoy annexed and united to the imperial Crown of this realm."[23] When Queen Mary assumed the throne of England, she repealed the Act of Supremacy, but continued to wear exclusively an imperial crown, and the monarchs of England have worn one ever since.

Although Henry VIII was the first king of England recognized by Parliament as an Emperor, the imperial crown was worn occasionally by earlier monarchs, starting with Henry V, likely in an attempt to visually assert imperial majesty in the wearer.[24] Late sixteenth and early seventeenth century audiences would have noticed the shape of a crown worn onstage and comprehended the specific meaning it suggested for the wearer. What makes this visual code particularly fascinating is how it was employed in production. Shakespeare's history plays frequently reference the "imperial crown" and "imperial throne" of England. In *2 Henry IV* (1598), when Hal believes his father is dead, he looks upon the crown and observes "My due from thee is this imperial crown" (4.5.41). In *Henry V* (1599), King Henry suggests the specific nature of the crown worn by the actor who plays the part when he lists "the crown imperial" along with the sword, the mace, and other accoutrements of royal ceremony. And in *Richard III* (1592–1593), Queen Elizabeth notes the shape of Richard's crown when she mentions "Th' imperial metal, circling now thy head" (4.4.382). It seems clear that in performance, the majority of Shakespeare's English monarchs wore imperial crowns, despite the fact that the majority of extant images of pre-Henry VIII kings present them appareled in royal crowns, and one of the kings, Henry IV, never wore an imperial crown at all.

The decision to present earlier English monarchs in imperial crowns may have been Shakespeare's alone. Other English history plays from the period offer no textual evidence at all to suggest that the crowns worn in production were imperial

---

[22]   J. J. Scarisbrick, *Henry VIII* (Berkeley and Los Angeles: University of California Press, 1968), 273.

[23]   Ellen Goodman, *The Origins of the Western Legal Tradition: From Thales to the Tudors* (Annandale, NSW: Federation Press, 1995), 298.

[24]   Dale Hoak, "The Iconography of the Crown Imperial," in *Tudor Political Culture*, ed. Dale Hoak (New York: Cambridge University Press, 1995), 59–60. This excellent essay details the history of the imperial crown in England.

instead of royal. The anonymously written play *The Famous Victories of Henry V* (1580s), for instance, mentions crowns over twenty times without referencing England's imperial stature once. It seems likely that the actor playing the king wore a royal crown. Shakespeare, on the other hand, seems to have chosen to dress his Henry in the crown that Queen Elizabeth wears in all of the extant pictures which present her with one. In this way, Shakespeare visually presents England's greatest military hero as the imperial predecessor to the current monarch. It is worth noting that one history play by Shakespeare that makes no mention of an imperial crown or England's imperial stature is *Richard II*, suggesting that the royal crown Richard wears and loses is fundamentally different from the imperial crown worn by the monarch that currently held the throne.[25]

Next to the crown, purple silk was the special purview of the most elite members of society and would have appeared only on the most aristocratic of characters on the stage. It is important to note that at the time, the appellations "purple," "scarlet," and "crimson" were sometimes used indiscriminately to refer to a range of colors between what we consider to be dark purple and bright red today. This explains references to "purple blood," "scarlet blood," or "crimson blood" that appeared commonly in plays and writings at the time. The blood did not change color, but the terms used to signify it varied. Thus, the royal scarlet of the English court fell within the guidelines of the color purple mentioned in sumptuary legislation and could legally be worn only by those who were earls or above, along with members of the Knights of the Garter in their mantles. Since the early modern stage frequently presented members of the aristocracy, it is not surprising that numerous examples of purple, scarlet, and crimson silks appear in Henslowe's diary. In almost every instance, the material is accentuated by opulent accessories that include gold or silver to highlight the social superiority of the wearer. For example:

- A purple velvett cut in dimonds Lact & spangels
- A scarlett cloke wth ij brode gould Laces: w^t gould buttens of the sam downe the sids
- A scarlett cloke Layde [the] downe w^t silver Lace and silver buttens
- A crimosin Robe strypt w^t gould fact w^t ermin[26]

Made of lavishly expensive material and richly adorned, the particular items must have been beautiful to behold on the English stage. When Orazio Busino, the Chaplain of the Venetian Embassy, attended the theatre in 1617, he could not understand the English the actors spoke, but he enjoyed gazing on the sumptuous

---

[25] History supports Shakespeare's decision to present Richard II in a royal crown. However, since the character Henry IV appears onstage in an imperial crown (who never actually wore one), it seems likely that Shakespeare was more interested in how he wished his kings to appear than in historical accuracy.

[26] Foakes, 291–2.

costumes of the actors.[27] To the English audience the theatrical apparel did not merely suggest magnificence and affluence, but also the wearer's particular social station.

In light of the high cost of clothing at the time, it is likely that the acting companies worked primarily to establish the illusion of the apparel appropriate to the elite nobility and did not make a regular practice of purchasing the exorbitantly expensive materials mentioned in the sumptuary laws, particularly those near the top of the social hierarchy. Dekker's *The Gull's Hornbook* (published in 1609) notes that by sitting on the stage, one may "examine the play-suits' lace, and perhaps win wagers upon laying tis copper."[28] Copper lace was widely used in the theatre to imitate gold lace either to embellish clothing or to make old clothes seem new.[29] And yet, the two property lists that survive from the period, Henslowe's 1598 entry into his diary and Edward Alleyn's undated catalog of theatrical apparel, show that the Admiral's Men also had a large collection of very expensive clothing that went beyond the illusion of sumptuousness. Jones and Stallybrass explain the presence of exorbitant apparel in theatre companies by noting the numerous, tight connections that existed between the theatre and the clothing industry.[30] Another way that expensive apparel made its way to the theatres was recorded in 1599 by Thomas Platter:

> it is the English usage for eminent lords or knights at their decease to bequeth and leave almost the best of their clothes to their serving men, which it is unseemly for the latter to wear, so that they offer them for sale for a small sum to the actors.[31]

Theatrical companies spent a great deal of money and effort working to expand the variety and quality of apparel they could present onstage.[32]

Particularly expensive and widely prohibited, purple silk could legally be worn only by those of at least the rank of Earl and also in the mantle of a Knight of the Garter. For the Knights of the Garter, the purple mantle was part of the visual presentation that marked and defined their membership in England's most prestigious knightly fraternity. A Knight of the Garter could be merely a knight or baron and thus be otherwise barred from wearing purple silk. For such an individual, the color and material of his mantle would signify greater nobility.

---

[27]   Qtd. in A. M. Nagler, *A Source Book in Theatrical History* (New York: Dover, 1952), 132–3.

[28]   Thomas Dekker, *The Guls Horne-booke* (London, 1609), 28–9.

[29]   Jones and Stallybrass, 190–91.

[30]   Ibid., 177–8.

[31]   Thomas Platter, *Thomas Platter's Travels in England*, trans. Clare Williams (London: Jonathan Cape, 1959), 167.

[32]   Jean MacIntyre considers the growing costume stores of the various theatrical companies in *Costumes and Scripts in the Elizabethan Theatres* (Alberta: University of Alberta Press, 1992).

Knights of the Garter additionally would have been recognizable by their *George* and by the distinctive garter from which the order derived its name. The George was a pendant that hung from a *collar* or chain of office. The pendant was made of gold and presented the figure of St. George fighting the dragon. The garter, which was made of blue velvet and worn below the left knee, was inscribed in gold letters with the phrase "Honi soit qui mal y pense," which translates as "Shame upon him who thinks evil of it." The order of the Knights of the Garter, Harrison states, was begun by King Edward III "after he had gained manie notable victories, taken John of France, and king James of Scotland (and kept them both prisoners in the Tower of London at one time) expelled king Henrie of Castile the bastard out of his realme, and restored *Don Petro* unto it (by the helpe of the prince of Wales and duke of Aquitaine his eldest sonne called the Blacke prince)."[33] The traits of nobility and valor associated with the Knights of the Garter were visually signified in the specific items that denoted the order.

We can say with certainty that the accoutrements of the Order of the Garter appeared on the English stage. Having seen Shakespeare's *Henry VIII* in 1613, Edmund Bacon remarked in a letter that the play was "set forth with many extraordinary Circumstances of Pomp and Majesty, even to the matting of the Stage; the Knights of the Order, with their Georges and Garter, the Guards with their embroidered Coats, and the like."[34] The assocations that attended the apparel worn by the Knights of the Garter are detailed in Samuel Rowley's *When You See Me You Know Me* (1605). As Prince Edward prepares to meet the Emperor and bestow upon him membership in the Knights of the Garter, King Henry enumerates the traits that make the Emperor worthy of such an honor:

> The Prince of *Wales* shall follow presently,
> And with our George and coller of estate,
> Present him with the order of the Garter:
> Great *Maximilian* his progenitour,
> Vpon his breast did weare the English Crosse,
> And vnderneath our Standerd marcht in armes,
> Receiving pay for all his warlike hoste;
> And *Charles* with knighthood shall be honored. (2724–31)[35]

The Emperor deserves to receive the "George and coller of estate" of the Knights of the Garter out of respect for the nobility and distinctively English courage of his line. The play suggests, likely to the London audience's approbation, that courage itself is an English trait. Talbot, in Shakespeare's *1 Henry VI* more fully explicates

---

[33] Harrison, 116.

[34] Qtd. in Andrew Gurr, *Playgoing in Shakespeare's London* (Cambridge: Cambridge University Press, 1987), 226–7.

[35] Samuel Rowley, *When You See Me You Know Me* (London, 1605).

the notion that the Knights of the Garter are Englishmen defined by their nobility, honor, and military prowess[36]:

> When first this order was ordain'd, my lords,
> Knights of the Garter were of noble birth,
> Valiant and virtuous, full of haughty courage,
> Such as were grown to credit by the wars;
> Not fearing death, nor shrinking for distress,
> But always resolute in most extremes. (4.1.33–8)

In English society and particularly in performance on the London stage, the traits Talbot highlights (English nobility, valor, virtue, and courage) were tightly grafted to the garter, George, and mantle that visually manifested one's membership in the Order of the Garter. The occasion upon which Talbot enumerates the key characteristics of a Knight of the Garter is the banishing of Falstaff (the historical Sir John Fastolf) from its membership for cowardice.[37] The manner in which Falstaff is banished deserves note. Accusing Falstaff of fleeing his post before battle, Talbot strips from him his garter, saying: "Shame to the Duke of Burgundy and thee! / I vow'd, base knight, when I did meet thee next, / To tear the Garter from thy craven's leg" (4.1.13–15). In this situation, Talbot's act of taking the garter from Falstaff does not *represent* his banishment from the Order of the Garter, but is, in fact, the act of banishment itself. The apparel, on a profound level, embodies the honor of a Knight of the Garter. When Falstaff is found deficient in the honor defined by his apparel, the action of the play works to divorce and dissociate him from it. Being stripped of his apparel, therefore, is not a representational act for Falstaff, but a dramatic, transformational one. Because the garter was understood to tie the wearer to notions of English nobility and English courage, it follows that once the wearer was banished from the order, he could not remain in the kingdom. Accordingly, after Talbot seizes Falstaff's garter, the King states "Stain to thy countrymen, thou hear'st thy doom! / Be packing therefore, thou that wast a knight; / Henceforth we banish thee, on pain of death" (4.1.45–7). On the English stage, the accoutrements of the Knights of the Garter were to be worn only by Englishmen who had the nobility and valor to deserve them. Those who did not would literally be divested of them through the course of the play and severed from English society. In this manner, the drama served to effect a sense of social justice through its presentation and treatment of costume.

---

[36]   The Order of the Garter carries with it a military dimension that hails back to Edward III who drew the majority of its members from among the nobility that fought with him at Crécy. For more, see Giorgio Melchiori, *Shakespeare's Garter Plays:* Edward III *to* Merry Wives of Windsor (Newark: University of Delaware Press, 1994), 115.

[37]   It is important to note that the Falstaff of *1 Henry VI* is not the same person as the fat, jolly knight from *1 & 2 Henry IV*. For a discussion of the use of the name, see Jean E. Howard's introduction to *1 Henry IV* in *The Norton Shakespeare*, 1184.

The critical importance of and connection between one's apparel and one's identity was acknowledged by the elite characters who appeared on the early modern stage. It is for this reason in *Richard III* (1592–1593) that Richard appeals to his noble and royal accoutrements when he is beset by Queen Elizabeth: "Now by my George, my Garter and my crown—" (4.4.366). Naming the items, Richard attempts to invoke on his behalf the English valor, honor, and royalty attached to them in the popular imagination. Elizabeth's response demonstrates that she understands the significance of Richard's apparel to his legitimacy and subverts his efforts:

Q. ELIZABETH: Profan'd, dishonor'd, and the third usurp'd.
K. RICHARD: I swear—
Q. ELIZABETH: By nothing, for this is no oath:
Thy George, prafan'd hath lost his lordly honor;
Thy Garter, blemish'd, pawn'd his knightly virtue;
Thy crown, usurp'd, disgrac'd his kingly glory. (4.4.367–71)

If Richard could ally himself to his attire, he could rule England successfully. Elizabeth, however, highlights the disconnect between the sartorial identity Richard has attempted to establish for himself and the one dictated by his actions. Once upon a time, Richard's personage was suitable to the George and the garter. By usurping the crown, however, he proved himself unqualified to wear the George, the garter, or the crown. The play then fittingly proceeds toward Richard's death at which time he is bereft of the apparel he was not fit to wear.

Costume figures similarly in *Macbeth* (1606). As Cleanth Brooks has noted, it is Macbeth's decision to wear clothes that sit upon him like poorly fitting garments that marks his improper assumption of rank in the play. Brooks writes "these are not *his* garments; in Macbeth's case they are actually stolen garments. Macbeth is uncomfortable in them because he is continually conscious of the fact that they do not belong to him."[38] A principal proponent of New Criticism, Brooks is primarily interested in the metaphor of apparel, but on the early modern stage, Macbeth's clothes would have served as a visible indication of his original social status and then his assumed rank. By seizing the crown and royal apparel when he has only recently donned the clothes of the Thane of Cowdor, Macbeth shows himself to be costumed inappropriately. Cathness mentions Macbeth's attempt to wear clothes that are beyond the scope of his mandate, saying "He cannot buckle his distemper'd cause within the belt of rule." Angus similarly states "Now does he feel his title hang loose about him, like a giant's robe upon a dwarfish thief" (5.2.15–22). Macbeth's attempt to dress outside his station is contained by the conventions of tragedy which makes him pay for his transgression with his life.

Marlowe's *Tamburlaine* provides further evidence of the ineluctable connection that existed on the English stage between character identity and the apparel one

---

[38] Cleanth Brooks, *The Well Wrought Urn: Studies in the Structure of Poetry* (New York: Harcourt, Brace, 1947), 34.

wears. The play begins with a discussion between Mycetes, the incompetent King of Persia and his attendants. Mycetes is described as a man "At whose birth-day Cynthia with Saturn joined, and Jove, the Sun, and Mercury denied to shed their influence" (1.1.13–5).[39] He is a weak, witless, indecisive king who wears the crown as a consequence of his royal birth, not because of noble worth. In performance, his character would not have been understood as weak in spite of his royal apparel but in juxtaposition with it.

Mycetes's fate is determined by his unworthiness to wear the clothes in which he appears on stage. Decked in the apparel of a king and speaking with the uncertainty of a servant, Mycetes is doomed to fall by virtue of the irreconcilable contradictions he encompasses. Like Richard III, he appeals to his royal attire as a source of his authority, as if the apparel a man wore alone could assert his nobility. When he is openly antagonized by his brother, Mycetes swears upon the greatness of his royal accoutrements that he shall have vengeance:

> MYCETES: Well, here I swear by this my royal seat—
> COSROE: You may do well to kiss it then.
> MYCETES:—Embossed with silk as best beseems my state,
> To be revenged for these contemptuous words. (1.1.97–100)

Wrongly assuming his clothes and accoutrements themselves contain royal puissance, the effete king attempts to draw on their majesty. Mycetes's appeal makes sense in light of the sumptuary laws that dictated that silk be worn only by the nobility. Although the action of *Tamburlaine* is set far from England and in the distant past, the play adheres to the visual codes of the time and place in which it was first performed. The opulent fabric Mycetes wears and that which covers his royal seat ought to mirror the royal worth of the man who employs it. By making special note of his silk accoutrement, Mycetes attempts to establish his royal authority. Instead, he merely highlights his inability, both figuratively and literally, to fit his station.

Quite the reverse, Tamburlaine enters upon the stage in the clothes of a shepherd. The specific clothes that would denote him as a shepherd are difficult to determine, but he probably wore simple, loose-fitting, rustic clothes made of wool and carried a shepherd's staff with a hook at the top such as those which are nearly ubiquitous in the extant images of shepherds from the period.[40] Most likely, Tamburlaine's occupation would have been clear to the audience when his apparel was first seen. And, just as Mycetes would have been understood according to the way his royal apparel contrasted with his diffident demeanor, so would

---

[39] Christopher Marlowe, *Tamburlaine* The Revels Edition, ed. J. S. Cunningham (New York: Manchester University Press, 1981).

[40] For some examples, see Phillis Cunnington and Catherine Lucas, *Occupational Costume in England from the Eleventh Century to 1914* (New York: Barnes and Noble, 1967), 23, 26, 30.

Tamburlaine's identity have been known according to the way his base clothing failed to match his imperial bearing. He states:

> I am a lord, for so my deeds shall prove,
> And yet a shepherd by my parentage.
> But lady [Zenocrate], this fair face and heavenly hue
> Must grace his bed that conquers Asia
> And means to be a terror to the world,
> Measuring the limits of his empery
> By east and west as Phoebus doth his course.
> Lie here, ye weeds that I disdain to wear!
> This complete armour and this curtle-axe
> Are adjuncts more beseeming Tamburlaine. (1.2.34–443)

Tamburlaine's transformation from shepherd to warrior and from commoner to nobleman occurs visually before the spectators. Jean MacIntyre has determined that full armor was most likely depicted onstage by the wearing of a *gorget*, a steel collar designed to protect the neck, and Tamburlaine likely donned one when he took up his cutlass and embraced his imperial potential.[41] Despite the power of Marlowe's mighty line, the dialogue that attends Tamburlaine's rise in status serves primarily to add emphasis to an aspect of the action that is intended to be seen and performed, and not merely heard.

When Tamburlaine and Mycetes meet on the field of battle, their contest appropriately centers on an article of clothing, Mycetes's crown. In this encounter, as the action rights what was previously wrong, the importance of costume to the fashioning of identity becomes central: Mycetes was born to the crown but lacks the inner worth that ought to accompany royal ancestry and Tamburlaine was born a shepherd but has imperial merit. Fearful that all of Tamburlaine's soldiers hunt the Persian King, Mycetes attempts to hide his crown so that he will be safe. Only when the battle is over will he risk retrieving it: "For kings are clouts [targets] that every man shoots at, our crown the pin [bull's-eye] that thousands seek to cleave; therefore in policy I think it good to hide it close . . . So shall not I be known, or if I be, they cannot take away my crown from me" (2.54.10–4). Mycetes believes that the crown itself holds the authority of the monarch and hopes that he can conceal it for a time and recover it later.

In early modern English drama, apparel in general and crowns specifically do not function as Mycetes thinks they do. Crowns are articles of clothing appropriate only to characters suitable to their worth. Those who are not worthy might wear one for a time, but eventually it will be struck from their head. Shakespeare's Richard II loses his throne because he is unworthy to wear the crown. As Alan Downer notes, in *Richard II*, "the visual symbolic exchange of the crown" from Richard II to Bolingbrook "gathers up, focuses and pictorially represents the downfall of a man whose nature was ill-suited to kingship, and who has to some extent come to

---

[41]   MacIntyre, 166.

realize the fact." [42] Tamburlaine understands the nature of this particular article of apparel. Mycetes, on the other hand, believes the physical crown and his title alone carry the power of his monarchy. Thus, when Tamburlaine threatens him, Mycetes states that he is the king and demands the respect that ought to accompany his title and apparel. Rather than simply take the crown, however, Tamburlaine lets Mycetes keep it until the time is right to simultaneously seize the physical crown and its metonymical extension, the throne of Persia: "Here, take it for a while, I lend it thee, till I may see thee hemmed with armed men. Then shalt thou see me pull it from thy head: thou art no match for mighty Tamburlaine" (2.4.38–41). Mycetes, unaware that crowns cling to those worthy of wearing them, is surprised that Tamburlaine did not simply pilfer his: "O gods, is this Tamburlaine the thief? I marvel much he stole it not away" (2.4.42–3). Tamburlaine knows that a crown cannot be kept if it is stolen. Its royal signification demands that the actions by which one obtains the crown are equal to its inherent worth.

Theatrical apparel prompted action on the early modern stage as it worked to find an appropriate wearer or separate itself from an unsuitable one. The crown that typically suggests greatness and royalty is an embarrassment when worn by Mycetes and demands the action that transfers it to an apposite master. When it attaches to Tamburlaine, it suits the individual and can remain in place. Tamburlaine's later apparel follows this notion of costume. After transferring from shepherd's clothing into armor, we know from Henslowe's diary, that he eventually puts on "Tamberlanes breches of crymson vellvet" and "Tamberlynes cotte with coper lace." [43] These clothes, including purple silk and the semblance of gold lace, fit the character of one who has achieved the most elevated rank in early modern English society. Visually, then, the play *Tamburlaine* proceeds from the point where the eponymous hero wears the apparel of the lowest commoner to the point where he appears in the clothes deemed in England to be the most sumptuous, elite apparel possible.

The fact that actors regularly appeared onstage in clothing that was far beyond their social station has led Amanda Bailey to conclude that the theatre was the site of significant social transgression: "By celebrating the profane logic of the marketplace rather than the dictates of established social codes, the theater promoted an ethos of irreverent conspicuous consumption." [44] David Scott Kastan has similarly argued that "the constitutive role-playing of the theater demystifies the idealization of the social order that the ideology of degree would produce. The successful counterfeiting of social rank raises the unnerving possibility that social rank is a counterfeit." [45] And yet, this is not necessarily the case. The theatre, far more than the rest of society, respected the social semiotics whereby the audience could understand the characters on sight. Although the actors wore

[42]   Alan S. Downer, "The Life of Our Design," *Hudson Review* 2 (1949): 251.

[43]   Foakes, 321–2.

[44]   Bailey, "Monstrous" 252.

[45]   David Scott Kastan, *Shakespeare After Theory* (London: Routledge, 1999), 154–5.

apparel on stage that was outside the realm of their social station, the characters they played carefully observed the dictates of social decorum. Moreover, those who failed to follow the dictates of social decorum were most often punished for their transgression. Thus, within the walls of the playhouses, social order was observed even more carefully than it typically was in normative society. And if an actor walked beyond the walls of the playhouse in his costume, he left himself vulnerable both to punishment for failing to obey the sumptuary laws and to a stiff fine for breaking the strict rules of the theatrical companies that forbid actors from leaving with their theatrical apparel.[46] Rather than suggesting that social rank is a counterfeit, it is more likely that the theatres worked as a conservative force, forwarding and bolstering the notion in England that particular apparel was the purview of specific social stations.

Despite the likelihood that a noble character's social station would have been clear when seen on stage in the late sixteenth and early seventeenth centuries, it becomes more difficult to determine the precise fabrics and articles of apparel worn to depict one's degree as we proceed down the social ladder. Crowns along with purple, scarlet, and crimson silk were typically worn to portray monarchs, dukes, marquises, and earls, but a wide range of silk fabrics and colors were employed for the array of noblemen that populated the early modern stage. Henslowe's diary lists silk, satin, damask, sarcenet, taffeta, and velvet items of a variety of colors that sumptuary legislation states would have been appropriate to members of the lesser nobility. It is certain that barons, viscounts, and knights appeared in the opulent fabrics appropriate to noblemen but greater specificity regarding how each rank differed visually from the other is difficult to establish.

Where we can again assert what was worn with some certainty is with swords. By the time the public theatres opened in England, it was widely maintained that swords could be worn only by those whose rank was no lower than knight or gentleman. The origin of this legislation dates to Edward III's sumptuary statute of 1363. Interestingly enough, as Frank Whigham has noted, this legislation does not actually mention the wearing of the sword.[47] And yet, from this beginning, the notion that swords were the province solely of gentlemen was embraced in the English imagination and found articulation on the stage. In the anonymously written *Arden of Faversham* (1588), when the low-born Mosby threatens the gentleman Arden with a sword, Arden swiftly takes it from him, citing the sumptuary law that prohibits the meaner sort from wearing them:

So, sirrah, you may not wear a sword!
The statute makes against artificers.
I warrant that I do. Now use your bodkin,

[46] *Henslowe Papers*, eds. Walter W. Greg, London: A. H. Bullen, 1907, 125.

[47] Frank Whigham, *Seizures of the Will in Early Modern English Drama* (New York: Cambridge University Press, 1996), 248. Also see Frank Whigham, *Ambition and Privilege: The Social Tropes of Elizabethan Courtesy Theory* (Berkeley : University of California Press, 1984), 155–69.

Your Spanish needle, and your pressing iron,
For this shall go with me. (1.310–14)[48]

Mosby wears his sword in an attempt to assert that he is a gentleman, but he
lacks the inner worth that warrants the outward show. Arden, on the other hand,
states "I am by birth a gentleman of blood" (1.36) and confirms his nobility by
courageously seizing Mosby's sword.[49] Arden's insulting suggestion that Mosby
limit himself to using a bodkin, needle, and pressing iron makes conspicuous and
contrasts the visual signs suitable to those who are born to labor for a living and
those who are of gentle birth. Much as the crown was appropriate only to the
wearer who demonstrated kingly merit, so could a sword only be worn by one
whom the play deemed to be truly a gentleman. Although Mosby could put on a
sword, he does not have the nobility, courage, and skill that would allow him to
keep it.

Because swords were the appropriate accoutrement to a gentleman, in *Twelfth
Night* (1601–1602), the conspicuously ignoble Sir Andrew Aguecheek is most
comical when he is forced into a duel. Sir Andrew proves himself undeserving
of his noble title upon his first entrance in the play, after Sir Toby Belch urges
him to woo the chambermaid Maria.[50] When Sir Andrew withdraws in failure,
Sir Toby says "And thou let part so, Sir Andrew, would thou mightst never draw
sword again" (1.3.61–2). Shakespeare's audience likely laughed at the phallic
implications of Sir Toby's statement. But they also would have understood the
sword and knighthood to be tightly grafted to one another. Accordingly, when Sir
Toby challenges Sir Andrew's right to draw the martial instrument, he questions his
birth and worth. In this way Sir Toby reifies and plays upon the connection that was
understood to exist at the time between the sword and phallic, masculine power.
The knight, who has the legal right to bear a sword, stands as an embodiment of
masculinity and becomes an appropriate object of ridicule when he falls far short
of the culture's expectations. Later in the play, after Sir Andrew has proven ever
more clearly that he does not deserve the title of knight, comedy is taken to the
extreme by pitting him in a duel against the cross-dressed Viola. Since the sword
is the appropriate weapon of the masculine knight, one can fall no lower than to
prove as poor in its usage as a woman.

Along with the sword, silk also served to signify gentility and nobleness on
the Shakespearean stage and in English society. Expensive, finely-crafted, and
ill suited to manual labor, silk was incompatible with the individual who worked
for a living. Sumptuary laws were unequivocal in their assertion that silk was to

---

[48]   *The Tragedy of Master Arden of Faversham*, ed. Martin White (London: A & C
Black, 1990).

[49]   Mihoko Suzuki notes that despite Arden's gentle birth, it is his marriage to Alice
that has provided him the majority of his fortune in "Gender, Class, and the Social Order in
Late Elizabethan Drama," *Theatre Journal* 44 (1992): 34.

[50]   Ibid., 39.

be worn by none but gentlemen and gentlewomen.[51] It is for this reason in *Arden of Faversham* that, in addition to taking away Mosby's sword, Arden begrudges how he "bravely jets it in his silken gown" (1.30). Born a commoner, Mosby is not fit to wear silk clothing. It follows that his efforts to keep his fine apparel and improve his financial situation (by courting a married woman and murdering Arden) contribute to his downfall. The silk clothing visually establishes Mosby's inappropriate pursuit of wealth, and the action of the play works to correct it.

The stable nature of silk as a signifier for gentility allowed dramatists of the period to reference it to distinguish between the common and the gentle. The quote that begins this chapter provides a clear example. In J. Cooke's *Greene's Tu Quoque or, The Cittie Gallant* (1611–1612), when the servant Bubbles comes upon a great fortune and takes it upon himself to become a gentleman, he does so first by purchasing the accoutrements appropriate to his ambition: taffeta, satin, and velvet. M. Channing Linthicum has identified a wide variety of silks that appeared in the plays and writing of the period: bodkin, tabine, tinsel, tissue, cypress, damask, plush, sarcenet, satin, taffeta, and velvet.[52] Each was deemed the province of gentility and would have been noted when worn by someone of inappropriate social station. Previously a servant, Bubble clearly is not fit to possess his newfound wealth. He has no noble traits and was not raised in wealth, but only lately inherited it from his uncle. The action of the play therefore works to divest Bubble of his money. When this happens and Bubble finds himself deeply in debt, he is able to save himself only by falling upon the mercy of his former master Staines. The action of the play then corrects Bubble's sartorial impropriety when Staines demands that he put on his former attire and accept his proper place in society.

> STA: Looke sir, heere is your livery,
> If you can put off all your former pride,
> And put on this with that humilitie
> That you first wore it, I will pay your debts,
> Free you of all incombrances,

---

[51] Queen Elizabeth's 1588 proclamation states:

ᴵtem, that no man under the said degrees [below the level of knight], saving such gentlemen as may dispend in yearly revenues as it is aforesaid £20 above all charges, shall wear any manner of silk in any apparel of his body, or of his horse or mule, except it be satin, taffeta, sarcenet, or damask in his doublet or coif, and camlet in his sleeveless jackets, or points, laces, or garters made in England or Wales.

Item, that no person under the same degrees, saving such as may dispend £5 by the year as is aforesaid above all charges, shall wear any silk in his doublets or jackets, nor any thing made out of the realm, saving camlet in their doublets and jackets.

Paul L. Hughes and James F. Larkin, *Tudor Royal Proclamations*, Vol. 3 (New Haven: Yale University Press, 1969), 5.

[52] M. Channing Linthicum, *Costume in the Drama of Shakespeare and His Contemporaries* (New York: Russell & Russell, 1963), 110–27.

And take you againe into my service.
BUBBLE: Tenter-hooke let mee goe, I will take his worships offer without
wages, rather then come into your clutches againe; a man in a blew coate may
haue some colour for his knauery, in the Counter he can haue none. (14.2893–
2902).[53]

Bubble was deemed unfit by the social order of the drama to be a gentleman, and
it is only after he commits to wearing the apparel of a servant that he can avoid
incarceration. It should be noted that *Greene's Tu Quoque* was first performed
at least seven years after the sumptuary laws were repealed in England. Legally,
Bubble could have continued to wear his silk apparel. According to the visual
codes of the theatre at the time, however, silk was only to be worn by gentlemen,
and Bubble needed to change his clothing to enjoy the play's happy ending.

It is because swords and silk belonged appropriately only to gentlemen that
Shakespeare's Sir John Falstaff is the ideal butt of comedy. As a knight, Falstaff
appeared on stage in fine apparel and wearing a sword. Taken on their own, this
attire signified to the English audience the nobility and courage that afforded
one the legal right to wear such clothing. In performance, however, this apparel
was juxtaposed with Falstaff's fundamentally diametrical character. On sight,
Falstaff's famous girth would have challenged the noble worth of the clothing that
attempted to restrain his enormous belly. In *1 Henry IV*, Bardolph says: "Why, you
are so fat, Sir John, that you must needs be out of all compass, out of all reasonable
compass, Sir John" (3.3.21–3). Bardolph's repetition of Falstaff's honorary "Sir"
underscores the speciousness of his title when it is coupled with the size of the
knight's stomach. Of course, Falstaff's dereliction of nobility only starts with too
much eating. He is also chronically lazy, a devoted drunk, one who habitually
visits prostitutes, and, most importantly, a coward, i.e., one who is determinedly
unfit to use his sword. For his transgressions against the cultural expectations of his
noble apparel, he is repeatedly ridiculed and humiliated. And yet, again and again
Falstaff manages to avoid being divested of his rank and its attendant sartorial
signifiers. Consequently, much of Falstaff's comedy in *1 Henry IV*, *2 Henry IV*,
and *The Merry Wives of Windsor* derives from the audience's continually deferred
question: when will he finally pay for his failure to live up to the expectations of
his sword and silk apparel and be bereft of them?

The stability of the sword and silk as signifiers for gentility throughout the
period does not mean that they were always employed in the same way or in a
simple manner. Because silk was understood on sight to belong exclusively to the
gentlemen and gentlewomen deemed worthy of wearing it, plays from the period
were able to employ the visual code in a variety of ways to negotiate complex
social issues of immediate significance. In *Eastward Ho!* (1605), co-written by
George Chapman, Ben Jonson, and John Marston, the languages of class and cloth
seem at first to intermingle easily and along conventional lines. The apprentice

---

[53]   J. Cooke, *Greene's Tu Quoque or, The Cittie Gallant*, ed. Alan J. Berman (New York
& London: Garland, 1984).

Golding loves his master's younger daughter Mildred and wishes to marry her but is concerned that she will refuse because her older sister is engaged to marry a knight. When Golding approaches Mildred with his romantic intentions, her response indicates the play's conservative politics regarding the mixing of the classes:

> GOLDING: But is it possible, that you seeing your sister preferred to the bed of a knight, should contain your affections in the arms of a prentice?
> MILDRED: I had rather make up the garment of my affections in some of the same piece, then like a fool wear gowns of two colours, or mix sackcloth with satin. (2.1.57–63)[54]

Mildred is the younger daughter of a wealthy goldsmith, Master William Touchstone. Despite her father's money, however, Mildred is earmarked for marriage to a commoner by virtue of being the younger child of a gentleman. Golding is similarly the younger child of a gentleman and also embraces his social station as a commoner. The play rewards their decision to embrace sackcloth and renounce satin by quickly promoting Golding to alderman's deputy. Like *Greene's Tu Quoque*, *Eastward Ho!* was also performed after the legal prohibition against the wearing of silk had been repealed—Golding and Mildred could legally wear satin in their apparel. Instead, in their dialogue here and in the apparel they no doubt wore in production, the two choose the cloth appropriate to their base social status and receive social and pecuniary approbation for doing so. In this way, the play works to tighten the connection between one's social station and the apparel one wears.

The play pursues its conservative politics further by strategically deploying fine apparel onto characters whom the play ultimately deems unworthy of wearing them. Quicksilver, like Golding, is an apprentice and the second son of a gentleman. At the start of the play he appears like a gallant in a cloak under which he wears "his hat, pumps, short sword and dagger, and a Racket," and is only identified as an apprentice in dialogue by Touchstone who rebukes him for his apparel. But Quicksilver defends his decision to appear in fine clothing, saying "my mother's a gentlewoman: and my father a justice of peace, and of quorum; and though I am a younger brother and a prentice, yet I hope I am my father's son" (1.1.26–9). The play's position on the issue is quickly made clear: Quicksilver is not a true gentleman, regardless of his parentage. Early on, Quicksilver tries to convince Golding to join him in his revelry and renounce a life of labor for a life of leisure. When Golding refuses, Quicksilver becomes angry and threatens to draw his sword. Golding then proves Quicksilver's commonness by physically restraining him and saying "in soft terms ye are a cowardly bragging boy; I'll ha' you whipped" (1.1.154–5). As in *Arden of Faversham*, Quicksilver's inability to employ his sword reflects his unworthiness to wear it. It logically follows that the

---

[54] George Chapman, Ben Jonson, and John Marston, *Eastward Ho!*, ed. R. W. Van Fossen (Manchester: Manchester University Press, 1979).

rest of the play sees him incrementally divested of his sword and fine apparel until finally he appears in rags and bemoans his decision to pursue a lifestyle beyond the dictates of his social station.[55]

Eastward Ho! presents its most complex use of apparel, the costuming of Sir Petronel Flash, to proffer its most reactionary view of social station. As a knight, Petronel was permitted and actually expected to appear in silk and wearing a sword. The play, however, sees him stripped of his fine clothing and accoutrements until he wears rags and is arrested as a masterless man. This seemingly radical break with the connection between social station and apparel actually further reveals the play's conservative politics as well as its determination to make one's outside accurately reflect one's inner worth. Petronel holds the title of knight, but the play makes it clear that he does not deserve the distinction. He did not earn his title by birth or noble feats. Instead, he purchased it. As historian Lawrence Stone has explained, the early seventeenth century saw the widespread sale of knighthoods in England. Upon acceding to the throne in 1603, King James bestowed no fewer than 906 new knighthoods in his first four months in power, almost tripling the number of knights that existed in England. James used the bestowing of knighthoods as a source of income, requiring all citizens worth £40 a year to pay for the increasingly dubious honor.[56] In *Eastward Ho!*, Petronel is insultingly referred to as a "thirty pound knight" (4.1.19198). The specific amount differs, but the play's assertion that not all knights are equal is clear.

Eastward Ho! employs the visual codes associated with knights to redefine the category of knighthood to include only those men who both hold the rank and deserve the distinction. Those who hold the rank and not the distinction become targets of ridicule by the sartorial logic of the play that readily employed costumes to respond to the changing social landscape in England.[57] Four years later,

---

[55]   Amanda Bailey disagrees. She believes that "Despite having narrowly escaped hanging at Tyburn, there is little indication that Quicksilver will cease wearing his clothes in a flamboyant manner." The evidence Bailey uses to support her conclusion, I believe, provides compelling support for the likelihood that Quicksilver has learned his lesson and wishes to serve as an example for the dangers of dressing beyond one's station. He says that he will continue to wear his prison clothes in the street as a "Spectacle, or rather an Example, to the Children of Cheaveside" (5.5.215–7). He backs away from the notion of being a spectacle (as he was in his gentlemanly apparel) in favor of being an example (in the clothes that mark his punishment). Amanda Bailey, *Flaunting: Style and the Subversive Male Body in Renaissance England* (Toronto: University of Toronto Press, 2007), 3–4.

[56]   Lawrence Stone, *Crisis of the Aristocracy*, Abridged Edition (Oxford: Oxford University Press, 1967), 41.

[57]   King James I's selling of knighthoods drew widespread criticism and even lampoons. One particularly relevant response is "Verses upon the Order for making Knights of such Persons who had 40 pounds per annum in King James I. Time," which appears in Alastair Bellany and Andrew McRae, eds., "Early Stuart Libels: an edition of poetry from manuscript sources." *Early Modern Literary Studies* Text Series I (2005). <http://www.earlystuartlibels.net/htdocs/early_jacobean_section/B3.html>. Among the suggestions

Ben Jonson similarly employed apparel to challenge contemporary notions of knighthood in *Epicoene* (1609–1610). There, Sir Amorous La Foole is marked for comic scorn by boasting of the "gold jerkin" he wore on the day he was knighted in Ireland (1.4.57–8).[58] By coupling garish clothing with the highly questionable location of La Foole's promotion, the play guarantees that the character bears none of the traits associated at the time with knighthood (he conspicuously lacks refinement and is a professed coward) and assures the audience that he will be thoroughly abused before the end of the play. In this manner, both *Eastward Ho!* and *Epicoene* employed the visual codes of the time in new and exciting ways to voice public resentment with James I's policy of selling and thereby cheapening knighthoods.

The conservative politics we find in *Eastward Ho!* naturally extend to the women. Just as Mildred is rewarded for embracing her social station and marrying a commoner, so is her sister Gertrude punished for attempting to climb the social ladder by marrying a knight. Her marital ambitions begin with a desire to socially surpass her mother, which she accomplishes by donning fine apparel for her wedding (purchased with the land that was her dowry). Her only source of income sold and her fortunes reversed, Gertrude has a chance to ruminate on the error of her ways after she is forced to sell her clothes for food: "Let me see; my jewels be gone, and my gowns, and my red velvet petticoat, that I was married in, and my wedding silk stockings . . . I'm sure I remember the time when I would ha' given a thousand pound, if I had had it, to have been a lady . . . my ladyship is little the worse for the wearing, and yet I would bate a good deal of the sum. I would lend it–let me see–for forty pound in hand" (5.1.58–60). In the London of *Eastward Ho!*, social climbing ought to be confined by the limitations of one's birth. Visually speaking, those born to wear sackcloth must not put on satin or they will be reduced to rags.

The visual codes governing gentlemanly apparel were not always presented in a manner that promoted conservative politics. Thomas Dekker's *The Shoemaker's Holiday* (1599) employs and contrasts silk and cloth apparel in support of progressive views regarding social station. Simon Eyre works as a shoemaker, but his financial and social advancement in the play do not result primarily from industry and hard work (as was the case with Touchstone and Golding in *Eastward Ho!*). Instead, Eyre advances as a result of his decision to impersonate an alderman

---

offered to those who can afford to become knights, the anonymous satirist recommends trading one's woolen cloth for fine apparel:

Bidd all your Home-sponne Russetts adue,
And sute yourselves in Fashions new:
Honour invits you to Delights:
Come all to Court, & be made Knights.

[58]   Ben Jonson, *Epicoene or, The Silent Woman*, ed. R. V. Holdsworth (New York: W. W. Norton, 1979).

in order to purchase a ship full of wares and take part in a capitalistic venture.[59] The play approves his actions by rewarding him with promotion. When the Lord Mayor, Oatley sees the newly wealthy Eyre, he welcomes him with "Good morrow, Master Eyre" (9.73), using the title reserved for gentlemen, and informs the shoemaker that he is to be promoted to sheriff. This promotion, quite naturally, occurs visually: when Eyre next enters, he wears a gold chain of office, and he notes that when he next goes to Guildhall, he will wear the appropriate "scarlet gown" of his new station. It can be inferred from the text that when Eyre later appears before the King, he wears the distinctive scarlet gown of the Lord Mayor.[60]

Throughout the period and to this day, the alderman's gown is black, while those of the two sheriffs and the Lord Mayor are scarlet. All three were typically made with silk, introducing an important distinction in notions of gentility that must be addressed. In the drama and the culture at the time, differentiation was made between the citizen gentleman and the gallant. The common born Eyre becomes a gentleman by making enough money to stop working, at which time he gives his shop to his foreman Firk. He then embodies the ideal of the citizen gentleman by investing his money back into London by assuming the administrative responsibilities and honor of being a sheriff and then Lord Mayor. He seals the goodwill of the city upon his promotion by paying for a feast that he throws for all of the apprentices of London. The good use to which Eyre puts his new fortune provides a strong argument for his social advancement and explains his success in assuming and maintaining the position and apparel of a gentleman.

The gallant, by contrast, seeks to accrue money primarily to purchase fine clothing and enjoy life. In city comedies, the gallant was typically a younger son who, despite his lack of resources, was known for sartorial extravagance.[61] He characteristically did not seek higher honors, titles, or nobility. The gallant attempted to accrue wealth and flaunted it primarily for selfish reasons. Ben Jonson's character Truewit in *Epicoene*, for instance, marks himself a prototypical gallant when he states that he values "good dressing" above all other beauties of the world.[62] In *The Shoemaker's Holiday*, Eyre distinguishes between the two categories of gentleman. Regarding the citizen gentleman, he states "it's a mad life to be a Lord Mayor. It's a stirring life, a fine life, a velvet life, a careful life" (17.37–8). Velvet is appropriate to the citizen gentleman as a sign of his success and devotion to the city. On the other hand, Eyre has little respect for the gallant. Speaking to the young Rose, Eyre warns her away from such a man: "A courtier?—wash, go by! Stand not upon pishery-pashery. Those silken fellows are but painted images—outsides, Rose; their inner linings are torn" (11.39–42). Silk is suitable apparel for one who serves the city and for whom fine clothing houses

[59]   Mark Thornton Burnett, *Masters and Servants in English Renaissance Drama and Culture* (London: Macmillan, 1997), 72.

[60]   MacIntyre 135.

[61]   Bailey, "Monstrous" 262.

[62]   Ibid., 272.

fine intentions. For those who wish merely to "brave it" in sumptuous apparel, Eyre offers only scorn.

And yet, the play rewards the character most known for his sumptuous apparel with a propitious marriage. Roland Lacy's tendency to appear in the richest, most garish clothing is noted in the play: "here 'a wore a scarf, and here a scarf, here a bunch of feathers, and here precious stones and jewels, and a pair of garters—O monstrous!—like one of our yellow silk curtains" (2.25–8). Thus appareled, Lacy seems even more farcical than Quicksilver in *Eastward Ho!*, and equally suited to a comic fall. However, Lacy is not necessarily a gallant. He has no titles, dresses sumptuously, and spends his time pursuing love instead of greater honors, but he also has a direct tie to nobility as the nephew and sole heir of Sir Hugh Lacy, the Earl of Lincoln. In this way, the young Lacy occupies a nebulous position between commoner, nobleman, and gallant: his actions in the play threaten to divest him of his inheritance and leave him to earn a living as a shoemaker; his relations offer the possibility of future nobility; his current situation and chosen apparel mark him a gallant. The very ambiguity of his social position contributes to the dramatic energy of the play, for the audience cannot easily determine whether Lacy will ultimately succeed in his designs or be punished. Only when the King enters late in the play and personally knights the young Lacy, do we see his choice of silk apparel and his questionable actions finally and fully sanctioned. Lacy's dramatic potential in Dekker's play hinges on his status as a gentleman who dresses in fine silk but could be bereft of his status, money, and sumptuous apparel at any time.

The social category of gentleman figured prominently in the city comedies precisely because it did not have a clear definition. It existed as a gray area between the more fully established categories of nobleman and commoner. When Harrison attempted to describe the term in the late sixteenth century, his definition demonstrated the difficulty people at the time had in classifying it: "Gentlemen be those whome their race and blood (or at the least their vertues) doo make noble and knowne."[63] Ralph Berry has considered early modern English notions of social station at length and concludes "*Gentleman* defies exact definition. Of all the social terms, it casts the widest net. . . . Only gentlemen exist in a state of tension and perennial re-definition, since there may be no title deeds. The real gentleman has to assert himself against the usurper, against the inferior classes, against all manner of challenges."[64] In the plays of the period, gentlemen could be citizens who had worked hard enough to earn the money to live without labor, second sons of nobility, or individuals whose parentage was uncertain but who had the wit to maintain high means of living without working. Because simple gentlemen were not members of the titular nobility, they were prohibited from wearing the items proscribed to those below specific ranks. However, an extraordinarily large

---

[63]   Harrison, 128.

[64]   Ralph Berry, *Shakespeare and Social Class* (Atlantic Highlands, NJ: Humanities Press International, 1988), xii–xiii.

range of sumptuous choices remained open to them including the use of exorbitant amounts of cloth, extravagant fashions, and costly materials.[65]

It was on the battlefield of swords, silk, and cloth that the category of gentility was negotiated in early modern drama. Over time, plays offered varying notions of who was fit to wear swords and silk and who was not, but the one thing that remained constant was the visual code itself. All the way up to the closing of the theatres in 1642, it was maintained that swords and silk belonged appropriately to those who were gentlemen, whoever they may be, and commoners were to restrict themselves to baser apparel.[66]

For female characters, the distinction between cloth and silk similarly demarcated gentility from commonness, but additional articles of apparel were understood to belong appropriately only to one or the other. Most significantly, the farthingale was to be worn only by the gentlewoman. In *The Shoemaker's Holiday*, when Eyre becomes a wealthy Sherriff, his wife Margery embraces their new prestige by seeking to purchase the clothes appropriate to gentility: "art thou acquainted with never a farthingale-maker, nor a French-hood maker? I must enlarge my bum—ha, ha! How shall I look in a hood, I wonder?" (10.35–7). Farthingales were clear signifiers of gentility for their design precluded the wearer from engaging in physical labor. Ben Jonson's *Poetaster* (1601) complicates the issue by suggesting that not all farthingales were respected equally. Having married below her station, Chloe laments her social decline by citing her transition from farthingales to bum rolls: "Nor you nor your house were so much as spoken of, before I debased myself, from my hood and my farthingale to those bum-rolls, and your whalebone bodies"(2.1.55–7).[67] It must be noted, however, that when we consider how difficult it would be to work in a stiffened bodice, it seems likely that the bum roll and the whalebone bodice were deemed the province of gentility, even if they were inferior to the farthingale. Thomas Killigrew's late play *The Parson's Wedding* (1637) makes it clear that the bum roll was understood to belong to the gentlewoman. Jolly notes a woman's social ascension by stating: "her beginning was simple and below stairs, till her Lady finding her to be a likely promising Baud; secret as the Key at her Girdle, obedient as her thoughts, those vertues rais'd her from the flat Peti-coat, and Kercher, to the Gorget and Bum-roll."[68] I am hesitant to suggest that Killigrew's play contradicts Jonson's with regards to the farthingale for the style had changed by then and gentlewomen in England

---

[65]   Bailey, "Monstrous" 259.

[66]   Although it may be a bit of an oversimplification to say so, it is this distinction that marks the broad social dichotomy embraced by social commentators who divided society into the "richer sort" or "better sort" and the "poorer sort," "inferior sort," or "meaner sort." Keith Wrightson, "Estates, Degrees, and Sorts," *History Today* 37.1 (1987): 21–2.

[67]   Ben Jonson, *The Complete Plays of Ben Jonson*, Vol. 2, ed. G. A. Wilkes (Oxford: Clarendon Press, 1981).

[68]   Act 3 Scene 5, Thomas Killigrew, *The Parson's Wedding* in *Six Caroline Plays*, ed. A. S. Knowland (London: Oxford University Press), 499–500.

rarely wore the large farthingales that were popular in earlier decades. What is abundantly clear from both quotations is that, as a rule, an enlarged bum signified the gentility of the woman who could wear the fashion and eschew working for a living.

In addition to seeking a farthingale, Margery in *The Shoemaker's Holiday* also wants a French hood. This makes sense because the headwear was typically made of silk and constructed with soft pleats, which made them easy to disarrange and thus unsuitable to working women.[69] Also, the French hood's name marked the distant origin of the fashion, and foreign apparel was the rage among the wealthy in early modern England. The presence of foreign fashions in early modern performances will be discussed at greater length in the next chapter.

At the playhouses, audiences expected non-gentle, common characters to refrain from wearing swords, silks, or farthingales. The base apparel that commoners wore consisted primarily of fustian, canvas, leather, and wool, and was usually defined by the wearer's occupation.[70] Craftsmen, for instance, typically appeared on stage wearing an apron over cloth apparel and carrying the accoutrements of their particular mystery. In *2 Henry VI*, the armorer Horner establishes the clothes he is wearing when, before going to fight, he says "Here, Robin, and if I die, I give thee my aporn [sic]; and, Will, thou shalt have my hammer;" (2.3.74–5). Shakespeare's *Julius Caesar* mentions the apparel worn by a carpenter:

> FLAVIUS: . . . what! know you not,
> Being mechanical, you ought not walk
> Upon a labouring day without the sign
> Of your profession? Speak, what trade art thou?
> FIRST COMMONER: Why, sir, a carpenter.
> MARULLUS: Where is thy leather apron and thy rule?
> What dost thou with thy best apparel on? (1.1.2–8)

The leather apron and the tools specific to one's guild defined the apparel in which an actor playing a craftsman most commonly appeared onstage. We can say with some certainty that in *The Shoemaker's Holiday*, when Lacy appeared onstage, he wore a leather apron and carried the shoemaker's tools, called St. Hugh's Bones.[71] Having appeared previously in the lavish silk apparel of a gentleman, Lacy would have been well disguised in this working attire.

We can determine the clothing worn by actors playing apprentices even more thoroughly than we can that which was worn by their masters. The tendency

---

[69] Linthicum, 232–3.

[70] Bailey, "Monstrous" 254.

[71] William Rowley's *A Shoemaker a Gentleman* (1608) lists the particular tools referred to as Saint Hugh's Bones: "all the tooles we worke with: as for example, the Drawer, Dresser, Wedges, Heele-block, hand and thumb-lethers, Shooe-thrids, Pincers, pricking-aule, and a rubbing-stone, Aule, Steele, and Tacks, shooe-haires, and Stirrups, whet-stone, and stopping-sticke, Apron, and Paring-knife, all these are Sir *Hughs* bones."

of apprentices in England throughout the early modern period to challenge the rules laid down for them prompted numerous regulations that established what they were permitted to wear.[72] From these regulations, we can develop a fairly clear picture of the simple and unadorned manner in which apprentices were typically expected to appear onstage. The City Ordinance of 1582 lays out ten rules, which state that no apprentice should presume:

1. To wear any apparel but what he receives from his Master.
2. To wear no hat within the City and liberty thereof, nor any thing instead thereof, but a woollen cap, without any silk in or about the same.
3. To wear no ruffles, cuffs, loose collar, nor other thing than a ruff at the collar, and that only of a yard and a half long.
4. To wear no doublets but what were made of canvas, fustian, sack-cloth, English leather, or woollen cloth, and without being enriched with any manner of gold, silver, or silk.
5. To wear no other coloured cloth, or kersey, in hose or stockings, than white, blue, or russet.
6. To wear little breeches, of the same stuffs as the doublets, and without being stitched, laced, or bordered.
7. To wear a plain upper coat of cloth or leather, without pinking, stitching, edging, or silk about it.
8. To wear no other surtout than a cloth gown or cloak, lined or faced with cloth, cotton, or bays, with a fixed round collar, without stitching, guarding, lace, or silk.
9. To wear no pumps, slippers, nor shoes, but of English leather, without being pinked, edged, or stitched; nor girdles, nor garters, other than of crewel, woollen, thread, or leather, without being garnished.
10. To wear no sword, dagger, or other weapon, but a knife; nor a ring, jewel of gold, nor silver, nor silk in any part of his apparel.[73]

Located near the bottom of the social ladder and subservient to other commoners, apprentices were legally obligated to abstain from all ostentatious show. In performance, the appropriately dressed apprentice was most identifiable by his small breeches, simple cloth coat, and ever-present flat cap.[74]

The strict rules governing what apprentices were permitted to wear lent themselves particularly well in the plays of the time to two common dramatic

---

[72] Bailey, "Monstrous" 257–8.

[73] John Nichols, *The Progresses and Public Processions of Queen Elizabeth*, 3 vols. (London: Printers to the Society of Antiquaries, 1823): 2.393–4.

[74] The London ordinance of 1582 stipulated that apprentices confine themselves to wearing a "most plaine" pair of breeches, a plain shirt, doublet, coat, cloak, and a woolen cap, all made from the poorest cloth and held together by "plaine stringes" and "plain white seame." Paul Griffiths, *Youth and Authority: Formative Experiences in England 1560–1640* (New York: Oxford University Press, 1996), 225–6.

scenarios: those instances when they were obeyed and those when they were flouted. In Thomas Heywood's *The Four Prentices of London* (1592), for example, the eponymous characters are dutiful apprentices: Godfrey to a mercer, Guy to a goldsmith, Charles to a haberdasher, and Eustace of Bulloigne to a grocer. Early in the play, all four leave their crafts to go to Jerusalem to fight in the crusades, but on their travels, each proudly continues to wear a flat cap and a shield bearing the insignia of the London guild to which he belongs. The play's original title page follows the dictates of the text in presenting the characters wearing their apprentice's headwear and guild insignia. For the London apprentices attending the show, the sight of their familiar apparel on the four heroic title characters likely drew particular approbation.

Plays of the period were able to make a clear moral statement by including apprentices who dressed according to their station alongside others who refused to be so confined. One such play has already been addressed; *Eastard Ho!* contrasts Golding's humble, apprentice's attire with Quicksilver's lavish, gentleman's clothing. The disparity between the two apprentices is so clear that the play could work as a dumb show: the action and the morals are advanced in the visual presentation of the costumes as vividly as they are in the dialogue. Massinger's *The City Madam* (1632) similarly engages the visual codes governing how apprentices were expected to dress when the wicked Luke Frugal tries to win over his brother's apprentices, both sons of gentry, by enticing them with fine apparel: "Are you gentlemen born, yet have no gallant tincture / Of gentry in you?" (2.1.51–2).[75] Luke continues to invoke the sartorial desires of apprentices, ultimately succeeding by suggesting that by merely donning the clothes of their betters, the apprentices will successfully assume their social status.

> Didst thou know
> What ravishing lechery it is to enter
> An ordinary, cap-a-pe, trimm'd like a gallant,
> (For which in trunks conceal'd be ever furnish'd)
> The reverence, respect, the crouches, cringes,
> The musical chime of gold in your cramm'd pockets
> Commands from the attendants, and poor porters—(2.1.79–85)

As we have seen, donning apparel incommensurate with one's social station does not transform one's identity. Rather, it precipitates the action that returns the wearer to the apparel deemed appropriate to the visual codes of the time. Luke ultimately turns on the apprentices when it serves his purpose and has them apprehended by the Sheriff for the very extravagances that he encouraged. When the two apprentices appear again near the end of the play, they wear the clothes of prisoners, seeking mercy and hoping for a chance to resume the occupation and wear the clothing that marked their social station at the beginning of the action.

---

[75] Philip Massinger, *The City-Madam*, ed. T. W. Craik (London: Ernest Benn, 1964).

Fig. 2.2   Title page of Thomas Heywood, *The Four Prentices of London* (1632), STC 13322. By permission of the Beinecke Library, Yale University.

Like apprentices, servants in early modern performances were also sartorially defined by their inferior position to those they served. The colored or marked apparel that servants were required to wear, termed *livery*, was intended to visibly and bodily tie the wearers to the household in which they served.[76] The actual clothing that constituted a servant's livery, however, can be difficult to determine because the position covered a great deal of social territory, ranging from those responsible for cleaning and cooking through those more socially advanced individuals who ran the household and kept constant company with the master. Additionally, the apparel servants wore might depend on the social significance of their master. Although servants might appear in simple clothing that signified low status, those who worked in great households had a long tradition of appearing in gentlemanly apparel that stood as a testament to the prominence of those they served.[77] Deemed extensions of their masters, servants were legally permitted to wear livery that included silk clothing and elite accoutrements that would otherwise be beyond the scope of their social station.

Perhaps the best example of such a servant is Malvolio in *Twelfth Night*, whose important role as steward to a countess's household would have made it inappropriate for him to appear in base apparel. Beyond the clothes he wears, the primary signifier of Malvolio's social position within the play is his gold chain of office. This item serves the double purpose of highlighting the wearer's importance to Olivia's household as well as his servitude to her nobility.[78] The chain circumscribes the fine apparel Malvolio wears and establishes it as a reference to Olivia's social superiority, not his own. It therefore follows that when he acts in a manner beyond the dictates of his visibly inferior position, he renders himself the appropriate butt of comic abuse. Malvolio's efforts to woo his mistress constitute a blatant disregard for the limitations signified by his chain. He is deemed mad for perpetrating so flagrant a transgression and incarcerated so that the threat he offers to the accepted social hierarchy can be safely contained.

Thomas Middleton's *A Mad World, My Masters* (1608) similarly presents a nobleman's steward in fine apparel and wearing a chain. Sir Bounteous's servant Gunwater asserts that he is a gentleman, and another character notes that he wears a velvet jacket. Clearly Gunwater is not a commoner, but his authority and social station is constrained by the duty he owes his master. And yet, it must be noted that Gunwater does not seek to escape his condition of servitude. The position brings in the estimable sum of fifty pounds per year as well as the fine clothes he wears. Consequently, he cherishes the chain that represents his subservient position. It

---

[76] Amanda Bailey, "Livery and its Discontents: 'Braving It' in *The Taming of the Shrew*," *Renaissance Drama* 33 (2004): 87.

[77] Felicity Heal, "Reciprocity and Exchange in the Late Medieval Household" in *Bodies and Disciplines: Intersections of Literature and History in Fifteenth Century England*, eds. Barbara A. Hanawalt and David Wallace (Minneapolis: University of Minnesota Press, 1993), 180.

[78] Hunter, 25.

follows that when he betrays the responsibility of his office by trying to have a sexual liaison with his master's mistress (who happens to be a cross-dressed man), Gunwater is fittingly punished by having his gold chain stolen. Costumed as a woman, Follywit explains "I'll teach the slave to be so bold yet, as once to offer to vault into his master's saddle," and takes the gold chain (4.3.34–5).[79] Since the chain serves as a visible reminder of the wearer's obligation to his master, Gunwater is fittingly punished by having it stolen when he betrays the confidence it represents.

Lesser servants, those that were not gentlemen, most commonly appeared in theatrical performances wearing a blue coat of service. In *A Mad World, My Masters*, when Follywit wishes to dress his friends as his servants in order to play the part of a great lord, he does so by purchasing blue coats for them. This demonstrates that the appropriate apparel for a servant is a blue coat, and also that the appropriate apparel for a nobleman includes a retinue of liveried servants. Like the apparel worn by other characters on the early modern stage, the blue coat was understood to signify and belong appropriately to the social station of the servant who wore it. Accordingly, when it was inappropriately doffed, the action of the play reacted to the social transgression. In *Greene's Tu Quoque*, as we have already seen, the servant Bubble fails in his efforts to become a gentleman and must once again put on his "blew cote" at the end of the play if he is to avoid going to jail. The sky-blue colored apparel so clearly signified service that servants were often termed blue-coats, blue-bottles, or members of the blue order throughout the period.[80] It seems likely that in the countless instances in which unnamed servants entered alongside noble characters, they were most commonly dressed in blue coats.

Shakespeare's *The Taming of the Shrew* (1590–1594) plays with the sartorial expectations of servants by having Lucentio choose to exchange apparel with his servant Tranio as part of a strategy to win the heart of Bianca. When Lucentio's father Vincentio sees Tranio dressed as his son, he is horrified and assumes that the servant has killed his master: "A silken doublet, a velvet hose, a scarlet cloak, and a copatain hat! . . . O, he hath murd'red his master!" (5.1.66–87). The trick is taken one step further after Vincentio calls for Tranio to be taken into custody. Rather than admit that he is actually a servant, Tranio instead calls for an officer to take the unknown Vincentio to jail. Before either is incarcerated, however, Lucentio enters and explains that he is the author of the plan to swap clothing, and master and servant return to their proper apparel. Considering how effectively Tranio imitates the role of the noble Lucentia before resuming his position as a servant, Amanda Bailey concludes that the play's disavowal of the treacherous implications of its comic subplot does not effectively contain the subversive scenario it develops. Consequently, despite the fact that Tranio appears at the end in the appropriate

---

[79]   Thomas Middleton, *A Mad World, My Masters*, ed. Standish Henning (Lincoln: University of Nebraska Press).

[80]   Linthicum, 27.

apparel of a servant, his previous actions serve to demonstrate that the social is nothing more than a fragile symbolic tissue that cannot be repaired by a return to accepted norms.[81]

I am not comfortable with this conclusion for it fails to consider comedy's extraordinary capacity to contain precisely these forces in performance. Tranio's success in playing the part of a gentleman is funny only because he is not one, and his ability to play the trick on Vincentio manages to extend the joke further. Much of an audience's pleasure in watching a comedy derives from the deferred reification of social norms that are challenged through the course of the action. Audiences know that Tranio is actually a servant, no matter how much he braves it in fine apparel, and enjoys his antics precisely because they know he will appear in the clothes appropriate to his real social station before the play concludes.

The possibility that a servant could effectively break with societal norms by assuming the authority of a lord (and not resume his prior position before the end of the performance) belongs appropriately to tragedy, and this is precisely what we find with DeFlores in Middleton and Rowley's *The Changeling* (1622) and Antonio in John Webster's *The Duchess of Malfi* (1614). In both, the servants were certain to appear in the apparel appropriate to their station (Antonio's chain is even mentioned) and yet act far outside the dictates of their livery. The finality of their actions, committing murder and having sex with a countess or marrying and have sex with a duchess, makes it impossible for the characters to resume their proper role as servants and contributes significantly to their downfall.[82] Studying *The Duchess of Malfi*, Frank Whigham has argued that the tragedy results significantly from the marriage that cuts inappropriately across social stations: "the class-endogamy pressure assigns to licit marriage an outer frontier, which the duchess trespasses."[83] Whigham's statement takes on additional significance when we note that the limits of licit marriage would have been immediately apparent to an early modern audience by virtue of the visual semiotics according to which the clothes each character wore established social hierarchy. For a liveried servant, a noblewoman's elite apparel marks her social station to be decidedly out of his star, and everyone in attendance at the early modern playhouse would have understood this on sight.

For the characters whose social station ranked below that of apprentice or servant, the apparel worn in production would have been defined primarily by its well-worn and threadbare quality. In early modern England, clothes were far too expensive for the lower classes to purchase new. Instead, it was common for

---

[81]   Bailey, "Livery" 100.

[82]   I am guilty of oversimplifying the issues relevant to both plays, but the basic thesis holds true that the breaking of the social norms signified by one's apparel lends itself to comedy when they are reified before the end of the play and to tragedy when they are repaired with the disastrous conclusion of the play.

[83]   Frank Whigham, "Incest and Ideology: The Duchess of Malfi (1614)," *PMLA* 100.2 (1985): 168.

clothes to be purchased second- and third-hand, even by those who had gainful employment. Vagabonds and beggars, consequently, would have been identifiable primarily by the shabby cloth articles that signified their inability to earn enough money to purchase clothes that registered at all in the hierarchy of social capital. Their clothes, defined primarily by their absence from the received categories of sartorial signifiers, rendered the wearer socially "nothing," a term which William Carol has noted was often associated with beggars.[84] Carol additionally notes that in early modern performances most of the beggars that appeared were not, in fact, beggars, but gentry and nobleman in disguise.[85] Since characters' identities were first and foremost understood by the clothing they wore, it follows that the perfect disguise for those defined by considerable social capital would be the apparel that signified social absence.

The actual transformation of a character from socially elite apparel to the clothing of the beggar or vagabond, without the hope of returning, belongs to tragedy. *King Lear* (1603–1606), as other scholars have noted, is the story of a king who is reduced to nothing through the process of being divested of the clothes that signified his regal status.[86] Lear's fine clothes and crown marked his identity as King on a profound level. Consequently, their removal signifies an equally profound transformation in Lear. He states "Does any here know me? . . . Who is it that can tell me who I am?" (1.4.226–30). When Lear later tears off the rest of his clothes, he connects the dissolution of his social identity with its visual cognate according to the sartorial dictates of the stage that equated nakedness with nothingness. The apparel of absence that marks the beggar and the vagabond exists in natural opposition to that of the king, validating the social hierarchy that defines its parameters.

Outside the standard parameters of social hierarchy on the Shakespearean stage are those who practiced what have come to be termed the professions, specifically academicians, lawyers, judges, physicians, and clergy. Writers at the time found these individuals difficult to categorize. They typically were deemed to exceed commoners in their social estimation, and yet they worked for a living and therefore were not gentlemen.[87] The clergy in England will be the subject of a later chapter, but here we will consider the clothes worn by actors playing the part of the other professionals. For academicians, lawyers, judges, and physicians, the apparel worn throughout the period and on stage derived largely from the academic gowns (often and indiscriminately referred to as robes) that signified university education. This can be explained by the fact recruits to all the professions had

---

[84]   William C. Carrol, *Fat King, Lean Beggar: Representations of Poverty in the Age of Shakespeare* (Ithaca: Cornell University Press, 1996), 11.

[85]   Ibid, 208.

[86]   Hunter, 32; Jones and Stallybrass, 198.

[87]   Wrightson, *English Society* 20.

a common experience having been reared and formally educated in the same tradition and the identical institutions.[88]

Marlowe's *Doctor Faustus* (1594) illustrates how tightly connected the professions were to one another by virtue of the similar educations that constituted each profession's training. At the start of the play, Faustus ruminates on his expansive learning and considers the various directions toward which he ought to focus his erudite attention: "Settle thy studies, Faustus, and begin / To sound the depth of that thou wilt profess" (1.1.1–2).[89] Having achieved the estimable status of a doctor of theology, Faustus finds himself suited to advanced work in analytics, physic, law, and divinity (1.1.3–47). He ultimately rejects them all in favor of magic, but the fact that each of the professions was a viable option open to the university educated individual had implications for how all the professions appeared on stage. We can get a sense of how Edward Alleyn likely dressed when he played the part of Faustus by looking at the title page of the second quarto (printed in 1616 and reprinted in 1619, 1620, 1624, 1628, and 1631), which includes a woodcut that closely fits the action of the play. There we find him in what appears to be a surplice, with a doctor's gown over it, and wearing an academic's hat. The gown that Faustus wears would have been scarlet, for that was the color appropriate to the distinction of the doctor of theology.[90] As Mosca states in Jonson's *Volpone* (1606), "Hood an ass with reverend purple . . . And he shall pass for a cathedral doctor" (1.2.112–13).[91]

In the image, Faustus's gown is clearly of a rich quality, likely consisting of satin with a fine border and asserting the quality of the person who was deemed worthy to wear the color scarlet and silk material, visual signifiers appropriate to only the most socially elite members of society.

The scarlet satin gown and velvet cap were similarly the typical garb of the early modern English judge and evidence from the drama makes it clear that they were regularly worn in performance by actors playing the part. In John Lily's *Mother Bombie* (1594), Halfepenie has a dream in which, he notes the quality of the material worn by judges, stating, "Mee thought there sate vpon a shelfe three damaske prunes in veluet caps, and prest satten gownes like Iudges" (3.4.176).[92] The scarlet color of the judge's gown is noted in George Chapman's *The Tragedie of Charles Duke of Byron*, by Bryon who laments "Must I be sat on now by

---

[88] Rosemary O'Day, *The Professions in Early Modern England, 1450–1800: Servants of the Commonweal* (Essex: Pearson Education Limited, 2000), 5, 16.

[89] Christopher Marlowe, *The Complete Plays*, ed. J. B. Steane (London: Penguin, 1969).

[90] It is worth noting that Faustus rose to the distinction of scarlet silk from modest origins. The Chorus states at the beginning of the play that Faustus comes from "parents base of stock" (0.11). His achievement highlights Faustus's ability to earn his greatness through extraordinary skill and not merely receive it by birthright.

[91] Ben Jonson, *Three Comedies*, ed. Michael Jamieson (London: Penguin, 1966).

[92] John Lily, *Mother Bombie* (London: William Stansby, 1632).

The Tragicall Hiſtorie of the Life and Death of Doctor Fauſtus.

With new Additions.

Written by CH. MAR.

Printed at London for *Iohn Wright*, and are to be ſold at his ſhop without Newgate. 1631.

Fig. 2.3   Title page of Christopher Marlowe, *Doctor Faustus* (1631), STC 17436. By permission of the Beinecke Library, Yale University.

petty Iudges? / These Scarlet robes, that come to sit and fight / Against my life;" (5.1.190–92).[93] The actual attire of the early modern judge was more elaborate than these quotes suggest,[94] and there is little way to know if the details were followed in performance. What we can say with certainty is that on the early modern stage, the distinctive gown and the cap served to signify the particular identity of the professions.

These items similarly appeared on the stage physician and the lawyer, who typically appeared in black instead of scarlet. Thus appareled, these characters exhibited both the social status that allowed one to wear silk as well as the gowns that suggested academic learning. What is worth noting is the nature of the academic learning suggested by the gowns, which consisted largely of the study of Latin. So significant was this aspect of university study that despite the specific skills required for the various professions, all were expected to be capable speakers of Latin. The drama of the time took advantage of this association, presenting capable doctors, lawyers, clergy, and judges as fluent speakers of Latin and charlatans as individuals who tried to convince others that they had greater facility with the language than they actually did. Accordingly, Faustus's dialogue makes frequent and correct use of Latin, establishing his preeminence in learning. In Jonson's *Epicoene* (1609), on the other hand, the characters Otter and Cutbeard are rendered comical when they disguise themselves in the gowns and caps of a divine and a canon lawyer and sputter forth in mangled Latin. The comedy of this scene (5.2) still lives in performances today, but must have been far greater when the apparel signified a competency that was so clearly beyond the capabilities of the men that tried to fake it.

To the early modern English audiences that attended the theatre, costumes engaged the issue of social station on a number of levels. Beyond simply marking a character's place in the hierarchy of a particular play, the clothes worn in

---

[93] George Chapman, *The Conspiracie and Tragedie of Charles Duke of Byron* (London: G. Eld, 1608).

[94] On 4 June 1635, English judges attempted to standardize the apparel they were to wear, stipulating:

The Judges in Term time are to sit at Westminster in the Courts in their Black or Violet Gowns, whether they will; and a Hood of the same colour put over their heads, and their Mantles above all; the end of the Hood hanging over behind; wearing their Velvet Caps, and Coyfes of Lawn, and cornered Caps.

The facing of their Gownes, Hoods, and Mantles, is with changeable Taffata; which they must begin to wear upon Ascension day, being the last Thursday in Easter Term; and continue those Robes until the Feast of Simon and Jude: And upon Simon and Jude's day, the Judges begin to wear their Robes faced with white furs of Minever; and so continue till Ascension-day again.

Although black could be worn, portraits of judges hardly ever show any robes other than the scarlet, and evidence from the plays uniformly supports the notion that scarlet was worn to portray judges. Quoted in J. H. Baker, "A History of English Judges' Robes," *Costume* 12 (1978): 32–3.

production also actively participated in establishing expectations, denoting power relations, delimiting freedom, prompting action, and more. Social station was crucial to the original early modern audience. We must consider how characters embodied social differences on stage if we hope to do justice to the complexity of early modern performance.

Chapter 3
Foreigners

There is no appearance of fancy in him, unless it be a fancy that he hath to strange disguises–as to be a Dutchman today, a Frenchman tomorrow, or in the shape of two countries at once, as a German from the waist downward, all slops, and a Spaniard from the hip upward, no doublet.

Much Ado About Nothing (3.2.31–7)

Non-English characters appeared regularly on the public stages in England throughout the early modern period. Outside the history plays, Shakespeare located only one of his works, *The Merry Wives of Windsor*, in contemporary England. The rest are set in France, Denmark, Italy, and elsewhere. This proclivity was shared by other playwrights who commonly situated their dramas in distant lands and populated them with distant peoples. And even in plays located in England (city comedies, for instance) foreign characters were commonplace. In just William Haughton's *Englishmen for My Money* (1598), we find French, Italian, and Dutch characters in London. What did actors wear when they played these foreign characters and what did their costumes say about the identities they personated?

The fullest considerations of this issue to date have been offered by Jean MacIntyre and Garrett Epp who argue that foreign fashions were a staple of the early modern playhouses. They contend that groupings of plays indicate that productions strategically shared resources, specifically costumes. For instance, they suggest that the Admiral's Men employed French apparel to costume the four plays they produced in 1598–1599 on the civil wars of France.[1] Further, they argue that because the King's Men produced at least three plays set in the Netherlands between 1617 and 1621, the performances "had to be costumed in the distinctive and well-known Dutch fashion." Also, the King's Men put on no less than eight plays set in Spain between 1620 and 1625, which suggests that each drew upon an inventory of Spanish dress.[2] MacIntyre has further argued that for *Othello* and *Volpone*, which emphasize a Venetian setting, the King's Men would have needed authentic costumes because Venetian dress was so well known in England.[3] Beyond noting the shared settings of plays, MacIntyre and Epp provide additional support

---

[1] Michael Drayton and Thomas Dekker's *Civil Wars of France*, parts 1, 2, & 3 (1598) as well as Thomas Dekker's *First Introduction of the Civil Wars of France* (1599).

[2] Jean MacIntyre and Garrett P. J. Epp, "'Cloathes Worth All the Rest': Costumes and Properties." *A New History of Early English Drama*. Edited by John D. Cox and David Scott Kastan (New York: Columbia University Press, 1997), 278.

[3] Jean MacIntyre, *Costumes and Scripts in the Elizabethan Theatres* (Edmonton: University of Alberta Press, 1992), 278.

for the use of foreign fashions on the English stage by citing Henslowe's diary, one of whose inventory lists includes sections titled "frenchose" and "venetians."[4] The names of the categories, they argue, denote the nationality of the articles listed and suggest that they were the appropriate apparel for productions set in France and Venice.

It is possible that foreign apparel was commonly presented on the English stage. Plays situated in France, Spain, Italy, and elsewhere may have offered opportunities for theatrical companies to display the fashions that were prominent throughout the world. But each piece of evidence supporting such a position is suspect. MacIntyre and Epp concede that there is no indication either in the plays or in extant documents from the period that any production's costumes were designed as a whole. Companies sometimes purchased special apparel for individual parts in new plays, but no professional company could afford to purchase specific costumes for all of the characters.[5] When not presenting a new work, companies typically performed different plays every day of the week (except Sundays) and costumed these productions with apparel drawn from the company's inventory. The lists provided in Henslowe's diary suggest that a company's stocks (or at least the Admiral's Men's, c. 1598–1602) were wholly incapable of costuming all of the characters of a production in the apparel of a foreign nation. Here is a complete list of the items in Henslowe's inventories that suggest foreignness:

> *Item*, j Spanerd gyrcken.
> *Item*, j senetores gowne, j hoode, and 5 senetores capes.
> *Item*, . . . ii Danes sewtes, and I payer of Danes hosse.
> *Item*, The Mores lymes . . .
> *Item*, . . . the sittie of Rome
> *Item*, j payer of whitte saten Venesons cut with coper lace.
> *Item*, j Mores cotte.
> *Item*, j payer of satten Venesyan satten ymbradered.
> *Item*, j payer of French hosse, cloth of gowld.
> *Item*, j payer of read cloth hosse of Venesyans, with sylver lace of coper.
> *Item*, j payer of pechecoler Venesyones uncut, with read coper lace.
> *Item*, j payer of mows coller Venesyans with R. brode gowld lace.
> *Item*, j read Spanes dublett styched.
> *Item*, j payer of crimson satten Venysiones, layd with gowld lace.
> *Item*, j Spanes casse dublet of crymson pyncked.
> *Item*, j Spanes gearcken layd with sylver lace.
> i blew damask cote the more

---

[4]   R. A. Foakes, ed. *Henslowe's Diary*, 2nd ed. (New York: Cambridge University Press, 2002), 291–4.

[5]   MacIntyre and Epp, 279. Court Masques, on the other hand, regularly included costumes specifically made for each character. The exorbitant cost of these costumes typically represented the largest expenditure in the production of the masques. For a list of the prices paid for costumes in specific masques, see Stephen Orgel and Roy Strong, *Indigo Jones: The Theatre of the Stuart Court*, 2 vols. (Berkeley: University of California Press, 1973).

Under the heading "frenchose," appear the following eleven entries:

1 blew velvet embr w^t gould paynes blew satin scalin
2 silver paynes lact w^t carnation satins lact over w^t silver
3 the guises
[4 Rich payns w^t Long *stok*ins
5 gould paynsw^t blak stript scalings of ca*nis*
6 gould payns w^t velvet scalings
7 gould payns w^t red strypt scalings
8 black bugell
9 red payns for a boy w^t yelo scalins
10 pryams hoes
11 spangled hoes

Under the heading "venetians" appear the following eight entries:

[1 A purple velvet cut in dimonds Lact & spangels
2 red velved lact w^t gould spanish
[3 a purpell velvet emproydored w^t silver cut on tinse*l*
4 green velvett lact w^t gould spanish
5 blake velvett
6 cloth of silver
7 gren strypt sattin
8 cloth of gould for a boye[6]

These thirty-six entries seem woefully inadequate to costuming any single production in foreign apparel, let alone a series of plays in different locations. Perhaps there are enough French hose and Venetians for actors performing in plays located in either France or Italy. After all, twenty-six of the items in this list are one or the other. However, it is important to note that aside from one "Danes hosse," no other leg–wear appears in Henslowe's inventories. It strikes me that the nearly complete absence of other breeches or hose indicates that the division of leg-wear into these two categories has more to do with groupings of like articles than with national association. French hose typically were rounder and reached only from the waist to the mid thigh. Venetians were longer, reaching to the knee, and were usually more tapered to the shape of the leg. In this context, French hose seems to correspond to trunk hose and Venetians suggests the longer breeches, including galligaskins. No matter what nationality an actor intended to present on stage, he was limited to choosing between these two broad types while dressing for a role.

And yet, the appellations "frenchose" and "venetians" did carry with them national associations that were sometimes noted in the plays of the period and

---

[6]   This list includes the apparel presented in both inventory lists in *Henslowe's Diary*, Foakes, 291–4 and 317–23. I list them together to note the paucity of distinctively foreign apparel. The items suggesting foreignness are not presented together in the inventories but appear randomly throughout.

deserve consideration. In Shakespeare's *Henry V*, for instance, the Dauphin mentions the Constable's French hose.[7] In the first productions of the play, the actor playing the Constable must have appeared in French hose, and, accordingly, we can extrapolate that the other actors playing Frenchmen in *Henry V* likely also wore short, round breeches. However, as Ann Jones and Peter Stallybrass have noted, the foreign fashions that appear in Henslowe's list were an established part of London tailoring.[8] A brief survey of portraits from the period shows that the English regularly and alternatively wore French hose and Venetians. Both were accepted as common apparel in England and readily appeared in plays with diverse settings without necessarily invoking French or Italian associations or causing confusion for an English audience.

Setting leg-wear aside, Henslowe's lists include only ten items to cover all of the nations represented in the Admiral's Men's performances. Neil Carson has noted that if the lists are taken to be complete and comprehensive, then the company maintained a surprisingly small stock.[9] So small, that it appears the lists are not comprehensive;[10] Jones and Stallybrass have identified gaps in the diary by noting that Henslowe lent money on a number of occasions for costumes that do not appear in their inventory list.[11] Consequently, the lists in Henslowe's diary provide important insight into the costume stores of a professional company, but do not account for everything that was worn in performance. We must be careful about the conclusions we draw from Henlowe's inventories, but that does not mean we should discount their usefulness altogether. For instance, it is hard to overlook the fact that at precisely the time that the Admiral's Men were performing a group of plays on the civil wars in France (1598–1599), their stores list almost nothing to suggest that the productions could have been costumed entirely and realistically in French apparel. Perhaps additional items were owned by the actors or further inventory was not listed, but the sheer dearth of French apparel cannot be ignored.

Ultimately, then, Henslowe's diary suggests that plays with foreign settings were not regularly costumed in foreign fashions. The Admiral's Men may have had enough French hose for all of the French characters onstage, but there is no mention of any other distinctively French apparel to cover the rest of the body. Nor are there enough foreign clothes listed to costume a play in the apparel of any other country. The absence of additional foreign articles makes sense when we consider that the primary purpose of theatrical costume is to highlight differences between characters. The first chapter addressed how apparel established different

---

[7] ". . . your French hose off, and in your strait strossers" (3.7.54–5).

[8] Ann Rosalind Jones and Peter Stallybrass, *Renaissance Clothing and the Materials of Memory* (New York: Cambridge University Press, 2000), 184.

[9] Neil Carson, *A Companion to Henslowe's Diary* (New York: Cambridge University Press, 1988), 52.

[10] Andrew Gurr, *The Shakespearian Playing Companies* (Oxford: Clarendon, 1996), 102–3.

[11] Jones and Stallybrass, 183.

genders on stage; one set of clothing is understood to be masculine only because it exists in contrast to feminine clothing. The second chapter demonstrated how clothes were used to differentiate between people of various social stations and professions. Along the same lines, if everyone in a play is of the same country, foreign fashion will do little to distinguish one character from another. It follows that plays were rarely, if ever, costumed entirely in foreign fashions. Furthermore, textual evidence from the plays themselves strongly supports the likelihood that the great majority of characters in plays set in foreign lands were costumed in apparel that was typically worn in England at the time. As such, their clothes did not serve notably as signifiers of nationality.

For instance, *Julius Caesar*, with its setting in ancient Rome, would seem to demand non-English apparel, specifically the toga, or at least Italian clothing. Shakespeare's primary source for the play, Plutarch's *Life of Caesar*, mentions togas numerous times. However, the translation Shakespeare used, by Thomas North, calls them "gowns." Whether Shakespeare abided by North's translation or, more likely, simply followed the convention of costuming foreign characters in English clothing, togas never appear in the play. Nor are they worn or referenced in any of the other plays situated in ancient Rome that were performed in the public theatres before 1642.[12] Any mention of distinctively Italian apparel is similarly absent from the play. Instead, *Julius Caesar*'s numerous references to costume all support the argument that, on the early modern stage, the dramatic presentation of ancient Rome was sartorially isomorphic to that of contemporary England. In the first lines of the play (quoted earlier on p. 67), we learn that the appropriate apparel of the Roman commoner is identical to that of an English commoner.

In Shakespeare's Rome on working days, a carpenter is expected to appear in the English apparel appropriate to his trade, replete with apron and ruler.

The use of English apparel in *Julius Caesar* is not limited to the lower class characters. We can be sure Caesar appeared in contemporary English apparel from Casca's explanation of how Caesar responded when he heard that the crowd was pleased when he refused the crown three times.

---

[12]   I should note that the Toga is mentioned once in George Ruggle's *Ignoramus*, an academic play performed in Latin in 1614/1615 at St. John's College, Cambridge for King James I. In Robert Codrington's 1630 translation of the play, when the title character appears without his lawyer's gown, his clerk, Dullman, asks "master Ignoramus do you come abroad without a toga vocata, a *Gown*?" Interestingly, even in its original Latin, the play defines the toga for the audience as a gown: "Magister Ignoramus, num tu venis foras sine toga, vocata *a gowne*?" George Ruggle, *Ignoramus: A comedy As it was several times Acted with extraordinary Applause, before the Majesty of King James: With a Supplement which (out of respect to the Students of the Common Law) was hitherto wanting. Written in Latine by R. Ruggles sometimes Master of Arts in Clare Colledge in Cambridge. And Translated into English by R. C. sometimes Master of Arts in Magdalen Colledge in Oxford* (London, 1630), 8.

> Marry, before he fell down, when he perceived the
> common herd was glad he refused the crown, he
> plucked me ope his doublet and offered them his
> throat to cut. (1.2.264–6)

Were Caesar wearing a toga, Casca's mention of a doublet would make no sense. The toga was sometimes worn over a tunic in ancient Rome, but a doublet would have been hidden beneath the folds of the larger article of clothing.

The well-known 1953 movie version of *Julius Caesar*, directed by Joseph Mankiewicz and starring Marlon Brando as Marc Antony, simply cuts the lines referring to English apparel to allow the actors to appear in togas. The movie is lavishly costumed in Roman apparel, but raises the notion of what it means to call a modern production "historically accurate." By dressing Roman characters in togas, the movie may have lost historical accuracy by moving away from the text and original practices of Shakespeare's theatre. On the other hand, one could argue that the production was more historically accurate because it was willing to depart from the strict dictates of the text to establish the world of ancient Rome that Shakespeare sought to create with his play. There is a third option. Perhaps the most historically accurate approach would be to use twenty-first-century clothing and follow Shakespeare's approach of using the apparel with which today's audience is most familiar to speak directly to the present moment. Shakespeare set his play in Rome and costumed its inhabitants in doublets. We might do the same by costuming our Romans in suits and ties. In this way, the politics of an ancient civilization are made immediately significant because we see the issues being negotiated in the present by our contemporaries.[13]

The use and referencing of distinctively English apparel is pervasive in *Julius Caesar*. In addition to the previously discussed apron and doublet, the play also includes hats, cloaks, robes, and night gowns. But there is a possibility that some elements of foreignness appeared in early modern presentations of Rome. The Henry Peacham sketch, dated 1595, depicts a Roman scene and includes items that seem to fall outside the realm of typical English apparel. As the only available pictorial evidence depicting costumes employed in what appears to be an actual Shakespeare production, *Titus Andronicus*, the Peacham drawing has been considered key to understanding what was worn at a particular moment on the early modern English stage. Recent scholarship, however, has questioned the nature of this evidence. June Schlueter suggests that the Peacham drawing does not depict a performance of *Titus Andronicus*, but instead presents a scene from the German play *Eine sehr klägliche Tragœdia von Tito Andronico und der hoffertigen Käyserin* (*A Very Lamentable Tragedy of Titus Andronicus and the Haughty*

---

[13] Of course, none of these issues concerned Shakespeare or his contemporaries since notions of historical accuracy only began to be seriously considered in the nineteenth century with Charles Kean's productions of Shakespeare at the Princess Theatre.

Empress).[14] Richard Levin has rebutted Schlueter's argument and resubmitted that the picture represents a conflation of scenes from Shakespeare's play.[15]

Regardless of which play is presented, the Peacham drawing's importance as a source of reliable information regarding early modern English costuming practices cannot be ignored. If Schlueter is correct, the picture presents a performance in Germany by English actors performing a translation of the lost *titus & vespacia* recorded in Henslowe's diary in 1592.[16] As such, it shows what was worn by traveling English performers at the time and may be representative of how Romans were depicted onstage in England in the late sixteenth and early seventeenth centuries. If Levin is correct, the play depicts the actual costumes worn in different scenes from Shakespeare's play.

Accepting Schlueter's argument that the scene presented here is not Shakespeare's, but rather Act 1 of *A Very Lamentable Tragedy*, the characters depicted are, starting on the left: Vespasian, Titus, the Emperor, the queen, the queen's two sons, and Morian, the blackamoor. If the scene is, instead, from *Titus Andronicus*, then the characters seen here most likely are: two of Titus's sons, Titus, Tamora, Tamora's two surviving sons, and Aaron. The costumes worn by these characters are of a diverse nature. The two on the left appear armed and in armor appropriate to the early modern period, although their outfits are quite different from each other. Martin Holmes states that one appears in the fashion of a Swiss mercenary infantry with a tall plumed bonnet in Spanish style, and the other is clad in late-fifteenth century German armor, which was out of use by 1595, the date of the drawing.[17] Taking into consideration the very limited costume stores available to a traveling company, the two appear in the attire of sixteenth-century soldiers.

The central character, however, appears in clothes that are unfamiliar to the late sixteenth century. Among those who have examined the picture, there is some disagreement as to what is presented here. R. A. Foakes states that this character appears "'bound with laurel boughs' (I.i.74), wearing a tunic, toga and sandals, and also with a sword at his side."[18] Holmes does not see a tunic or a toga in this picture. Rather, he sees the central character wearing "a laurel wreath, a venerable beard, a classical-looking cuirass and buskins, and a military cloak knotted on the left shoulder, and carries a tasseled spear."[19] I find myself most interested in how this figure would have appeared to a sixteenth-century audience. The article worn by the central character that would have been most clearly understood was the

---

[14] June Schlueter, "Rereading the Peacham Drawing," *Shakespeare Quarterly* 50 no. 2 (1999): 171–84.

[15] Richard Levin, "The Longleat Manuscript and *Titus Andronicus*," *Shakespeare Quarterly* 53 (2002), 323–40.

[16] Schlueter, 176–8.

[17] Martin R. Holmes, *Shakespeare and His Players* (London: J. Murray, 1972), 150–1.

[18] Foakes, *Illustrations*, 50.

[19] Holmes, 150.

Fig. 3.1   Peacham drawing, by permission of the Marquess of Bath, Longleat
              House, Warminster, Wiltshire, Great Britain.

character's laurel wreath. Laurel was well known as a sign of military distinction
and nobility, and is mentioned or worn in numerous plays from the period,
including three by Shakespeare.[20] Appearing with a laurel wreath on his head and
standing at the center of the stage, this character would have visually asserted
his social superiority to a contemporary audience. Beyond the laurel headwear,
however, this character's most distinctive visual feature is not to be found in any
specific article of apparel, but in the general "foreignness" and "ancientness" that
define the rest of his attire. He appears in clothes that are different from those of
every other character in the play and unfamiliar to contemporary Englishmen. It
is in that difference that their purpose is fulfilled—the clothes serve to situate the
play's action in a distant land and in the distant past. The character's distinctive
clothing makes him stand out visually and asserts the play's Roman setting.

With limited costume stores (even more limited when on the road[21]),
playing companies dressed most characters from plays with foreign settings in
contemporary English apparel, but often dressed the most significant individual
part or parts in distinctive costumes suggestive of the play's setting. The inventories
in Henslowe's diary strongly support this likelihood by including a surprisingly
large number of articles that are earmarked for specific roles, far more than are
allocated to particular nationalities. Included in that list are a "payer of hosse for
the Dowlfen," that we can assume appeared in the plays that dramatized the civil
wars in France. The apparel worn by the Dauphin in these productions would have

---

[20]   *Antony and Cleopatra* (1.3.100), *3 Henry VI* (4.6.34), and *Titus Andronicus*
(1.3.107).

[21]   See S. P. Cerasano, "'Borrowed Robes,' Costume Prices, and the Drawing of *Titus
Andronicus*," *Shakespeare Studies* 22 (1994): 45–57.

determined the wearer's singular importance and the play's French setting even though other characters did not wear French clothing or fashions.

Beyond establishing one's social superiority and the location of the action, a particular costume could also signify the wearer's national character. While most characters in plays set in foreign lands wore English apparel, the individuals specially costumed for the production often appeared in "foreign" fashions that carried particular associations. I put cautionary quotation marks around the word "foreign" to highlight the fact that the Shakespearean stage was not attempting to display genuine foreign apparel. Rather, the playing companies presented *English understandings* of how people from other countries dressed. Among the higher classes in Europe, it actually would have been difficult to determine the country of origin for genuine foreign fashions since the aristocracy from various countries frequently shared styles. As Francis Kelly explains, "among the better classes the fashions in civilized Europe were broadly the same, especially for men. In fact, very often it is not possible to determine the nationality of contemporary portraits from the mere costume, which might belong indifferently to England, France, the Netherlands, Spain, or Italy"[22] On the other hand, the costumes worn on stage to depict members of various countries clearly spoke their national associations to an audience that had shared understandings of how people from various locations appeared and what their apparel said about them.

The best sources of evidence for how foreign characters appeared are the play scripts from the period. While the plays with foreign settings provide little information in this area (since they dressed most characters in typical English apparel), the works set in England made a common practice of costuming foreign characters in apparel that was understood to be appropriate to the individual's country of the origin. Looking at the plays situated in England, we find that the professional theatre had a well established visual vocabulary determining the particular articles of apparel in which citizens of various nations were supposed to appear, and what those items represented.

Such a study has important ramifications for the plays set in England as well as those located in other countries. Shakespeare's *Hamlet* (1601) provides an example. When Hamlet confronts his mother in 3.4 with a list of Claudius's faults, he includes an insult that has caused readers some confusion in the past. After denigrating the new King as "A murtherer and a villain," "a vice of kings," and more, Hamlet calls Claudius "A king of shreds and patches" (3.4.95–102). The *Riverside Shakespeare* glosses this with "clownish (alluding to the motley worn by jesters) (?) or patched-up, beggarly (?)." The *Arden Hamlet*, third edition, notes that this line suggests "ragged patchwork (as contrasted with the paragon of *your*

---

[22]   Francis M. Kelly, *Shakespearian Costume*, Revised by Alan Mansfield (New York: Theatre Arts Books, 1970), 61. Also see James Laver, *Costume of the Western World: Fashions of the Renaissance* (New York: Harper and Brothers, 1951), 3.

precedent lord)."[23] However, this line carries other possibilities in light of the visual presentation of Danes on the early modern stage.

Danish, German, and Low Country Citizens

It is most likely that Hamlet calls Claudius a "king of shreds and patches" to reference the *pludderhoser* in which he most likely appeared. Pludderhoser are extra wide breeches with slashed fabric that were stuffed with different colored material and ribbons that would peek through the openings in the apparel.[24] The contemporary poet Thomas Nashe noted the tendency of the Danish to appear in such apparel in *Pierce Penilesse*, where he states

> his [the Dane's] apparel is so puft vp with bladders of Taffatie, and his back like biefe stuft with Parsly, so drawn out with Ribands and deuises, and blisterd with light sarcenet blastings, that you would thinke him nothing but a swarm of Butterflies, if you saw him a farre off.[25]

Hamlet has previously referred to Claudius as "A very pajock" (3.2.278), where "peacock" is likely intended. By identifying Claudius' "shreds and patches," Hamlet goes beyond mocking the King's garish visual presentation to reference his oversized breeches and invoke the apparel's most negative and common association: dipsomania.

Danes were frequently targeted for their tendency toward excessive drinking. As Hamlet himself notes:

> This heavy-headed revel east and west
> Makes us traduc'd and tax'd of other nations.
> They clip us drunkards, and with swinish phrase
> Soil our addition, and indeed it takes
> From our achievements, though perform'd at height,
> The pith and marrow of our attribute. . . .
> . . . the dram of [ev'l]
> Doth all the noble substance often doubt
> To his own scandal. (1.4.17–38)

The Danish are so well known for their drinking, Hamlet says, that their other, more laudable traits are eclipsed. Further mention of the Danish penchant for drinking appears in *Othello*, where Iago mentions it to highlight the Englishman's

---

[23]   William Shakespeare, *Hamlet*, eds. Ann Thompson and Neil Taylor (London: Thomson, 2006).

[24]   Cay Dollerup, "Danish Costume on the Elizabethan Stage," *The Review of English Studies* 25, no. 97 (1974): 54.

[25]   Thomas Nashe, *Pierce Penilesse, his Supplication to the Divell*, ed. G. B. Harrison (London, 1924), 35–6.

own drinking problems: "I learned it [drinking deeply] in England, where indeed they are most potent in potting; your Dane, your German, and your swag-bellied Hollander–Drink ho!–are nothing to your English" (2.3.76–9). According to Iago, the yardstick for determining the Englishman's tendency to drink excessively is set by the Danish, the Germans, and the Dutch. Not by coincidence, the appropriate apparel for all of these characters on the professional English stage is the extra wide breech. It was also the typical article found on the stage Swiss and likely the stage Fleming as well. Located in the same geographical region, these nations shared an identifying visual signifier on the English stage and were understood on sight to be defined primarily by their proclivity toward bibulousness.

By all dramatic accounts, the Danish, Germans, Dutch, Swiss, and Flemish were costumed identically. The large, baggy breeches of the Danish mentioned in *Pierce Penilesse* find their German equivalent in Benedict's strange fashions in Shakespeare's *Much Ado About Nothing* when Don Pedro accuses him of being "a German from the waist downward, all slops" (3.2.35–6). Large Dutch breeches appear in Haughton's *Englishmen for My Money* when Frisco, wanting to hide, wishes he "had the Dutchmans Hose, that I might creepe into the Pockets" (1612–3). Likewise, in Thomas Middleton's *No Wit, No Help Like a Woman's* (1612), when the Dutch Merchant enters with his son, the text reads "Enter Dutch Merchant with a little Dutch Boy in great slops."[26] It is not altogether clear from the text whether both wear large slops or just the boy, but the costuming convention of the Dutch suggests that they were similarly appareled.

Appearing on the English stage in oversized breeches, these characters were understood to have a common affinity for alcohol. The Danish penchant for drinking to excess has already been noted. The German's drunkenness appears as his definitive trait in *A Merchant of Venice* in which Portia mentions it as the reason she hopes she will not have to marry him (1.2.86–91). Virtually every play that includes Dutch characters throughout the period makes mention of their tendency to drink immoderately. From all of these characters we can infer a connection between a common attire and a predilection to drink excessively. But the link between baggy breeches and dipsomania is made overt in George Wither's 1633 poem, "Abuses Stript and Wipt: or, Satyricall Essays."[27] Ridiculing the English tendency to mimic the apparel of other nations, he writes that they often choose the "fashion for the drunken *Switzers slops*." With confidence we can assert that the Fleming, who was similarly defined by his tendency to drink and by an accent that was indistinguishable from stage-Dutch, also appeared in the baggy breeches appropriate to these characters.[28]

---

[26] Thomas Middleton, *No Wit, No Help Like a Woman's*, ed. Lowell E. Johnson, Regents Renaissance Drama Series (Lincoln: University of Nebraska Press, 1976), stage direction at 1.3.46–7.

[27] George Wyther, *Abvses Stript and Wipt, or Satirical Essayes* (London, 1613).

[28] Sometimes the characters were literally interchangeable. In Middleton's *No Wit, No Help Like a Woman's*, the Dutch Merchant is referred to as a Fleming. Savourwit says

And yet, just because these characters regularly appeared in clothes that carry a particular association, I do not mean to suggest that the theatre of the time dealt exclusively or even predominantly in simple stereotypes. Certainly there are instances in which the drama straightforwardly presents characters in large, baggy slops as alcoholics. As early as 1554, *An Enterlude of Welth and Helth* presents the Fleming Hance Berepot with garbled speech and a predilection for alcohol. He enters drunk, singing a Dutch song, and is an appropriate target for ridicule. Similarly John Marston can joke in *The Malcontent* (1604) that "amongst a hundred Dutch-men, [one finds] fourscore drunkards."[29] And, as late as 1635, Henry Glapthorne reviles the Dutch in *The Hollander* by presenting the title character, Jeremiah Sconce, falling on his face during a drinking scene.[30] But the plays also make more complex use of these characters' tendency to be associated with drunkenness.

Middleton's *No Wit, No Help Like a Woman's* specifically mentions the large slops in which the Dutch regularly appear, but does not present the wearers as drunkards. The Dutch Merchant in the play is sober, well mannered, and able to speak perfect English. Rather than an object of ridicule or comedy, he is the good Sir Oliver Twilight's loyal friend. However, the play does not dismiss the popular association of large, baggy breeches with alcoholism. Rather, it employs the convention in a new way to forward the plot. When the immoral servant Savourwit wants to discount the words of the Dutchman and sour his relationship with Sir Oliver Twilight, he accuses the Merchant of being a drunk and a liar. In this manner, the connection between drunkenness and Dutch apparel is reified even as it is employed here to condemn national stereotypes. Similarly, Dekker and Webster's *Westward Ho!* (1604) includes the Dutch tapster Hans. This character exhibits the broken English characteristic of the stage-Dutch and serves alcohol, but does not drink any himself. Rather, drinking appears as an English vice. The play presents the national association of the Dutch with alcohol to provide a contrast in which the English appear in a most unfavorable light.[31]

Dekker makes different use of Dutch apparel in *The Shoemaker's Holiday* (1599). In this play, the Englishman Lacy takes on the disguise of a Dutchman in order to avoid going to war and stay in London where he can woo his sweetheart Rose. Dekker's choice of costume for this character offers considerable room for comedy. Born the nephew of an Earl, Lacy is a nobleman whose fine apparel is as

---

"Would that Flemish ram / Had ne'er come near our house!" Thomas Middleton, *No Wit/ Help Like a Woman's; or, The Almanac*, in *Thomas Middleton: The Collected Works*, eds. Gary Taylor and John Lavagnino (Oxford: Clarendon Press, 2007), 5.8–9.

[29]   John Marston, *The Malcontent*, ed. George K. Hunter (Manchester: Manchester University Press, 1999), 3.1.19–20.

[30]   For a detailed discussion of the presentation of the Dutch in this play, see A. J. Hoenselaars, *Images of Englishmen and Foreigners in the Drama of Shakespeare and His Contemporaries* (London and Toronto: Associated University Presses, 1992), 203–5.

[31]   Hoenselaars, 115.

different from the working Dutchman's clothes as can be conceived. Previously, Lacy was seen in the most garish of ensembles: "here 'a wore a scarf, and here a scarf, here a bunch of feathers, and here precious stones and jewels, and a pair of garters—O monstrous!—like one of our yellow silk curtains" (2.25–8).[32] When he next appears, he sports the humble apparel of a shoemaker, including an apron and tools. But he also almost certainly wears the Dutchman's oversized, baggy breeches, for he enters singing a drinking song and is identified by Firk as one who can "give a villainous pull at a can of double beer" (4.94). Lacy's disguise is threefold, for he trades his noble, gentlemanly, English clothing for common, laborer's, drunken Dutch apparel.

Returning to *Hamlet*, we can see that the association of drunkenness with the large breeches worn by stage Danes serves to clarify the character of Claudius and establish important differences between him and his nephew. Hamlet notes early in the play that Claudius has this very night followed the Danish custom of excessive drinking:

> The King doth wake to-night and takes his rouse,
> Keeps wassail, and the swagg'ring up-spring reels;
> And as he drains his draughts of Rhenish down,
> The kettle-drum and trumpet thus bray out
> The triumph of his pledge. (1.4.8–12)

Taken together, Claudius's Danish nationality and his bibulousness provide compelling evidence that he appeared onstage in baggy breeches. Additionally, as the highest ranking character on the stage, Claudius would have been appropriately costumed in the apparel associated with the Danish (even if other characters did not wear baggy breeches). Consequently, Hamlet's indictment that he is a "king of shreds and patches" references his particular attire and accuses him of being both the leader of a conglomeration of drunks and the chief drunkard.

Although Danish himself, Hamlet makes a point of distancing himself from the national proclivity to drink immoderately. When Horatio asks if it is a local custom, Hamlet responds,

> Ay marry is't,
> But to my mind, though I am native here
> And to the manner born, it is a custom
> More honour'd in the breach than the observance. (1.4.12–6)

Hamlet's aversion to the practice appears not merely in his spoken words, but also in his visual presentation. In his choice of clothing, Hamlet opts for a suit that is not only of "solemn black," but also of sober black. On stage, Hamlet's black apparel would have struck a meaningful contrast to Claudius's festive pludderhoser, which

---

[32] Thomas Dekker, *The Shoemaker's Holiday*, ed. Anthony Parr (London: A & C Black, 1990), 2.25–8.

were marked by their size and the brightly colored fabric that would have shown through in celebration of his recent nuptials.[33] As one of the highest ranking people on stage and the eponymous hero of the play, Hamlet would have been earmarked for a distinctive costume as much as would Claudius. His chosen apparel marks his sobriety and positions him in contrast to the King's Danish presentation.

Beyond large, baggy breeches, plays from the period occasionally associate a few other articles with characters from this geographical region. I will only make short mention of them here because they appear sporadically and did not carry much significance for early modern audiences. Cay Dollerup argues that Danish characters on stage regularly appeared in the hats that were typical of the Danish at the time: elongated, dark fur hats without brims that were reminiscent of eggs.[34] He contends that in *Hamlet*, Osric likely wore such a hat, for Horatio says "This lapwing runs away with the shell on his head" (5.2.185–6). Hats are also mentioned in *The London Prodigal* (1605), in which the Englishwoman Frances praises Luce's Dutch headwear (although there is no way to say for certain what she wears). A Dutch cloak appears in *Englishmen for My Money*, worn by the Dutch character Vandalle and stolen by the clown Frisco who puts it on and says "now looke I as like the *Dutchman*, as if I were spit out of his mouth."[35] Jean MacIntyre suggests that the Dutch cloak had a distinctive collar unlike those of other nations, but there is no textual evidence to say for sure how the article appeared on stage.[36] The Danish hat and the Dutch cloak differ from the wide breeches in that the first two carry the totality of their significance in establishing the foreign origins of the wearer, while the oversized slops also suggest dipsomania. To varying degrees, all three served to materialize national difference in the theatre.

Moors

Particular articles of apparel spoke to an audience as clearly as a character's dialogue to establish the wearer's nationality and assert distinctive associations. Nowhere is this more true than in the dramatic presentation of Moors, whose

---

[33]   Claudius suggests that the court is simultaneously in a state of mourning for the death of King Hamlet and in a state of celebration for his marriage to Gertrude: "With an auspicious, and a dropping eye, / With mirth in funeral, and with dirge in marriage, / In equal scale weighing delight and dole" (1.2.11–4). And yet, as G. K. Hunter has noted, there can be no balanced attitude in one's choice of apparel. Claudius speaks of being equally happy and sad, but his clothes are almost certainly festive and contradict his words, G. K. Hunter, "Flatcaps and Bluecoats: Visual Signals on the Elizabethan Stage" *Essays and Studies* 33 (1980): 33–4.

[34]   Dollerup, 56. Dollerup also suggests that distinctive, crude gold chains that were regularly worn by Danes who visited England may have appeared on stage as well. However, this item is not mentioned in any play from the period.

[35]   William Haughton, *Englishmen for my Money, or A Woman will have her Will* (London: W. White, 1616), F2.

[36]   MacIntyre, 132.

skin color invoked a history of negative associations for early modern audiences. Virginia Vaughan clarifies the personation of Moors, "the black characters that populated early modern theatres tell us little about actual black Africans; they are the projections of imaginations that capitalize on the assumptions, fantasies, fears, and anxieties of England's pale-complexioned audiences."[37] Shakespeare invokes these assumptions, fantasies, fears, and anxieties in the opening scene of *Othello*. The play begins not with the Moor, but with Iago and Roderigo who appear before the house of Brabantio and inform him that his daughter is being ravished by Othello:

> IAGO: Your heart is burst, you have lost half your soul;
>   Even now, now, very now, an old black ram
>   Is tupping your white ewe. Arise, arise!
>   Awake the snorting citizens with the bell,
>   Or else the devil will make a grandsire out of you. (1.1.87–91)

The Venetian senator is at first unwilling to believe the two or even listen to them since he knows their character to be highly suspect and believes that his daughter lies safely in her room. When he learns that she is gone, however, he flip-flops, completely accepting the veracity of their allegations and acknowledging that before him is "nought but bitterness," for he believes in his heart that his daughter is in the lascivious arms of the Moor. Her absence from the house provides the "ocular proof" necessary to substantiate all of his anxieties about Othello who has not yet appeared on stage, but has been thoroughly prefigured for Brabantio and the audience by Iago's invocation of the Moor's black visual presentation. Othello gets no chance to establish his own identity on the English stage; he can only work against the prescriptions imposed by entrenched notions of blackness that had been firmly established in England and promulgated in the public playhouses.

It is important to remember, however, that the Jacobean audience that saw the black *Othello* in the next scene did not see before them an actual Moor. Rather, they saw the white actor Richard Burbage in blackface. The exact manner in which Burbage personated a Moor is open to some speculation, but historical precedent offers persuasive suggestions. Roughly fifty years before, King Edward took part in a masque of young Moors for which the participants wore face masks as well as elbow gloves of black velvet, and leggings of black leather. The hair of the Moors was simulated by means of "cappes made with Cowre budge."[38] A similar presentation of Moorish hair was seen during the reign of Elizabeth when masquers wore "Corled hed Sculles of black Laune."[39] It appears that actors

---

[37] Virginia Mason Vaughan, *Performing Blackness on English Stages, 1500–1800* (New York: Cambridge University Press, 2005), 5–6.

[38] Eldred D. Jones, "The Physical Representation of African Characters on the English Stage During the 16th and 17th Centuries," *Theatre Notebook* 17 (1962): 18.

[39] Albert Feuillerat, ed. *Documents Relating to the Revels at Court in the Time of Queen Elizabeth* (Louvain, 1914): 41.

on the public stages continued the tradition of using black gloves and leggings: Henslowe's diary lists "The Mores lymes,"[40] and the Peacham drawing presents the Moor with black arms and legs. Black paint would have been impractical for one's extremities because of the risk of getting it on one's apparel. Staining one's costume could discolor expensive clothes and threaten to break the stage illusion by accidentally drawing attention to the whiteness of the actor underneath the paint.

Over time, however, paint replaced the masks as the primary means by which a Moor's black face was presented on the stage.[41] In *The Masque of Blackness* (1605), the female masquers eschewed the traditional vizards and opted to blacken their skin. As Sir Dudley Carleton noted at the time:

> Instead of Vizzards, their Faces and Arms
> up to the Elbos, were painted black, which
> was Disguise sufficient, for they were hard
> to be known;[42]

It is interesting to note that here, the masquers used black paint on their arms as well. The use of paint to blacken one's face is mentioned in plays written for the popular stage, but no mention is made of also painting one's arms or legs. In *Lust's Dominion, or the Lascivious Queen* by Dekker, Haughton, and Day (1599–1600), to take on the disguise of the murdered Moors, Isabel recommends that Philip and Hortenzo "put the moors habits on, and paint your faces with the oil of hell (5.2.167–72)."[43]

The "oil of hell" alludes to the way that blackface was achieved on the early modern stage. Vaughan explains,

> Tallow or a similar grease was probably mixed with some sort of black powder, such as the color bases outlined in Nicholas Hilliard's manuscript, "The Arte of Limning" (ca. 1601). Hilliard describes black pigments made from burnt cherry stones, date stones, peach stones or charcoal, but for velvet black, he recommends a powder manufactured from ivory burnt in a crucible, ground with gum water.[44]

Vaughan goes on to suggest that the move from masks to black paint occurred in the late 1580s when black Moors began to have speaking roles that required an

---

[40]   Foakes, *Henslowe's*, 318.

[41]   The exception to this rule is those instances when a quick revelation of identity required the use of a mask that could be easily removed. See Jones, 19.

[42]   Sir Ralph Winwood, *Memorials of Affairs of State*, Vol. 2 (London, 1725), 43–4.

[43]   Thomas Dekker, *Lust's Dominion*, in *The Dramatic Works of Thomas Dekker*, ed. Fredson Bowers, Vol. 4 (Cambridge: Cambridge University Press, 1961).

[44]   Vaughan, 11.

actor to have a range of expressions that a vizard would hamper.[45] Starting with George Peele's *The Battle of Alcazar* (1588–1589), then, the "oil of hell" was likely the norm on the English stage and the primary means by which Burbage took on the visual identity of a Moor in *Othello*.

The appellation "oil of hell" for black face paint is particularly apt at this time in theatre history, for there was both a homiletic and a dramatic tradition presenting blackness as the identifying skin color of the devil. The mystery cycles in England presented blackness as a religious sign indicating that the bearer was a fallen soul. Interludes in the sixteenth century carried on and reified the practice, with the devil, Judas, and others being understood to be damned according to the well-known chromatic symbolism.[46] The association of blackness with the devil was well established at the beginning of the early modern period and remained strong throughout. The opening lines of Peele's *The Battle of Alcazar* invoke this association as the defining trait of the Moor:

> Blacke in his looke, and bloudie in his deeds,
> And in his shirt stained with a cloud of gore,
> Presents himself with naked sword in hand,
> Accompanied as now you may behold,
> With devils coted in the shapes of men. (1–20)[47]

In *Titus Andronicus*, when the Nurse brings forth Tamora's child, she acknowledges the baby's color in terms familiar to the audience of the time:

> NUR. She is delivered, lords, she is delivered. . .
> AAR. Well, God give her good rest! What hath he sent her?
> NUR. A devil.
> AAR. Why, then she is the devil's dam: a joyful issue.
> NUR. A joyless, dismal, black, and sorrowful issue! (4.2.61–6)

Similarly, in *Lust's Dominion, or the Lascivious Queen* by Dekker, Haughton, and Day (1599–1600), the Moor Eleazer is called a "fiend; / That damned *Moor*, that Devil, that Lucifer" (2.1.50–1), a "true stamp'd son of hell" whose "pedigree is written in thy face" (4.1.40–1), and one who "hath damnation dy'd upon his flesh" (5.2.20). And in *Othello*, Iago warns Brabantio that without quick action, "the devil will make a grandsire out of you." The association of black skin with the devil remained constant until 1642. The academic play *Sicily and Naples* (printed in 1640) calls the Moor Zisco "A Moore! A divell! A mere divell! His very lookes spake him so, but for his club-foote, his damnable club-foote (Asse that I was not

---

[45]   Ibid.

[46]   For a survey of the medieval tradition of presenting the damned as black, see Vaughan, particularly chapters 2 and 3.

[47]   George Peele, *The Battle of Alcazar*, in *The Dramatic Works of George Peele*, Vol. 2, ed. John Yoklavich (New Haven: Yale University Press, 1961).

to see it, I'me sure I feel it now,) 'tis an infallible sign" (8).[48] In these plays, skin color itself, versus some notion of racial identity, was crucial, for it alone served to signify damnation. *Titus Andronicus* draws attention to this fact. Aaron's black kinsman has had a child with a white woman, and the issue is white. Accordingly, we see that in the theatre, the Moor's black skin color is the corollary of evil, not its cause or effect. A white child, even one born to a black parent, does not bear the chromatic signifier of evil and dodges the negative association. On the contrary, "Aaron will have his soul black like his face" (3.1.204–5). As Sujata Iyengar has noted, the innate wickedness that attended black skin was widely understood by the inability of its wearer to blush modestly.[49] Thus, it was the proper visual identifier of the fallen soul.

Arden Othello editor E. A. J. Honigmann has raised the issue of the actual color of the stage Moor: "Should the Moor of Venice be played as a black, or as an Olive-coloured' Moor of north Africa?" He concludes that Othello did not appear as black, but was likely performed as an olive colored, "tawny" moor, citing an extant painting from 1600 of the Moroccan Ambassador to England, Abd el-Ouahed ben Messaoud, who appears with dark, but not black skin.[50] Robert Hornback counters this suggestion by noting that this painting provides the only evidence that Othello may have appeared as tawny, and faces an enormous number of references from the period that identify the Moors, even "tawny" ones, as identifiably and distinctively "black."[51] As Dympna Callaghan has convincingly argued, "black skin persisted as the most conspicuous marker of racial difference despite burgeoning distinctions between peoples of other races, such as 'white Moors,' 'blackamoors,' 'tawny Moors,' and 'savage m[e]n of Inde.' . . . blackface concealed under the sign of negritude a host of ethnicities ranging from Eskimo to Guinean."[52]

Appearing in blackface, the Moor was understood by the color of his skin to be evil. As Vaughan notes, "Blackness and villainy are originary conditions, not effect and cause."[53] But additional meaning accrued to the skin color. Muly Mahamet in *The Battle of Alcazar* is defined by his deceitfulness and cruelty, but later dramatic presentations of Moors established lasciviousness as a distinctive trait of black skin as well. Both Aaron in *Titus Andronicus* and Eleazar in *Lust's Dominion* establish their power through sexual relationships with royal white

---

[48]   Samuel Harding, *Sicily and Naples, or the Fatall Union. A Tragedy* (Oxford, 1640).

[49]   Sujata Iyengar, *Shades of Difference: Mythologies of Skin Color in Early Modern England* (Philadelphia: University of Pennsylvania Press, 2005), chapters 4 and 5.

[50]   This painting appears in Vaughan on page 58.

[51]   Robert Hornback, "Emblems of Folly in the First *Othello*: Renaissance Blackface, Moor's Coat, and 'Muckender,'" *Comparative Drama* 35 (2001): 72–6.

[52]   Dympna Callaghan, *Shakespeare Without Women: Representing Gender and Race on the Renaissance Stage* (New York: Routledge, 2000), 78.

[53]   Vaughan, 42.

women, with the second play very likely building upon the precedent of the first,[54] and both potentially drawing upon the earlier, now lost, *titus & vespacia.*

As a result of these previous dramatic presentations of Moors, early audiences of *Othello* would have understood Brabantio's anxieties regarding the sexual threat that Othello offered his daughter. And, it is against this predetermination that Othello's nobility stands in strongest relief. As G. K. Hunter notes, *Othello* is "the most magnificent specimen of the dramatic 'inversion of expected racial values' [for] before *Othello* there are no Moor figures who are not either foolish or wicked (or both)."[55] In contrast to a tradition of cruel, mendacious, lascivious Moors, Othello distinguishes himself as a peaceful, honest, and temperate Venetian citizen. Upon first entering the stage, Othello invokes a history of noble service to Venice to support his marriage to Desdemona, and his first action is to urge non-violence and patience when his party is confronted by the outraged Brabantio and his armed attendants.

Before he delivered any lines, however, Othello would have been identified on sight by two contrasting visual signifiers. The first is his black skin, which would have invoked the threat that earlier stage Moors had established and which Brabantio felt upon hearing that his daughter was alone with the Moor. The second would have been the Venetian apparel appropriate to a high ranking citizen. Although the play provides no details by which we can deduce specifically what Burbage wore to play the part, Othello's clothing would have marked him as a distinguished member of Venetian society and, when in Cyprus, a military general. It is most likely that English clothing was worn by everyone in the play, and that costumes served primarily to distinguish the individual characters' social stations. Robert Hornback has argued to the contrary that Othello appeared in a "Moor's coat."[56] Although such an item appears in the inventory of Henslowe's diary, and was probably the apparel in which earlier stage Moors appeared, I find it highly unlikely that Burbage wore one when he played the part. Not only does Othello break strongly with earlier presentations of Moors, he is also the only one to have a clear national association in the west. As Emily Bartels explains, "Othello *is*, as the subtitle announces, 'the Moor of Venice' . . . a figure defined by two worlds."[57]

---

[54]   Ibid., 51.

[55]   G. K. Hunter, *Dramatic Identities and Cultural Tradition* (Liverpool: Liverpool University Press, 1978), 29.

[56]   Hornback argues that the Moor's coat was a long piece of apparel that would have aligned Moors with fools and highlighted the characters' comic aspects. I find this argument unconvincing. Although a long coat was regarded by many as the proper apparel of fools at the time, there are too many others who also wore long coats to draw any immediate parallels. Contrary to Hornback's claim, Henslowe's diary suggests that the coat is the appropriate apparel of a horseman much more frequently than a fool, Hornback, 83–7.

[57]   Emily C. Bartels, "*Othello* and Africa: Postcolonialism Reconsidered," *William and Mary Quarterly*, 3rd ser., 54 (1997): 61.

These two "worn worlds" exist in Othello's visual presentation and would have spoken his dual identity to an early modern audience.[58]

The argument of *Othello*, visually speaking, is that these two worlds are mutually exclusive. Othello inverts the audience's expectations of a Moor in the first act of the play by realizing the promise of his Venetian apparel—the Duke notes Othello's Venetian merits and seeks to allay Brabantio's anxieties by saying "If virtue no delighted beauty lack, / Your son-in-law is far more fair than black" (1.3.280–90). Then, through the course of the rest of the play, Othello reverts or converts to the stereotype of the Moor, finally strangling the woman he loves and committing suicide. Daniel Vitkus has argued that Othello essentially "turns Turk" in the play, assuming the cruel, irreligious identity that he posits on the Ottoman enemy he is originally called upon to defeat.[59] There is much truth in Vitkus's observation, but it is important that we draw a distinction between the stage Moor and the stage Turk.

Vitkus correctly notes that Othello would not have been "identified with a specific, historically accurate racial category; rather he is a hybrid who might be associated, in the minds of Shakespeare's audience, with a whole set of related terms—*Moor, Turk, Ottomite, Saracen, Mahometan, Egyptian, Judean, Indian*— all constructed and positioned in opposition to Christian faith and virtue."[60] On the English stage, however, distinctions existed between the dramatic presentations of Moors and of Turks that made them discrete theatrical identities. The key feature distinguishing the two was their headwear. The chief identifying article worn by Turks is the turban, which I will discuss at length in the next chapter. The Moor, on the other hand, was repeatedly presented with distinctive black, curly hair. Since both a turban and one's hair both appear on the head, the two could not have been seen at the same time. The theatrical use of Moorish hair seems to have remained unchanged from the time of the masque of King Edward to the writing of *Othello* and beyond. In *Titus Andronicus*, Aaron the Moor mentions his hair, stating:

My fleece of woolly hair that now uncurls,
Even as an adder when she doth unroll
To do some fatal execution (2.3.34–6)

---

[58]   Peter Stallybrass coined "worn worlds" in the titles of two essays he has written regarding the ability of apparel to imprint the wearer in English society and on the English stage: "Worn Worlds: Clothes and Identity on the Renaissance Stage," in *Subject and Object in Renaissance Culture*, eds. Margreta de Grazia, Maureen Quilligan, and Peter Stallybrass (New York: Cambridge University Press, 1996) and "Worn Worlds: Clothes, Mourning, and the Life of Things," in *Cultural Memory and the Construction of Identity*, eds. Dan Ben-Amas and Liliane Weissberg (Detroit: Wayne State University Press, 1999).

[59]   Daniel J. Vitkus, "Turning Turk in *Othello*: The Conversion and Damnation of the Moor," *Shakespeare Quarterly* 48.2 (1997): 170–6.

[60]   Ibid, 159–60.

These lines would have made little sense in performance unless the actor playing Aaron appeared with a wig or with his hair styled to match the text. We find further evidence in the Peacham drawing, which clearly shows the Moor's short, curly, black hair. It is quite possible that the actor appears in a wig, with the band around his head being used to hold the hairpiece in place.

The early modern stage clearly differentiated the stage Moor and the stage Turk. However, the distinctions between these character types do not contradict John Gillies argument that "the sharper, more elaborately differentiated and more hierarchical character of post-Elizabethan constructions of racial difference are inappropriate to the problems posed by the Elizabethan other."[61] I do not wish to suggest that the theatres offered more astute representations of genuine Moor or Turk identities than has been previously asserted. However, I want to stress that the two were distinct entities on the English stage, separated by their particular costumes and defined significantly by theatrical precedent.

Vitkus's desire to conflate stage Moors with stage Turks is understandable since the stereotypical attributes of the two overlap considerably—both were understood to be vicious, iniquitous, and lascivious. However, the specific apparel of the Turks connected the wearer to a powerful nation that threatened the Christian world.[62] The Moor's black skin, on the other hand, identified him on the English stage as a fundamentally dislocated creature.[63] Muly Mahamet in *The Battle of Alcazar* is a powerful leader, but other Moors on the English stage are solitary figures in plays dominated by white characters. Such is the case with Othello, whom Roderigo calls "an extravagant and wheeling stranger / Of here and everywhere" (1.1.136–7). Consequently, we should be careful not to ignore the different costumes and character associations of Moors and Turks on the English stage. Taken together, the evidence regarding the stage Moor's visual presentation is extensive, revealing how they appeared and were originally received to a high degree of specificity.

Italians and Spaniards

In contrast to this superfluity of evidence, little exists to suggest how stage Italians were costumed. For plays set in Italy, this is to be expected, for the costumes most likely consisted of English apparel. Such is the case with *Othello*, which mentions numerous articles of apparel, all of which were appropriate to English fashion.

---

[61] John Gillies, *Shakespeare and the Geography of Difference* (Cambridge: Cambridge University Press, 1994), 32.

[62] Vitkus, 168–9.

[63] See Barbara Everett, "'Spanish' Othello: the making of Shakespeare's Moor" in *Shakespeare and Race*, eds. Catherine M.S. Alexander and Stanley Wells (New York: Cambridge University Press, 2000), 71, and Michael Neill, "'Mulattos,' 'Blacks,' and 'Indian Moors': *Othello* and Early Modern Constructions of Human Difference," *Shakespeare Quarterly* 49.4 (1998): 362.

But for those plays that are set in other countries and include Italian characters, insufficient evidence exists to assert what articles of apparel specifically signified Italian national identity on the English stage. Some items are noted to be associated with Italy; for instance, we find mention of "Italian doublets" and "Italian cloaks" in plays from the period. But these articles of apparel pose a new problem: they are not worn by Italians. Portia mentions an Italian doublet in *The Merchant of Venice*, but it does not appear on a Venetian. Rather it is part of the ridiculous ensemble worn by an Englishman who appears in clothes drawn from numerous locations.

Italian cloaks similarly appear on non-Italian characters in an attempt to show the inappropriateness of the wearer's chosen apparel. In *Richard II or Thomas of Woodstock* (1592), the English King Richard and his court appear in

> French hose, Italian cloaks and Spanish hats,
> Polonian shoes with peaks a handful long,
> Tied to their knees with chains of pearl and gold
> Their plumed tops fly waving in the air
> A cubit high above their wanton heads. (2.3.91–5)[64]

The Italian cloak serves as just one item among many marking the wearer's absurd visual presentation. At least two other plays make the same use of Italian cloaks. In Christopher Marlowe's *Edward II* (1591–1593), Gaveston draws others' ridicule for his bejeweled and absurdly gaudy "short Italian hooded cloak" (1.4.415),[65] and, in Thomas Tomkins' *Lingua: Or The Combat of the Tongue* (1602–1607), Phantastes mocks the "fantastical gulls" who appear wearing "a Spanish felt, a French doublet, a Granado stocking, a Dutch Slop, an Italian cloak, with a Welch freeze jerkin" (3.5.41–43).[66] In each of these plays, the Italian article of apparel does not serve to identify the wearer with Italy, nor does it bestow a particularly Italian association.

Another article associated with Italy (and sometimes with Spain), yet worn predominantly by others is the *chopine*, a woman's shoe with a long, raised cork sole. The base of the shoe could be anywhere from four inches long to nearly a foot and a half, requiring the wearer to walk with the help of another to avoid falling.[67] Thomas Coryate mentions chopines in his popular travel book *Coryats Crudities* (1611), stating that they were worn by all Venetian women.[68]

---

[64]   Peter Corbin and Douglas Sedge, eds., *Thomas of Woodstock or Richard the Second, Part One* (Manchester and New York: Manchester University Press, 2002).

[65]   Christopher Marlowe, *Edward II*, in *Christopher Marlowe: The Complete Plays*, ed. J. B. Steane (New York: Penguin, 1969).

[66]   W. Carew Hazlitt ed. *A Select Collection of Old English Plays*, vol. 9 (London: Reeves and Turner, 1874).

[67]   M. Channing Linthicum, *Costume in the Drama of Shakespeare and His Contemporaries* (Oxford: Clarendon Press, 1936), 248–50.

[68]   Thomas Coryate, *Coryat's Crudities*, 2 vols. (London: 1611). Coryat observes that "chapineys," which are "so common in Venice," are "not to be observed (I thinke) amongst any other women in Christendome" (1.400).

When these distinctive shoes appear in the drama, however, they are noted to be worn by non-Italians. In Philip Massinger's *The Renegado* (1623), Donusa, niece to the Ottoman Emperor, wears a pair.[69] Thomas Heywood mentions the "Italian in her high chopeene" in a song in *Challenge for Beauty* (1634–1636),[70] that is about the penchant of the English to steal fashions from other countries. Hamlet notes that a boy actor has grown by saying he is "nearer to heaven . . . by the altitude of a chopine" (2.2.425–6). The frequency with which chopines are mentioned in the drama of the period suggests that Italian women may very well have been portrayed wearing them on the English stage. However, the article does not seem to have carried any greater associations for them than an Italian nationality.

More suggestive is the likelihood that actors personating Italian women wore dresses that suggested lasciviousness. As Andreas Mahler has noted, English audiences believed Italian women to be driven by lust and desire, striving to keep up a façade of virtue.[71] An example of this stereotype can be seen in Edward Sharpham's comedy *The Fleire* (1606), in which the sisters Florida and Felicia find themselves poor and destitute upon arriving in London and decide to become prostitutes to support themselves. They state that they would rather be courtesans, for "your whore is for euery rascall but your Curtizan is for your Courtier" (sig. D2v).[72] Whether prostitutes or courtesans, however, the two were earmarked for their profession by their nationality which was likely manifested in the wearing of suggestive apparel. The cover of *Coryats Crutidies* provides a telling English pictorial representation of an Italian woman's lustfulness, depicting her in a dress that reveals her breasts. Across from her is a French woman who displays ample décolletage but appears positively modest compared to the Italian woman. The third woman in the picture is German and appears, fittingly, with a tankard on her head and vomiting.

We must not assume that this picture provides an accurate example of how a boy would have appeared on stage when dressed as an Italian woman. However, it does depict widely-held English stereotypes that would have influenced both how female Italian characters were presented in the theatre and the manner in which they were received.

The likelihood that Italian women were presented wearing evocative apparel is suggested in John Webster's *The Duchess of Malfi* (1612–1614). After becoming

---

[69] Philip Massinger, *The Renegado*, in *Three Turk Plays From Early Modern England*, ed., Daniel J. Vitkus (New York: Columbia University Press, 2000).

[70] Thomas Heywood, *The Dramatic Works of Thomas Heywood Now First Collected with Illustrative Notes and a Memoir of the Author*, Vol. 5 (London: G. Pearson, 1874), 66.

[71] Andreas Mahler, "Italian Vices: Cross–Cultural Constructions of Temptation and Desire in English Renaissance Drama," in *Shakespeare's Italy: Functions of Italian Locations in Renaissance Drama* (Manchester and New York: Manchester University Press, 1993), 60.

[72] Edward Sharpham, *The Fleire* (London: 1607).

Fig. 3.2   Title page of Thomas Coryate, *Coryats Crudities* (1611), STC 5808.
              By permission of the Huntington Library.

pregnant, the Duchess begins to wear clothing that will hide her condition from others. Bosola notes "She wanes i'th'cheek, and waxes fat i'th' flank; / And, contrary to our Italian fashion, / Wears a loose-bodied gown" (2.1.69–71).[73] This line offers the possibility that it was common for Italian women to be performed in form fitting dresses. And yet, the fact that Bosola goes so far as to note that wearing loose gowns contradicts Italian fashion suggests that the tighter clothing may not have been widely understood by English audiences to be appropriate apparel for them. In either configuration, the action of Webster's play moves forward—the Duchess's situation becomes more urgent—as a result of her visible change of clothing from tighter apparel to a loose gown. But larger arguments regarding the Italian woman's costumes are difficult to construct with certainty.

A greater understanding of stage Italians could perhaps be gleaned by employing a broader definition of an actor's visual presentation, one that also considers a character's deportment. Keir Elam notes that "the areas of behaviour particularly associated with Italy were the courtly disciplines or arts of the body, such as genteel modes of walking (Harrison's 'going up and down'), curtseying, dancing, and fencing."[74] Elam references William Harrison's *Description of England* in which he deprecates the practice of some Englishmen to go to Italy and mimic their affectations upon returning to England, particularly their manner of walking: "Such men as this last are easily knowen; for they haue learned in Italie, to go vp and downe also in England."[75] The notion that Italians carried themselves in a proud manner that identified their nationality was almost certainly employed on the stage. A full consideration of modes of deportment falls outside the scope of this book, but for just one example, we can look to Haughton's *Englishmen for My Money*. The Italian merchant Alvaro is ideally suited to an overly and overtly haughty demeanor. Full of classical learning and national pride, Alvaro's character called for a deportment that signified his sense of superiority despite the fact that he is a merchant, not a courtier. Moreover, his pretentiousness would have contributed to the comedy in the play when the ridiculous foreigner tried (and failed) to win the heart of an Englishwoman.

Pride and a sense of superiority were not unique to stage Italians, but were even more appropriate to stage Spaniards. In Marston's *The Malcontent*, Bilaroso notes that "amongst a hundred Spaniardes, [you will find] threescore braggarts" (3.1.19–20), supporting the English conviction that arrogance was the defining feature of the Spaniard. This haughtiness found clear articulation in the stage Spaniard's typical costume, which included an oversized ruff, a short, wide cloak that entirely

---

[73] John Webster, *The Duchess of Malfi*, ed. Elizabeth M. Brennan (New York: W W Norton, 1993).

[74] Keir Elam, "English Bodies in Italian Habits," in *Shakespeare, Italy, and Intertextuality*, ed. Michele Marrapodi (Manchester and New York: Manchester University Press, 2004), 32.

[75] William Harrison, *Description of England*, 2 vols., ed. L. Whitington (London, Walter Scott, 1899), vol. 2, 130.

covered the top half of the body, large breeches, and a wide-brimmed hat. Such is the apparel in which Surly appears in *The Alchemist* (1610) when he disguises himself as a Spanish Don. Upon seeing him, Subtle says "He looks in that deep ruff like a head in a platter, / Served in by a short cloak upon two trestles." (4.3.24–5).[76] When the puritan Ananais sees Surly, he mentions a distinctly Spanish hat while ridiculing Surly's entire ensemble: "That ruff of pride / About thy neck betrays thee . . . Thou look'st like Antichrist, in that lewd hat" (4.7.51–5).

The oversized ruff, broad cloak, large breeches, and wide-brimmed hat were well known visual codes for the Spaniard throughout the period. When Horatio Busino, chaplain to the Venetian Embassy, witnessed the Lord Mayor's Show in 1617, he saw an Englishman play the part of a Spaniard for the audience's derision and delight, and recorded the event: "Among the figures represented was a Spaniard, wonderfully true to life, who imitated the gestures of that nation perfectly. He wore small black moustachios and a hat and cape in the Spanish fashion with a ruff round his neck and others about his wrists, nine inches deep."[77] These individual articles of apparel, along with Spanish breeches, received frequent mention in the drama of the period, and were tightly associated with Spanish pride. Hoenselaars notes that pride was presented in the literature of the period as originally coming to England from Spain: in the ballad titled "The lamentable fall of Queen Elnor," Queen Elinor of Castile is introduced as "the first that brought this land the deadly sinne of pride." George Peele's dramatic rendering of Queen Elinor's story, *Edward I* (1591), presents her scoffing at English "freeze" and preferring more expensive and luxurious tissues.[78]

English contempt for Catholic Spain was rabid throughout the early modern period and found in Spanish apparel, particularly the ruff, a focus for its scorn. An examination of portraits from the period shows that large ruffs were not the sole province of the Spanish but appear often and with roughly equal frequency in paintings of the English, French, Dutch, and Italians as well.[79] And yet, large ruffs were popularly derided in England as the distinctive and prideful fashion of Spain, this despite the fact that the wearing of oversized ruffs was disparaged for its pridefulness in English religious texts and sermons. The religious zealot Phillip Stubbes devotes considerable attention in his discussion of the "Pride of Apparel" to the sinfulness of wearing large ruffs, noting that some people in Ailgna (England) wear them "a quarter of a yard deep, yea some more, very

---

[76] Ben Jonson, *The Alchemist*, in *Five Plays*, ed. G. A. Wilkes (New York: Oxford Univerity Press, 1981).

[77] Allen B. Hinds, ed. *Calendar of Papers, Venetian*, Vol. 15 (London: HMSO, 1909), 62.

[78] Hoenselaar, 33.

[79] Laver's survey of the fashions worn across Europe demonstrates the pervasiveness of large ruffs at the time.

few lesse."[80] The wearing of oversized ruffs was also widely decried from the pulpit in "The Sermon Against Excess of Apparel" (first published in 1563), which criticized those who "hang their revenues about their necks, ruffling in their ruffs."[81] Repeatedly, the English looked beyond their own proclivity to wear enormous ruffs and posited that vice on the Spanish. In *The Alchemist*, the puritan Ananais attacks the immorality of Surly's Spanish apparel, but uses language drawn directly from religious condemnations of English excesses of apparel.

Beyond the plays and the Lord Mayor's Show that Busino witnessed, English pictorial representations of the Spanish frequently presented them in enormous ruffs and distinctive, wide-brimmed hats. The title page of George Carleton's *A Thankful Remembrancer of God's Mercie* (1624) includes sixteen images of Spanish-inspired Popish plots against Queen Elizabeth and King James that present the Spanish clothed in giant neckwear and distinctive hats.[82] In these pictures, the unvarying visual presentation of Spanish characters acts as a natural and necessary corollary to the insidious individuals that would carry out such evil deeds against the English.

The Alchemist demonstrates this understanding of the Spanish and Spanish apparel in Dame Pliant's response to the suggestion that she marry with the Spanish Don (Surly in disguise): "Truly I shall never brook a Spaniard. . . . Never sin' eighty-eight could I abide 'em, / And that was some three year afore I was born, in truth" (4.4.28–30). Dame Pliant agrees to marry the Spaniard when her brother threatens her with violence, but her reasoning demonstrates the suggestiveness of Spanish apparel and the associations it carried when presented onstage. She mentions the threat offered to England in 1588 by the Spanish Armada, but the fear that the English felt in the face of the most powerful Catholic country in Europe existed before that time and continued unabated beyond the interregnum, and was invoked by the disguise Surly wears onstage.

Surly goes beyond the staple components of a Spanish costume, to also color his beard and darken his skin, "To dye your beard, and umber o'er your face" (5.5.52). Perhaps the facial hair he tinted came to resemble the "small black moustachios" that Bussino saw on the man playing a Spaniard in the Lord Mayor's Day festivities, but there is no way to be sure. The darker skin Surly affects references Spain's history of having been occupied by the Moors until 1492 and serves the action of the play by concealing the fact that he is fat when the Spanish were expected to be lean. After Subtle says "he does look too fat to be a Spaniard," he accepts Surly's Spanish identity saying "Your scurvy, yellow, Madrid face is welcome"

---

[80]   Phillip Stubbes, *Phillip Stubbes's Anatomy of the Abuses in England in Shakespeare's Youth, A.D. 1583*, part 1, ed. Frederick J. Furnivall (London: The New Shakespeare Society, 1877–1879), 51.

[81]   *Certain Sermons or Homilies Appointed to be Read in Churches in the Time of Queen Elizabeth and Reprinted by Authority from King James* (Philadelphia: Edward C. Biddle 1844), 278.

[82]   This picture appears in Michael Duffy, *The Englishman and the Foreigner* (Cambridge: Chadwyck-Healey, 1986), 61.

(4.3.28–32). Other plays note that Spaniards were expected to be thin,[83] but I have not found other instances where the actor's skin was likely darkened for the role. When Lovewit assumes the disguise of a Spaniard by donning Hieronimo's cloak, hat, and ruff, we can assume he did not have time to also darken his skin, and yet he succeeded in establishing his disguise and marrying the Widow Pliant.

The fact that Lovewit's Spanish disguise is purchased from players and was supposedly the costume for Hieronimo in Thomas Kyd's *The Spanish Tragedy* (1589) would seem to suggest that the large ruff, wide cloak, and broad brimmed hat that appear in *The Alchemist* were worn in the earlier production. This is unlikely, however, since Kyd's play is set in Spain. Were all of the characters dressed in the apparel of the stage Spaniard, distinguishing between them would have been difficult. Not surprisingly, then, *The Spanish Tragedy* makes no mention at all of the articles of apparel that were associated with Spanish identity and pride. Moreover, Hieronimo is one of the more humble characters in the play and would have been earmarked for a smaller ruff than the Spanish King, the Duke, or Lorenzo. Interestingly, the illustration that appeared on the title page of the 1615 edition of the play (and subsequent editions) mirrors the likelihood that in production, *The Spanish Tragedy* was largely costumed in English apparel: the ruffs are not oversized; the breeches are not so large as to denote Spanish excess; and none of the hats have extraordinarily wide brims.

R. A. Foakes notes that "the illustration as a whole may have no direct connection with stage performances, and certainly no attempt has been made in it to suggest a stage, but it is not unreasonable to assume that . . . the costumes, were something like those represented on the 1615 title page."[84] The fact that the characters in the picture appear in largely English apparel supports the likelihood that the drawing is derived from an actual production. In *The Alchemist*, Jonson's mention of Hieronimo's costume does not reference an actual set of apparel previously worn on the stage. Instead, it plays on the nature of character and identity in performance. By referencing a costume associated with another play, Jonson highlights the fact that the clothes worn by all of the characters currently on stage are also merely costumes. Each performer's act of personation is challenged even as the action of the play proceeds through the use of a metatheatrical conceit.

French

Like the stage Spaniard, French characters on the English stage were similarly identifiable by a few specific articles of apparel. However, they were also broadly expected to appear in the most fashionable apparel worn at the time, even as the times and fashions changed. Accordingly, in *Hamlet*, when Laertes prepares to

---

[83]   Richard Brome's *The Northern Lass* (1629) mentions that "They [the Spanish] are a People of very spare dyet, I haue heard, and therefore seldome fat." Richard Brome, *A Critical Edition of Brome's* The Northern Lass, ed. Harvey Fried (New York: Garland, 1980), (5.8.155–6).

[84]   Foakes, *Illustrations*, 105.

Fig. 3.3   Title page of Thomas Kyd, *The Spanish Tragedy* (1623), STC 15093. By permission of the Huntington Library.

go to France, his father Polonius urges that he purchase the finest apparel he can afford lest he stand out as inferior by virtue of his poorer dress:

> Costly thy habit as thy purse can buy,
> But not express'd in fancy, rich, not gaudy,
> For the apparel oft proclaims the man,
> And they in France of the best rank and station
> [Are] of a most select and generous chief in that. (1.3.70–4)

The English believed that the French manner of dress reached and often overreached the height of fashion, exceeding the limits of decorum to appear overly extravagant or gaudy in appearance. In his *Crudities*, Coryate criticizes the lavishness of English dress by comparing it to the French: "we weare more phantasticall fashions then any Nation under the Sunne doth, the French onely excepted."[85] Similarly, in James Shirley's *The Ball* (1632), the French dancing master Le Frisk is introduced as a "Court Dancing weesill" whose overelegant way of dressing is considered "a sinne

---

[85]   1.398.

oth' state."[86] Chapter two noted that fashionable apparel and rich fabrics typically served either to establish one's high class or to mark the wearer as undeserving of what he or she has on. As we see in *The Ball*, the English stage took advantage of the comic potential endemic to the Frenchman's choice of apparel. By wearing garish clothing that would be inappropriate for even the most aristocratic of characters, the Frenchman's role in the drama is clear: Le Frisk is earmarked for comic derision on sight and deserves the abuse he receives throughout the play.

The French character's proclivity to wear lavish clothing additionally served to highlight the wearer's vanity. Marston's *The Malcontent* states that "amongst a hundred French-men [one finds] forty hot-shottes" (3.1.19–20). Typifying the Frenchman's gaudy apparel and serving as a visual signifier for vanity was the wearing of feathers. In *The Jew of Malta* (1589-1590), when Barabas disguises himself as a French musician, he appears with a lute and a nosegay in his hat (4.4.39).[87] He likely wore other clothes to establish his disguise, but the nosegay serves as the quintessential item identifying his new nationality. Similarly, in *Henry VIII*, Sir Thomas Lovell laments the fact that English gallants have embraced French fashions and urges them to "leave those remnants of fool and feather that they got in France" (1.3.24–5). Unlike the articles of clothing that signified other nationalities in early modern drama, the wearing of feathers fulfilled no utilitarian purpose, serving only to render one's overall ensemble more ostentatious. Moreover, a direct connection between vanity and the wearing of feathers appears in English drama in the interlude *The Contention between Liberality and Prodigality* (1567–1568 and performed again by the Children of the Chapel Royal in 1601). In this play, the character Vanity appears onstage "all in feathers." Other characters on the English stage also wore feathers,[88] but the embellishment was particularly appropriate to the vain French.

In addition to appearing vain with their choice of apparel, French characters asserted their lascivious leanings in their visual presentation. Hoenselaars has dated the origin of the English association of the French with lechery and amorous pursuits to the thirteenth century and noted that it runs throughout the early modern period.[89] The French hose, although a popular style throughout Europe and able to be worn without comment, was employed in drama to reference the wearer's sexual proclivities. In *Henry V* (1599), the Dauphin mentions the Constable of France's French hose when he insults him to suggest that he both lacks sexual vigor and has an old mistress: "O then belike she [your mistress] was old and gentle, and you rode like a kern of Ireland, your French hose off, and in your strait strossers" (3.7.52–4). The notion here is that the Constable has

---

[86]   Hoeselaars, 205. *The Ball: A Comedy; As It Was Presented by Her Majesties Servants at the Private House in Drury Lane. Written by George Chapman and James Shirley* (London, 1639), sig. A4r.

[87]   Christopher Marlowe, *The Complete Plays*, ed. J. B. Steane (New York: Penguin, 1969).

[88]   See Linthicum, 221.

[89]   Hoenselaars, 16.

relinquished his French hose, and in doing so, divested himself of his distinctly French sexual competence. Moreover, by trading his French hose for the Irish "strait strossers," he would have exchanged his stylish French apparel for the most unfashionable clothes conceivable. The French hose was the appropriate breech for a lover because it reaches only from the waist to the middle of the thigh and allows the shape of the rest of the leg to be appreciated because of the skin-tight nether stocking. In *Henry VIII*, the article is described as "tall stockings, short blist'red breeches" (1.3.30–31).

On the English stage, the French hose was able to carry its amorous association beyond French characters. In *Romeo and Juliet* (1595), Mercutio mentions Romeo's French hose as the culmination of a lengthy lampoon of Romeo's overly romantic disposition:

> [Here comes Romeo] Without his roe, like a dried herring: O flesh, flesh, how art thou fishified! Now is he for the numbers that Petrarch flow'd in. Laura to his Lady was a kitchen wench (marry, she had a better love to berhyme her), Dido a dowdy, Cleopatra a gipsy, Helen and Hero hildings and harlots, Thisby a grey eye or so, but not to the purpose. Signior Romeo, *bon jour!* there's a French salutation to your French slop. You gave us the counterfeit fairly last night" (2.4.43–5).

The "counterfeit" Romeo gave his friends, Mercutio suggests, was to slip away for a secret sexual liaison. Romeo's French hose, appearing in a play set in Venice, stands out as a distinctively foreign article of apparel and signifies the wearer's passionate inclinations. Robert Daborne's *A Christian Turned Turk* (1612) makes similar, if not even more bawdy use of French hose. While Gallop is in the act of having sex with another man's wife, a pair of Sailors discovers the pile of clothes left behind by the lovers. Upon finding the article of apparel that marks Gallop's successful tryst they exclaim: "S'hart, a French slop!" The wearing of French hose to signify one's amorous desires naturally invoked the early modern belief that lust effeminates.[90] Wearing the distinctive apparel of the lover, Romeo refuses to fight Tybalt and Mercutio dies. Afterward Romeo berates himself in highly suggestive terms: "O sweet Juliet, / Thy beauty hath made me effeminate, / And in my temper softened valor's steel!" (3.1.113–5). This connection between French hose, libidinous desire, and effeminateness suggests that the French, and those who appear in their apparel, were understood by English audiences to be emasculate.[91]

---

[90] Stephen Orgel, *Impersonations: The Performance of Gender in Shakespeare's England* (New York: Cambridge University Press, 1996), 25–6.

[91] The English additionally associated French fashion with the pox, syphilis. As Roze Hentschell has argued, "*Morbus Gallicus* was regarded as both a venereal disease and an obsession with French clothing and manners. Often these two 'maladies' were seen as one; overt preoccupation with French fashions was taken as a symptom of the disease and vice versa; vanity and venery were thus interchangeable." Roze Hentschell, "Luxury and Lechery: Hunting the French Pox in Early Modern England" in *Sins of the Flesh: Responding to Sexual Disease in Early Modern Europe*, ed. Kevin Siena (Toronto: Centre for Reformation and Renaissance Studies, 2005), 134.

Like French men, French women were similarly understood by the English to be lascivious, and dressed the part on the English stage.[92] The title page of Coryate's *Crudities* presents a French woman in a dress displaying ample décolletage. This representation of French women appears in Richard Brome's *The Damoiselle* (1638), in which the Englishman Frank impersonates a French lady, Frances, and suggests how a woman ought to dress, saying one ought to "set forth . . . Head, Face, Neck, Breast . . . To cover, or discover any part--- / Unto de best advantage."[93] Among her recommendations, Frances provides advice for how the English Mrs. Bumpsey can win the love and sexual desire of both her husband and of all other men.

In addition to wearing dresses that revealed the wearer's chest to suggest sexual availability, female French characters also likely appeared in French farthingales and French hoods. These fashionable items were well known and widely worn by English women, but may very well have been exploited on the stage for the national association invoked by their appellations. Because their name ties them to French women, mention of French hoods appears most frequently when they are worn by Englishwomen striving to assert a recent rise in social station. Thus, in *The Shoemaker's Holiday*, Margery celebrates her husband's financial success and election to Sheriff by seeking out a "French-hood maker" (10.36). Similarly, in George Chapman's *Eastward Ho!* (1605), Gertrude enters in 1.2 wearing "French head attire and a Citizens gown."[94] and accompanied by a tailor who carries items culled from the fashions of other countries. For men, "French doublets" receive mention in a number of plays, and refer to a distinctive cut that was considered highly stylish, but carried no greater associations on the stage.

Before we move beyond the French, one special instance deserves mention. In Shakespeare's *Henry V*, the French Montjoy enters and announces his identity by referencing his apparel: "You know me by my habit." King Henry's reply makes it clear that he does indeed know him and suggests that the audience was similarly familiar with Montjoy's visual presentation: "Well then, I know thee" (3.6.114–5). However, it is unlikely that Montjoy's identity was primarily defined by his French apparel. Rather, as a herald, he would have appeared in distinctive apparel that served to identify both his nation and his function. Most likely, Montjoy would have worn a *tabard*, or *herald's coat*. Falstaff suggests how a tabard would have appeared in *1 Henry IV*, when he says "two napkins tack'd together and thrown

---

[92]   Shakespeare's most famous French woman, Joan De Pucelle (Joan of Arc) in *1 Henry VI* appears not in French apparel, but in armor. Nevertheless, she serves as an archetype of negative English attitudes toward French women, depicted in the play, Deanne Williams concisely explains, as "a vilified whore." Deanne Williams, *The French Fetish from Chaucer to Shakespeare* (New York: Cambridge University Press, 2004), 189.

[93]   Richard Brome, *The Damoiselle, or The New Ordinary*, in *Five New Playes* (London: 1658), G1v.

[94]   George Chapman, Ben Jonson, and John Marston, *Eastward Ho*, ed. R. W. Van Fossen (Manchester: Manchester University Press, 1979).

over the shoulders like a herald's coat without sleeves" (4.2.43–5). The tabard was traditionally emblazoned with a coat of arms, and Montjoy would have appeared wearing that of the King of France, thereby defining his allegiance and his duty on sight.

Irish, Scottish, and Welsh

On the early modern stage, depictions of the foreigners closest to England, specifically the Irish, Scottish, and Welsh, highlighted national differences as vigorously as they did with citizens of other nations. Christopher Highley has noted that the English tended to see connections among its borderlands, and to merge Ireland, Scotland, and Wales into a single territorial and ethnographic zone, with common linguistic and cultural ties.[95] Accordingly, the Shakespearean stage registered the sense that Celts were members of a different nationality (or at least ethnography) than the English by costuming them in non-English apparel. However, notions of Celtic unity did not keep stage Irishmen, Scotsmen, and Welshmen from each having distinctive costumes that highlighted the wearer's country of origin and asserted one's national character.

Of the three, we can determine the apparel worn by Irish characters on the English stage with most certainty. Pictorial evidence along with references from plays support the likelihood that stage Irishmen appeared wearing items drawn from the following: a *brat*, a *leine*, an *ionar*, *trowsers*, *bróg*, a *dart*, and a *scian*.[96] The brat was a large semicircular mantle made of rough hairy cloth that bore a fringe all around. It was the topmost article of apparel worn by the Irish. The leine was a tunic or shirt that was typically dyed yellow; it seems to have gone out of use by the end of the sixteenth century.[97] The ionar was a jacket that sometimes had a short pleated skirt and could reach either to the waist or knee. Trowsers were tight, straight breeches that hugged the leg and were of variable length. Bróg was a rough, rawhide shoe. The dart was a light throwing spear, and the scian was a large dagger.

Mention of any of the Irish articles of apparel on stage served to invoke the commonly held English association of the Irish with incivility and wildness.[98] In Beaumont and Fletcher's *Coxcomb* (1608), when Antonio appears disguised as

---

[95]   Christopher Highley, *Shakespeare, Spenser, and the Crisis in Ireland* (New York: Cambridge University Press, 1997), 68.

[96]   For my lists and descriptions of Irish, Scottish, and Welsh articles on the English stage, I draw heavily on J. O. Bartley, *Teague, Shenkin and Sawney: An Historical Study of the Earliest Irish, Welsh and Scottish Characters in English Plays* (Cork: Cork University Press, 1954), particularly 9–11, 50–1, 80–1.

[97]   Ibid, 10.

[98]   Ibid, 39, and Thomas Healy, "Drama, Ireland and the Question of Civility," in *Early Modern Civil Discourses*, edited by Jennifer Richards (New York: Palgrave, 2003), 131. For instance, in *2 Henry VI*, Shakespeare speaks of "the uncivil kerns of Ireland" (3.1.310).

an Irish footman, he says "I hope I am wilde enough for being knowne" (2.3.1).[99]
The brat was likely the most recognizable sartorial signifier of the Irish. Edmund
Spenser commented on the item, saying it is 'a fit house for an out-law, a meet bed
for a rebel, and an apt cloke for a thiefe.'[100] The drama supports this view of the
brat. In *Sir John Oldcastle* (1599–1600), the Irishman MacChane is a murderer
who escapes by stealing Harpool's clothes. Forced to don the Irishman's apparel,
Harpool seeks help, yelling "this *Irish* rascal that lodg'd with me all night, hath
stollen my apparel, and has left me nothing but a lowsie mantle, and a pair of
broags" (19.40–42).[101] Of course, when Harpool is seen wearing the Irish brat, he
is apprehended as a criminal himself. Later in the play, it becomes clear that the
Irishman had also been wearing trowsers. When the Irishman is confronted with his
crime and faces death, he asks for his clothes back and for an Irish style execution:
"let me have mine own cloathes, my strouces there, and let me be hang'd in a wyth
after my country the *Irish* fashion" (22.123–5). With this request, the Irishman
reifies the association between his crime and his Irish attire, and suggests the two
are ineluctably connected in the minds of both the English who sought to arrest the
man wearing the apparel and the Irish who proudly claim the clothes as their own.

John Speed's 1610–1611 map of Ireland includes pictures of six Irish natives,
divided into three pairs: Wild Irishman and Wild Irishwoman, Civil Irishman and
Civil Irishwoman, Gentleman of Ireland and Gentlewoman of Ireland.[102] All six
appear in brats, with social class most clearly distinguished by the quality of the
mantle that each wears. However, the Wild Irish also appear different from the other
two pairs by not wearing hats or other headwear, and having long, unkempt hair.
Although Speed provides three classes of Irish, the early modern stage represented
only the Wild Irish when it costumed Irish characters, consistently presenting them
without hats and commenting on their disheveled hair. As early as 1587, Thomas
Hughes's *The Misfortunes of Arthur* presents a dumbshow including a man who
appears "bareheaded, with blacke long shagged haire downe to his shoulders,
apparailed with an Irish Iacket and shirt, hauing an Irish dagger by his side and a
dart in his hand."[103] The text explains that this character represents Revenge and
Fury. More than forty years later, the visual presentation of the Irish remained the
same. John Ford's *Perkin Warbeck* (c. 1633) includes a masque with Warbeck's

[99]   Francis Beaumont and John Fletcher, *The Works of Beaumont and Fletcher; The
Text Formed from a New Collation of the Early Editions*, ed. Alexander Dyce (Boston:
Phillips, Sampson, and Co, 1854).

[100]   Edmund Spenser, *A View of the State of Ireland*, eds. Andrew Hadfield and Willy
Maley (Oxford: Basil Blackwell, 1997), 57.

[101]   *The Oldcastle Controversy:* Sir John Oldcastle, Part I *and* The Famous Victories of
Henry V, eds. Peter Corbin and Douglas Sedge (Manchester: Manchester University Press,
1991.

[102]   John Speed, *Theatre of the Empire of Great Britaine* (London, 1612).

[103]   Thomas Hughes, *The Misfortunes of Arthur*, eds. Harvey Carson Grumbine, Francis
Flower, and William Fulbeck (Berlin: E. Felber, 1900), 133–4.

followers disguised as "four wild Irish in trowses, long-haired, and accordingly habited" (3.2.111–12).[104] In early modern England, headwear was deemed the appropriate apparel of all civilized people. The practice of presenting the Irish with heads bare and long, scruffy hair would have asserted their wildness clearly to a contemporary audience. It is interesting to note that in the Peacham drawing, the two characters on their knees on the right appear without hats. Perhaps their headwear was merely taken from them when they were captured, but it is possible the Queen's sons, whose cruel actions mark their wildness, were understood on sight as the villains they prove to be.

Along with the brat and long hair, trowsers also deserve additional attention when considering Irish costume. Trowsers were noticeably different from French hose or Venetians, both of which had width to them and gathered at the leg. Additionally, and more importantly, the trowsers were frequently worn without nether stockings. Unlike all other nationalities depicted on the English stage, Irish characters often appeared with bare lower legs and sometimes without shoes. In Dekker's *Old Fortunatus* (1599), Andelocia takes on the disguise of an Irish costermonger and says "I weare out my naked legs and my footes, and my tods" (4.2.63–4).[105] The practice of going without nether stockings was practical for the Irish who had to walk among the bogs.[106] However, on stage, the incivility of appearing with bare legs marked the nation that embraced the fashion.

Thomas Healy has argued that "it is wrong to imagine simple definitions of savagery and civility performed on the stage any more than it was to find them in real life."[107] Certainly he is correct, but in the case of Irish costumes we have an exception. The English stage invested their distinctive apparel with broad, straightforward associations that could be manipulated in the drama, but remained essentially unchanged throughout the period.

We cannot make such certain conclusions about the costumes worn to portray Scotsmen and Welshmen as we can about Irishmen. Certainly they would have also been identifiable on stage, but they were not characterized as negatively as the Irish. Scottish characters pose the greatest challenge, offering no consistent "type" before 1642 and offering few associations with their distinctive apparel.[108] Only two articles of clothing specifically belonged to the stage Scotsman: the blue bonnet, and the *whinyard*, a short sword or hanger. It is important to note

---

[104] John Ford, *The Chronicle History of Perkin Warbeck, A Strange Truth*, ed. Peter Ure (London: Methuen, 1968).

[105] Thomas Dekker, *The Dramatic Works of Thomas Dekker*, Vol. 1, ed. Fredson Bowers (Cambridge: Cambridge University Press, 1962).

[106] Jones and Stallybrass analyze how the practice of the Irish to go with bare legs and feet was employed as iconography in the portrait of Captain Thomas Lee made by Marcus Gheerhaerts in 1594, 50–1.

[107] Healy, 144.

[108] For a discussion of how Scotland was broadly understood in the English imagination, see William C. Carroll, *Macbeth: Texts and Contexts* (Boston: Bedford/St. Martin's, 1999).

that when we discuss Scottish characters we mean Lowland Scotland, which was non-Gaelic, Protestant, and oriented toward England. Highland Scotland, along with the Anglo-Scottish Marches, and the Western Isles were thoroughly Gaelic and oriented toward Ireland.[109] The drama of the period did not draw from this demographic, limiting its nationalized speaking characters to Lowlanders.[110]

The tendency of Scottish characters to wear blue bonnets maintained throughout the period and became a means to reference Scotsmen. In *1 Henry IV* (1596–1597), Falstaff mentions a force of Scotsmen by saying "a thousand blue-caps" (2.4.357). Similarly, in *The Valiant Scot* by J. W. (Gent.) (1625–1626), Wallace appears with a "blew bonnet" and carries a whinyard. When a force of Scotsmen arrive, a line note identifies them only by stating that they wear "blew caps."[111] The whinyard also appears in Robert Greene's *James IV* (1590–1591) in the hands of the Scotsman Bohan who threatens Obero, the King of the Fayries: "Thou wilt not threape me; this whiniard has gard many better me[n] to lope the[n] thou. but how now? Gos sayds; what, wil't not out? whay thou wich, thou deele! gad's fute, may whiniard!" (1.1.34–8).[112] In addition to blue bonnets and whinyards, J. O. Bartley has suggested that Scottish characters might have also appeared in gray apparel. His evidence for this possibility, however, is drawn solely from Fynes Morson's observations while traveling through Scotland and has no necessary connection to how the Scottish were depicted in performance on the professional stage. Perhaps gray apparel was worn by actors playing Scottish characters, but the color did not garner mention in the plays or influence how the characters were received at the time.

A bit more can be determined regarding the apparel worn by Welsh characters on the English stage. One important visual signifier is the leek that Fluellen wears in his cap in *Henry V* as a sign of his Welsh national pride and that he forces Pistol to eat. It appears Fluellen did not wear the leek all the time, for Gower questions why he wears one when St. Davy's day is past (5.1.1–2). However, Welsh characters in other plays may very well have typically worn leeks, for in Thomas Randolph's *Hey for Honesty, Down with Knavery* (1626–1628), the Welsh beggar Caradock is called a "true Leek of Wales" and later swears "by this leek," suggesting he had one with him. Additionally, Bartley has identified only one pictorial illustration of a Welshman from the period, and it presents the character with a leek in his hat, suggesting the vegetable was understood in

---

[109] Highley, 69.

[110] Bartley, 80.

[111] J. W., *The Valiant Scot by J.W.: A Critical Edition*, ed. George, F. Byers (New York: Garland, 1980).

[112] Robert Greene, *Robert Greene's* The Scottish History of James IV: *A Critical, Old-Spelling Edition*, ed. Charles H. Stein (Salzburg: Inst. f. Engl. Sprache u. Literatur, Univ. Salzburg, 1977). The play notes that Bohan is "attired like a rid-stall man," but there is no way to be sure how a ridstall man might have appeared. See Bartley, 83 and 93, n. 16.

England to be the common accoutrement for someone from Wales.[113] The origin of the Welsh practice of wearing a leek in one's hat on Saint David's Day, March 1, is explained by Fluellen: "the Welshmen did good service in a garden where leeks did grow, wearing leeks in their Monmouth caps, which your Majesty know, to this hour is an honorable badge of the service" (4.7.98–101). Fluellen is talking about the apocryphal story of King Cadwallader who ordered his Welsh soldiers to wear leeks on their helmets when they fought the Saxons in a leek field. On the English stage, the leek suggested Welsh pride and their quickness to get into a quarrel. King Henry notes that Fluellen is "valliant / And touch'd with choler, hot as gunpowder / And quickly will return an injury" (4.7.180–1). When Fluellen appeared with a leek in his hat, the audience would have known that he was a Welshman prepared to fight.

Welsh characters also likely had *monmouth caps*, carried *Welsh hooks*, and wore apparel made of *frieze* or Welsh flannel. The monmouth cap was a round brimless hat with a high tapering crown that served as an identifiable piece of headware for the Welsh in much the same way that the blue bonnet served the Scottish.[114] It was widely noted to be worn by Welshmen, but did not carry greater significance. The Welsh hook was a halberd like weapon that had a hook on the back of the metal head and was known to be the appropriate weapon of the Welsh. Mention of the Welsh hook appears in several plays. In George Peele's *Edward I* (1590–1593), Welsh military strength is called upon against the English to "scowre the marches with your Welshmens hookes, / That Englishmen may thinke the divell is come." (616–17).[115] The Welsh hook also appears in the pictorial representation of a Welshman that Bartley found from the period.

Frieze and Welsh flannel are mentioned interchangeably throughout the period as the appropriate fabric of the Welsh. Both frieze and flannel came in a variety of qualities in English society, but when worn on stage by the Welsh, they tended to appear unpretentious and suggested that the wearer was of a lower class. In *The Merry Wives of Windsor*, Falstaff refers to the Welsh Parson Evans as "The Welsh Flannel" (5.5.162–3), and the Clown in Thomas Dekker's *The Welsh Embassador* (1623) notes that the Welsh love "freeze and goates and welsh hookes and whay and flannel and fighting" (4.2.115–16).[116] In *Edward I*, frieze serves a greater purpose for the play. At the conclusion of their armed conflict, the Welsh offer a "mantle of frize" to the English, as a sign of peace, to be given to the new-born English prince. The proud, Spanish-born queen entreats King Edward to refuse the gift, but Edward embraces the frieze mantle. By offering to clothe the English prince in Welsh frieze, the play offers a visual signifier of England's eventual mastery of Wales.

---

[113] Bartley, 51.

[114] Linthicum, 226.

[115] George Peele, *Edward I*, ed. Frank S. Hook, in *The Life and Works of George Peele*, Vol. 2, ed. Charles Tyler Prouty, (New Haven: Yale University Press, 1961).

[116] Dekker, *Dramatic Works*, Vol 4.

In Shakespeare's *Henry V*, the costumes specific to Irish, Scottish, and Welsh characters would have offered a very potent message of British unity under English rule. By presenting the Irish Macmorris, the Scottish Jamy, and the Welsh Fluellen as loyal members of Henry's army, the play suggests that the conflicts between England and its closest neighbors have been resolved. However, the nature of that resolution is determined by the manner in which these characters are presented on stage. MacMorris poignantly asks "what ish my nation?" suggesting that he sees himself as English. And yet, the play mentions Irish trowsers, and MacMorris almost certainly appeared in them, along with a brat and a dart. Fluellen and Jamy likely also appeared in the clothes appropriate to their nation. In this situation, however, all of the rebellious potential that their apparel suggests for the English is expurgated. *Henry V* envisages a world in which the Celtic nations willingly serve the English throne but do not figure as equals. They wear clothes and speak with accents that highlight their difference and inferiority even as they fight for the power that dominates them.

English

Having surveyed the costumes appropriate to foreigners on the early modern English stage, it remains to consider how English characters would have appeared in performance and determine what their costumes said about them. Surprisingly, this is a difficult question to answer. Although English apparel and fashions were the most commonly worn clothes in performance, their very Englishness rendered their national associations invisible before an English audience. An English style doublet or cloak would serve to establish the wearer's gender and social station on sight, but it said little about one's national character, particularly on a stage that frequently costumed both English citizens and those of foreign nations in the same clothing.

Yet, we can draw some conclusions about the apparel that was worn by English characters. It is almost certain, for instance, that much of the clothing worn by the English on the stage (and in the audience) was made of wool cloth, for it was vastly less expensive than silk and, as we noted in the last chapter, it was the appropriate apparel of those were not of the nobility. Wool held a preeminent place in the English economy throughout the early modern period and, as a result, carried particular cultural associations. Foremost, the wool cloth industry was deemed ancient and illustrious, representing humble, virtuous English labor and financial stability.[117] Despite this widely held opinion of wool, by the time the professional playhouses were opening in the latter half of the seventeenth century, the cloth industry in England was in a serious state of decline, to the point of

---

[117]   Roze Hentschell, *The Culture of Cloth in Early Modern England* (Burlington, VT, 2008), 1.

crisis, from which it never fully recovered.[118] Literature of the period records both understandings of wool cloth: English virtue and financial decay.

Robert Greene's *A Quip for an Upstart Courtier* (1592) engages both cultural associations. This work presents a dream sequence in which a jury is compiled to determine whether English cloth breeches or Italian velvet breeches are of more worth and which has the greater prerogative in England. In the story, Cloth-Breeches and Velvet-Breeches appear and speak for themselves to argue about who can preside over their case. Cloth-Breeches makes a strong argument for an "ancient knight" who appears wearing russet, a type of wool cloth. In the angry response from Velvet-Breeches, the positive cultural associations of wool are enumerated:

> Why, you may guess the inward mind by the outward apparel, and see how he is addicted by the homely robes he is suited in. Why, this knight is mortal enemy to pride, and so to me; he regardeth hospitality, and aimeth at honour, with relieving the poor: you may see, although his lands and revenues be great, and be able to maintain himself in great bravery, yet he is content with homespun cloth . . .[119]

Wool cloth thus signifies humility and "homespun" English virtue.

Later in the work, a draper appears and we learn that whereas those who wear wool are virtuous and humble, those who work the cloth often are not. Tellingly, the immoral draper dresses beyond his social station, wearing damask, an expensive silk.[120] In the description of the draper, we learn that he often pulls and lengthens his wool far beyond the point to which it should be stretched, creating an inferior product, and then darkens his shop so that consumers cannot see the poor quality of the work:

> he hath so dark a shop that no man can well choose a piece of cloth: it so shadows the dye and the thread, a man shall be deceived in the wool and the nap, they cause the clothworker so to press them; beside, he imposeth this charge to the clothworker, that he draw his cloth, and pull it passing hard when he sets it upon the tenters, that he may have it full breadth and length till thread and all tear and rent a-pieces.[121]

In the early modern imagination, cloth represented English virtue, but it also was understood to inspire vice in the Englishmen who prepared it for sale.

Both cultural associations of wool cloth find articulation in the drama of the period. In *Love's Labour's Lost*, the notion that wool represented honesty and

---

[118] Ibid., 5.

[119] Robert Greene, *A Quip for an Upstart Courtier*, ed. Charles Hindley (London: Reeves and Turner, 1871), 58–9.

[120] Linthicum, 120.

[121] Robert Greene, 69–70.

humility is forwarded in Berowne's conversion from flowery romantic poetry to honest and earnest protestations of love:

> Taffata phrases, silken terms precise,
> Three-pil'd hyperboles, spruce affection, . . .
> I do forswear them, and I here protest, . . .
> Henceforth my wooing mind shall be express'd
> In russet yeas and honest kersey noes. (5.2.406–13)

Like russet, kersey was a common and widely worn type of English wool cloth. Berowne engages the notion that wool represented honesty and humility to the London audience as he deploys that understanding of English cloth to woo Rosalind.

The negative associations that attended those who worked English wool appear in Thomas Middleton's *Michaelmas Term* (1605–1606). This play presents the character Quomodo, a villainous draper who seeks to cheat people out of their money through false business practices.[122] Like the draper in *A Quip for an Upstart Courtier*, Quomodo overstretches his wool and keeps his shop dimly lit in order to trick customers into purchasing his inferior product. Indeed, Quomodo's assistants are named Shortyard and Falselight, carrying their immoral business practices in their very appellations. The play happily concludes with Quomodo punished and his assistants banished from England. In this manner, Middleton's play invokes the dangers associated with those who work wool and then circumscribes them within the purview of English law and the conventions of comedy.

As we see in *Love's Labour's Lost* and *Michaelmas Term*, English drama had recourse to both cultural understandings of wool cloth. And yet, I am not convinced that woolen apparel served as a *visual* signifier of English morality or corrupt business practices on the early modern stage. When wool was worn in performance, it served overwhelmingly as a visual signifier of class, not of English morality or immorality.[123] Because woolen cloth was so widely worn on stage and off, its particular cultural associations were only engaged when they were specifically mentioned in the dialogue of the play. The decidedly English notions concerning wool were important to early modern drama, but could not be invoked by its visual presentation alone.

The apparel worn by English characters drew much more attention when it was of foreign design or fashion. As we saw with the French hose, the putting on of an article of apparel that carried particular national associations could serve to identify those qualities in a wearer from another nation. What has not been discussed is those instances, and there are a number of them, in which English characters wore

---

[122]   Roze Hentschell convincingly argues that Quomodo's profession as a draper (and not merely an immoral merchant) is crucial to the play's topicality. Hentschell, *The Culture of Cloth in Early Modern England*, 132.

[123]   On occasion, as we will see in the next chapter, wool cloth could also suggest that the wearer was a Puritan.

the apparel of several nations at once. For instance, in *The Merchant of Venice*, Portia laments the Englishman who has come as a suitor, saying "How oddly he is suited! I think he bought his doublet in Italy, his round hose in France, his bonnet in Germany, and his behaviour everywhere" (1.2.73–6).

The notion that Englishmen frequently appeared in the fashions of other countries, often several countries at once, was denigrated and lampooned throughout the period in English plays, writings, and sermons. In his description of England, William Harrison wrote:

> sithence such is our mutabilitie, that to daie there is none to the Spanish uise, tomorow the French toies are most fine and delectable, yer [ere] long no such apparell as that which is after the high Alman [Almaine] fashion, by and by the Turkish manner is generallie best liked of, otherwise the Morisco gowns, the Barbarian sleeues [the mandilion worne to Collie weston ward, and the short French breches] make such a comelie vesture, that except it were a dog in a doublet, you shall not see anie so disguised, as are my countrie men of England.[124]

So many foreign fashions were embraced in England, Harrison notes, that a proper painting of an Englishman must present him naked with scissors so the he may carve the clothes that please him that day.[125] The "Sermon Against Excess of Apparel" that Elizabeth I commanded to be preached in churches throughout England repeats Harrison's argument and includes mention of Englishmen appropriately being pictured as naked.[126] Roze Hentschell has identified numerous other instance in which the English tendency to wear foreign fashions was aspersed, demonstrating that these works bring to light the widespread English anxiety that the importing of foreign fabrics was disrupting England's most important industry, the manufacture and sale of cloth.[127] What deserves further consideration are the multiple ways that the theatre contributed to the notion that wearing foreign apparel from other nations was inappropriate.

One way that the stage attacked the practice was through straightforward commentary. In some instances, characters more or less step outside the action of the play to lampoon the English tendency to wear foreign clothes. For instance, Heywood's *A Challenge for Beauty* includes a lengthy, comic song that does little to forward the drama, but that mentions the fashions and practices of numerous nations, noting that rather than have its own customs or predispositions, the English take part in everyone else's. Edward Sharpham's comedy *The Fleire* (1606) does the same thing, including a song that particularly mocks the English appreciation

---

[124] Harrison, Vol. 2, 168.

[125] In making his statement, Harrison notes that he draws on an illustrated anecdote by the Tudor physician and writer Andrew Boorde that was published in 1542, Vol. 2, 167–8.

[126] *Certain Sermons*, 278.

[127] Hentschell, *The Culture of Cloth in Early Modern England*, chapter 4. Also see Jones and Stallybrass, 115–6.

for French apparel. In these instances, the plays ridicule the English tendency to wear foreign clothing, but do not actually provide examples of it.

In performance, the wearing of fashions drawn from several foreign nations served to mark the wearer in particular ways. It did not, surprisingly, tend to suggest the particular associations invoked by the individual articles that were worn. Rather, it suggested a state of mental imbalance or moral corruptness. In *Much Ado About Nothing*, Benedict's tendency to dress as a German from the waist downward and a Spaniard from the hip upward marks a mental imbalance caused by being in love. Claudio realizes this to be the cause of his infirmity and notes "If he be not in love with some woman, there is no believing old signs" (3.2.40–1). Benedict is not English (nor is anyone else in the play), but he almost certainly would have been costumed as an Englishman and appeared ridiculous when he changed his apparel for a composite ensemble drawn from several countries.

A far darker example of the inappropriateness of wearing foreign fashions appears in *Richard II or Thomas of Woodstock* (1592). King Richard's poor leadership and growing disconnect from his country finds visual emphasis in his and his court's new chosen apparel:

> Wild and antic habits
> Such as this kingdom never yet beheld:
> French hose, Italian cloaks, and Spanish hats,
> Polonian shoes with peaks and hand full long,
> Tied to their knees with chains of pearl and gold.
> Their plumèd tops fly waving in the air
> A cubit high above their wanton heads. (2.3.89–95)

The immorality of the court's outlandish apparel stands in contrast to the modest clothes worn by the noble Woodstock. To render this comparison more clearly, Richard mocks Woodstock's plain attire before putting on his "wild and antic habits." Rather than take offense, Woodstock proudly embraces his choice of "plain breeches," suggesting that his apparel is made of wool and invoking the positive, associations that English cloth held at the time. The play's tragic conclusion is therefore mapped out through the court's sartorial transformation according to broadly held English notions regarding the wearing of foreign apparel.

The effort expended to keep Englishmen from wearing foreign apparel reified the general notion that articles of clothing appropriately belonged to specific wearers. The English ought to appear in English apparel because clothes do, in fact, proclaim the man. Jones and Stallybrass argue that to study the Renaissance "we need to undo our own social categories, in which subjects are prior to objects, wearers to what is worn."[128] In other words, in English society one's clothes served to fashion a character deeply, marking the wearer's identity by establishing one's country of origin and national allegiances. On stage, this argument proves even

---

[128] Jones and Stallybrass, 2.

more true; for the actor, there is no identity that goes deeper than the apparel that is appropriate to one's particular role.

As we consider the role of costume on the English stage, we must not lose sight of the fact that theatre works in conventions. The foreign apparel that appeared in performance did not accurately represent the fashions prevalent in other nations. Additionally, plays set in foreign locations did not costume all of the characters in apparel deemed appropriate to the drama's settings. When we understand the conventions that were employed at the time, we can begin to appreciate how notions of nationhood and foreignness were negotiated through the use and manipulation of costume in performance.

Chapter 4
Religion

I charge thee to return and change thy shape.
Thou art too ugly to attend on me.
Go, and return an old Franciscan friar:
That holy shape becomes a devil best.

Christopher Marlowe, Doctor Faustus (1.3.23–6)[1]

On 16 May 1559, a mere six months into her reign, Queen Elizabeth issued a proclamation declaring it illegal for plays to include religious subject matter: "none to be played wherein either matters of religion or of the governance of the estate of the common weale shalbe handled or treated."[2] The haste with which the Queen addressed this issue makes sense in light of the religious conflicts that surrounded the country's move from Catholicism to Protestantism, back to Catholicism, and finally back to Protestantism during the previous thirty years.[3] Despite the unequivocal language of the Queen's decree, religious characters continued to populate English drama. All the way up to the opening of the public playhouses, interludes included friars, monks, priests, bishops, cardinals, and popes. Moreover, the plays performed by the new professional companies also included religious characters, and in the works of Shakespeare alone we find numerous members of the clergy.

In post-reformation England, however, religious figures did not carry the same associations that they previously held. Similarly, the apparel they wore also came to carry very different associations as the clothes deemed appropriate to the clergy in England diverged from what was worn by Catholics. The first half of this chapter will explore the changing definition and role of Christian religious apparel in early modern English theatre and culture. In addition to exploring how Catholics and Protestants were visually constructed onstage and in the English imagination, we will also consider the apparel worn by the new stage Puritan.

---

[1]   Christopher Marlowe, *The Complete Plays*, ed. J. B. Steane (New York: Penguin, 1969).

[2]   E. K. Chambers, *The Elizabethan Stage*, Vol. 4 (Oxford: Clarendon Press, 1923), 263–4.

[3]   Queen Elizabeth's edict referred specifically to interludes. The religious cycle or mystery plays were already in decline at this time and were finally outlawed in England in 1576. Chester stopped producing its cycle dramas in 1574.; Wakefield and York suppressed theirs in 1576; Coventry held out until 1581. Glynne Wickham *The Medieval Theatre*, 3rd ed. (New York: Cambridge University Press, 1987), 221.

The second half of this chapter will examine the costumes worn to depict the other religions that were regularly depicted in early modern English drama: Mahometans (Muslims) and Jews.

Christians

Ecclesiastical apparel, although rarely considered in histories of the early modern period, had its own Reformation and was the subject of considerable interest and anxiety following Henry VIII's separation from the Catholic Church. The first change in the English understanding of religious clothing resulted from Archbishop Cranmer's 1533 *Articles*, which refused to acknowledge the pope as the head of the church, referring to him only as the bishop of Rome.[4] In this statement and its general acceptance throughout England came the disavowal of the sanctity of the pope's particular vestments. Among the Catholic clergy, only the pope wore a *tiara*,[5] a triple-crown processional headgear in a cone shape, and a white *cassock*, an ankle-length, sleeved tunic that can be held at the waist by a narrow belt, or buttoned from neck to foot. The cassock was the article of apparel that Catholic clergy regularly wore outdoors and underneath the vestments for performing the Eucharist. By the sixteenth century, cardinals wore red cassocks, bishops wore purple, priests wore black, and the pope wore white.[6] Once the pope had been relegated in the eyes of the English to the rank of bishop, the particular apparel by which he was known ceased to identify the wearer as God's premier representative on Earth and came instead to be understood as the symbol of his impiety. The literature of the time and throughout the period we are examining consistently refers to the pope as the Antichrist, and his unique clothing served as an easily identifiable visual signifier. Consonant with Henry VIII's rejection of the pope's ecclesiastical preeminence in England was his denial of the authority of the cardinals. Accordingly, the distinctive, scarlet apparel worn by the cardinals and their *cardinal's hat*, a scarlet, wide-brimmed, low-top hat, became symbols of the immorality of Catholicism.

Interestingly enough, even before Henry VIII had separated from the Catholic Church, at least two plays recorded discontent with the English cardinal Wolsey. John Skelton's *Magnificence*, dated variously at 1516 and 1520–1522, lampoons the cardinal's pretensions and his string of better-than-royal palaces. The play ultimately lightens its moral attack to make a less contentious argument

---

[4]   Roger Lockyer, *Tudor & Stuart Britain, 1471–1714* (London: Longman, 1964), 61.

[5]   For descriptions of the items of religious apparel, I draw upon Janet Mayo's *A History of Ecclesiastical Dress* (London: B. T. Batsford, 1984) and R. A. S. Macalister's *Ecclesiastical Vestments: Their Development and History* (London: Elliot Stock, 1896).

[6]   Also particular to the pope, although nearly impossible to see by observers, was the *orale*, a thin veil or mantle fastened around the neck when he celebrated pontifical High Mass, and the *subcingulum*, which was an ornamental addition to the girdle which hung down upon the left side.

supporting fiscal moderation, but the playwright's aversion to the prelate's secular endeavors is clear. For Christmas 1526, a play written by John Roo (or Rouse) was produced at Gray's Inn. In this performance, Lord Governance was ruled by Dissipation and Negligence, by whose misgovernance Lady Public Weal was separated from Governance, which caused Rumor Populi, Inward Grudge, and Disdain of Wanton Sovereignty to rise with a great multitude and restore Lady Public Weal to her proper place. According to the historian Edward Hall, who was present, the play was well received by all but Cardinal Wolsey who saw enough of himself in the performance (despite the playwright's assurance that the work included only historical personages) to order the arrest of the author and one of the actors.[7] English disdain for cardinals in general and Wolsey in particular provided material for drama all the way up to the interregnum.

Following the passage of the Act of Supremacy (November 1534), in which King Henry was recognized as the head of the Church in England, anti-Catholic performances became less subtle in their condemnation of cardinals and the pope. For instance, in June 1539 a water entertainment was performed in which two barges entered the Thames and met in the middle. One was manned by a crew representing the king and his council, the other by men dressed up as the pope and cardinals. The two boats met in combat, fighting until the "papal" barge was beaten and its contents pitched into the river.[8] Dialogue was unnecessary to this performance for the visual codes alone were more than sufficient to forward both the action and the ideology of the performance. John Doebler has noted that "the average Renaissance Englishman knew a language of images, an iconography, whether he encountered those images in graphic form, in literature, or on a stage."[9] In the case of religion, which played such an enormous role in the life of the entire commonweal, this is particularly true. The apparel worn by those aboard the papal barge was understood as a visual marker of the profane according to the newly transformed cultural definition of what constituted the sacred in England.

With the dissolution of the monasteries (largely completed by 1540), the apparel particular to monks, nuns, and friars joined that of the pope and the cardinals as representative of the Catholic Church and its iniquities. Long after the monastic houses were confiscated by the crown and the money gained thereby had been spent, the clothes particular to these clergy remained symbols of greed and sexual license on the stage. The origin of this opinion lies in the public estimation of the monasteries before they were dissolved. At the beginning of the sixteenth century, many saw the monks as idle, corrupt individuals, living off the fat of the land.[10]

---

[7]   Robert Potter, "The Cardinal's New Clothes: Politics and Morality in the 1520s," *Research Opportunities in Renaissance Drama* 31 (1992): 62–3.

[8]   J. J. Scarisbrick, *Henry VIII* (Berkeley: University of California Press, 1968), 367.

[9]   John Doebler, *Shakespeare's Speaking Pictures: Studies in Iconic Imagery* (Albuquerque: University of New Mexico Press, 1974), 6.

[10]   Rosemary O'Day, "The Anatomy of a Profession: the Clergy of the Church of England," in *The Professions in Early Modern England*, ed. Wilfrid R. Prest (New York: Croom Helm, 1987), 32.

There was reason for this opinion. After the plague, the number of monks was halved with some communities being entirely wiped out. Monastic revenues were so large relative to the number of monks, that they encouraged worldliness. Feasting had replaced fasting and services were often poorly attended.[11] Additionally, dress had grown extravagant, despite rigid rules that ordered monks to wear a long tunic made of wool, a belt or girdle, a hood, and perhaps a *scapula*, a rectangular piece of fabric that went over the tunic and provided extra protective covering for the monk when he worked or traveled abroad. As a result of the monks' wealth, the humble attire that was supposed to be the sign of their devotion to a life of simplicity and prayer became instead a symbol of their hypocrisy. The fact that the majority of English society could only speculate on the activities that actually took place in the secluded monasteries only added to public mistrust of the monks.

The nuns were the subject of fewer moral attacks than were the monks, but their distinctive apparel and the isolated conditions in which they lived similarly marked them for public suspicion. A nun typically wore a white undertunic, a gown, a hood, a veil, and a *wimple*, a piece of fabric that went around the face and neck. Additionally, they could also wear a scapula. The colors of a monk or nun's habit were determined by his or her religious order and could be of a wide variety.[12] Ostensibly devoted to a life of celibacy, both the monk and the nun, after the Reformation, were figured to be notoriously libidinous behind their cloistered walls, and convents became synonymous with brothels. Thus, when Hamlet tells Ophelia to "get thee to a nunnery," he is simultaneously recommending to her a life of chastity and one of prostitution.

Friars dressed nearly identically to monks and were treated much the same in drama until the 1590s when their particular identities were made the subject of theatrical consideration. The friar's orders were created in the twelfth century (first entering England in the thirteenth) in an attempt to reform what they saw as the increasing immorality of the monastic orders. The friar typically wore a wool tunic, a scapula with a hood, and a cord around the waist, with slight differences in style and color marking the different orders. For instance the Franciscan friars were called the "gray friars" because of the color of their original habits. However, beginning in the fifteenth century, they typically wore brown apparel. Additionally, they wore a distinctive cord around their waist that had three knots representing their vows of poverty, chastity, and obedience. With this in mind, we can begin to understand how Mephistopheles might have appeared in the original production of *Dr. Faustus* after Faustus tells him he is "too ugly to attend on me," and that he should "Go, and return an old Franciscan friar: That holy shape becomes a devil best" (1.3.24–6).[13] In order to appear in the semblance of a Franciscan friar

---

[11]   Lockyer, *Tudor & Stuart Britain,* 69–70.

[12]   For a list of the orders of monks and nuns, and the particular colors of their apparel, see Macalister, *Ecclesiastical Vestments,* 235–53.

[13]   Christopher Marlowe, *Doctor Faustus,* in *Christopher Marlowe: The Complete Plays,* 259–339 (New York: Penguin, 1969).

such as those who resided in England at the beginning of the sixteenth century, Mephistopheles would have reentered wearing a brown tunic, a hood, and a cord around his waist. However, since friars had not been admitted into England for almost fifty years when *Doctor Faustus* was first performed (c.1588), it is possible that Mephistopheles entered in the gray apparel appropriate to a "gray friar." In Henslowe's list of costumes and properties from 10 March 1598, among the six friar's gowns that are mentioned, only one is identified by color: "*Item,* i freyers gowne of graye."[14]

In the English drama performed between the Reformation and the opening of the first professional public playhouse in 1567, popes, cardinals, monks, and friars found repeated theatrical representation, particularly in the newly transformed morality plays. Whereas the pre-Reformation morality taught its audience that the way to heaven was to take part in the sacraments of the church and be obedient to the authority of the priest who administered them, the post-Reformation morality taught the tenets of Protestantism and stressed the evils of Catholicism.[15] During this time, it became the practice in England to have the Vice characters played as Catholic clergy (reversing the earlier practice of having the seven virtues dressed as Catholic clergy).[16] In this capacity, they would admit their own impiety to the audience while dressed in religious apparel, thereby furthering the aims of Protestantism by highlighting the evil of Catholicism and the hypocrisy of its ceremonies. Quite naturally, the characters we have addressed thus far were the ideal ones to play the part of Vice, for their apparel immediately identified them as Catholics and as enemies of the newly emergent English Church.

Recognizing the frequency with which this costuming convention was used, T. W. Craik has stated that "scarcely a single anti-Catholic play in this period fails to introduce some such character as Flattery disguised as a friar (*Ane Satyre of the Thrie Estaitis*) or Ignorance as an old Popish priest (*Enough is as good as a Feast, The longer thou livest the moor Fool thou art, New Custom*)."[17] Craik's statement, although a fair generalization for the period reaching from 1540 (*Ane Satyre*) to 1570 (*New Custom*), fails to acknowledge the rapid changes that were

---

[14] Philip Henslowe, *Henslowe's Diary,* 2nd edition, ed. R. A. Foakes (New York: Cambridge University Press, 2002), 323. The fact that there is an entry for "faustus Jerkin his clok" in a roughly contemporaneous list in Henslowe's diary increases the likelihood that the apparel worn by the actor playing Mephistopheles is, indeed, one of the friar's gowns listed here (294).

[15] Rainer Pineas, "The English Morality Play as a Weapon of Religious Controversy." *Studies in English Literature* 2.2 (1962): 157, 180.

[16] Although the ecclesiastical apparel employed in early modern drama has not received thorough study before, its use in medieval drama has. See Dunbar Ogden, *The Staging of Drama in the Medieval Church* (Newark: University of Delaware Press, 2002), chapter 4 (123–40); and Clifford Davidson, *Technology, Guilds and Early English Drama* (Kalamazoo, MI: Medieval Institute, 1996), chapter 4 (57–118).

[17] T. W. Craik, *The Tudor Interlude: Stage, Costume, and Acting* (Leicester: Leicester University Press, 1967), 56.

taking place in moralities during this thirty-year period. He notes that the Vice characters in the post-Reformation moralities were regularly dressed as Catholic clergy, but overlooks the fact that this period can be divided into two parts, each defined by trends in choice of character. Upon examining the plays and the dates when they were written, we find that the earlier works include primarily popes, cardinals, monks, and friars, and the later ones prefer "Popish priests." The most likely explanation for these tendencies can be found in the changes in religious apparel that occurred during this time. When *Ane Satyre of the Thrie Estaitis* was first performed circa 1540, dressing Flattery as a friar would have been more potent than dressing him as a priest because, at the time, the English priesthood was appareled in much the same way as the Catholic. Indeed, the religious vestments worn by the Catholic clergy were reaffirmed for use in the English Church in the early years of the reign of Edward VI.

The Book of Common Prayer, first published in 1549, stipulated the apparel that the priest should wear while administering Holy Communion. The introductory section of "The Order for the Administracion of the Lordes Supper or Holye Communion" states:

> Upon the date and at the tyme appoincted for the ministracion of the holy Communion, the Priest that shal execute the holy ministery, shall put upon hym the vesture appoincted for that ministracion, that is to saye: a white Albe plain, with a vestement or Cope.[18]

These are the primary articles of apparel required by the Catholic Church for performing the Eucharist. The *alb* is a white, linen, ankle-length tunic with sleeves and is held in place at the waist by a girdle. The term "vestement" implies the *chasuble*, the principal attire used by the priest, including bishops and archbishops, for the celebration of the Mass. The chasuble was a large, round piece of fabric, worn over the shoulders, with a hole in the center to pass the head through while putting it on. The *cope* was a semicircular, ceremonial version of an outdoor cloak which was most often worn at non-Eucharist ceremonies (e.g., baptism, marriage, and procession) in place of the chasuble. Four items not listed, although they were likely to have been tacitly understood to accompany those mentioned, are the *stole,* the *maniple*, the *mitre*, and the *crozier*. The stole is a long, narrow strip of material worn on top of the alb and draped over the shoulders in various ways to indicate the rank of the wearer. A priest would wear the stole crossed over the breast while the bishop would wear his uncrossed, and both would have them held in place by the girdle. The maniple was a small strip of linen that was draped over the left forearm. The mitre worn in the sixteenth century was a tall divided hat and was worn primarily by bishops and archbishops. The crozier was a pastoral staff

---

    18   *Book of Common Prayer,* Society for Archbishop Justus, http://justus.anglican.org/resources/bcp/1549/Communion_1549.htm (accessed 5 April 2004).

carried by bishops. A similar staff, but topped with a cross instead of a hook, was carried by archbishops.[19]

Since Protestant religious apparel for the priest was indistinguishable from the Catholic vestments, it made sense for the moralities of the time to present the more conspicuously Catholic clergymen as the Vice characters.[20] Thus, in John Bale's *King Johan* (c.1540), Usurpyd Power appears as the pope, Private Welth enters dressed as a cardinal, and Treason is a monk. In the year of the play's original presentation, each of these characters would have been immediately identifiable as Catholic and the play would have forwarded its ideological agenda in its visual presentation as well as with its dialogue. When characters portrayed other members of the Catholic clergy, they required introductions in the dialogue in order to be understood.

The apparel worn by English priests was not officially altered until 1552. In *The Book of Common Prayer* published in the fifth year of Edward VI's reign, the 1549 rules governing vestments were removed from the segment addressing the Holy Communion. The only place in which apparel is mentioned at all is in a prohibitory rubric at the beginning of the section addressing Morning Prayer:

> And here is to be noted, that the minister at the tyme of the Communion and all other tymes in his ministracion, shall use neither albe, vestment, nor cope: but being archbishop or bishop, he shall have and wear a rochet; and being a preest or deacon, he shall have and wear a surplice onely.[21]

The *rochet* worn at this time was a large, white overgarment that reached the floor, was gathered at the waist, and had full lawn sleeves. Typically, Anglican bishops wore it with a *chimere* and a *tippet*. The chimere was a silk or satin sleeveless gown that was open at the front. The tippet was a long black scarf. The *surplice* was similar to the rochet except that it was shorter and, as a result, not gathered at the waist. Both the bishop and the priest would typically wear the cassock underneath their Communion apparel.

The change of religious apparel mandated in the 1552 *Book of Common Prayer* was anything but superficial. While the new wording might seem to assert only a minor sartorial adjustment in the practice of Christianity, it carried with it enormous ecclesiastical significance marking some of the chief variances in

---

[19] Over the chasuble, archbishops could be distinguished from bishops by their *pallium*, a long woven band or scarf of white wool marked with six dark crosses, that was placed around the neck and shoulders, with a strip hanging down the front.

[20] By 1540, nearly all of the monasteries, nunneries, and friaries in England were closed, and their tenants provided with government pensions to guarantee that they could support themselves without pursuing their previous, Catholic vocation. Consequently, no provision at all was made for the apparel worn by monks, nuns, or friars, who were not welcome in the newly Protestant country.

[21] *Book of Common Prayer,* Society for Archbishop Justus, http://justus.anglican.org/resources/bcp/1552/MP_1552.htm (accessed 5 April 2004).

Fig. 4.1   Generalized Catholic Priest and Bishop, drawn by Adam West.

belief systems that separated Protestantism from Catholicism. The vestments visually asserted the fact that, in the Catholic Church, the clergy served a mystical function essential to the salvation of the congregation. By donning the appropriate vestments and speaking the right words, the Catholic priest was understood to literally transform bread and wine into the body and blood of Christ for his congregation. By changing the apparel that priests are to wear when administering Holy Communion, the 1552 prayer book rejected the validity of transubstantiation, positing instead the Protestant belief that the Eucharist was merely a reaffirmation of the Christian's belief in God. The altering of religious apparel denied the very status of the priest as an intermediary between God and man, suggesting that the clergy were no different from commoners. Accordingly, the priest's ability to absolve his parishioners of their sins was also challenged.

If the Catholic vestments were not efficacious in transubstantiation, what purpose did they serve? According to the post-Reformation morality plays written in England, they were worn to trick people into giving their money and their faith to a religion that secretly worshipped the devil. Thus, in N. Woodes's *The Conflict of Conscience* (c.1572) Hypocrisie tells how he fools people into the Romish

Fig. 4.2   Generalized English Priest and Bishop, drawn by Adam West.

faith, while Cacones, a priest, finds that the sacraments are the greatest source of revenue for the clergy, especially the Eucharist.[22]

Despite the significance of the change in apparel made by the 1552 prayer book, a significant number of English clergy did not believe it went far enough. According to the newly emergent Protestant faith in England, the priest's role was not mystical but pedagogical. The Protestant parishioner could not save his soul by performing good deeds, attending church, and taking part in ecclesiastical ritual. Rather, as Christopher Haigh explains, "Protestantism was not a works religion, it was a Word religion: the Word preached, the Word read, the Word sung to the Lord, the Word applied to life, the Word wrestled with in the heart

---

[22]   Pineas, "The English Morality Play as a Weapon of Religious Controversy," 172.

of a sinner yearning for grace."[23] Apparel that distinguished the priest from the members of his congregation drew attention from his real purpose which was to teach the word of God. Even the surplice and the rochet, divorced as they were from the vestments of the Catholic Church, were considered idolatrous by some because they suggested that the wearer held a special providence and place in God's design. Disagreements regarding the appropriate apparel for the English clergy resulted in what has come to be termed the "vestments controversy," and marks the beginning of the split in England between Protestants and Puritans.

The origin of the vestments controversy can be dated to 1550, when John Hooper was appointed to the bishopric of Gloucester and declined the position on the grounds that he refused to wear the vestments mandated by the *Book of Common Prayer*.[24] At this time, clergy were expected to wear the alb and the chasuble or cope. When the requirements changed two years later, the more extremist Protestants remained unappeased. However, their discontent was silenced the following year, 1553, when King Edward died and Queen Mary attempted to convert the country back to Catholicism. The vestments that had only recently been discarded were once again taken up by the English clergy with the uncompromising Protestants either fleeing the country or facing punishment (more than 300 were executed). Mary's death in 1558 was understandably cheered by the Protestants who subsequently returned to England from abroad en masse, expecting Queen Elizabeth's accession to usher in a new era of religious purity.

The high expectations for Elizabeth's reign were dampened, however, when the *Book of Common Prayer* was reissued in 1559 calling for a return to the alb, cope, and chasuble required in the prayer book of 1549. The new "Act of Uniformity" stated "that suche ornaments of the Churche, and of the ministers therof, shalbe reteined and be in use as was in this Churche of England, by aucthority of Parliament, in the second yere of the raygne of Kyng Edward the vi."[25] This issue, which had drawn fire during Edward's reign, became a major point of contention. After all, those who fled England during Mary's reign had largely spent their time in the Protestant churches on the continent where even the surplice had been completely abandoned.[26] To return and find that England was prepared to take a step backwards rather than embrace a more purified form of Protestantism was unacceptable and sparked a war of words that stands as the opening salvo between Puritans and the Church of England. This point of contention was not resolved in March 1566 when Archbishop Parker circulated his "Advertisements" which

---

[23]   Christopher Haigh, *English Reformations: Religion, Politics, and Society under the Tudors*. (Oxford: Clarendon Press, 1993), 287.

[24]   Hooper ultimately agreed to wear the vestments after he had spent some time mulling the issue in jail. J. H. Primus, *The Vestments Controversy* (Kampen: J. H. Kok, 1960), 64.

[25]   *Book of Common Prayer,* Society for Archbishop Justus, http://justus.anglican.org/resources/bcp/1559/front_matter_1559.htm (accessed 5 April 2004).

[26]   Primus, 75.

discarded the unrealistic demand of Eucharistic vestments and required merely that the surplice be adopted and that specific outdoor apparel be worn: "a square cap, a scholar's gown priest-like, a tippet, and in the church a linen surplice."[27]

The year 1566 marks the height of the vestments controversy, for after Parker presented his "Advertisements," he called a conference of all London pastors and curates where he demanded that the attendees declare whether they would follow his guidelines or not. Of those present, sixty-one agreed and thirty-seven refused. The latter were suspended and their livings sequestered. As might be expected, this action prompted some of the most strident antivestment polemics, the mere titles of which make clear the position of the authors. For just two examples: *A briefe discourse against the outwarde apparell and Ministring Garmentes of the Popishe Church* and *To my lovynge brethren that is troublyd about the popishe aparrell, two short and comfortable Epistels.*[28]

The events of 1566 solidified the notion that the general clergy in England were visually identifiable by the surplice or the rochet and a square cap, and that Puritans were unwilling to be seen in Parker's prescribed apparel. Moreover, drama records the significance of this visual code. In *New Custom*, the title character dresses as a Genevan minister "With a gathered frocke, a powlde head, and a broad hatte, An vnshaued bearde, a pale face" and (according to Perverse Doctrine in the opening scene, where he is a trustworthy witness) inveighs against the square caps and white surplices of priests as superstitious trifles.[29] Puritan revulsion for the surplice also appears in a number of plays. For instance, in William Rowley's *A Match at Midnight* (1633) Sim states it "H'as turn'd his stomacke, for all the World like a Puritanes, at the sight of a surplesse."[30]

In the year before the first public playhouse opened in London (the Red Lion in 1567), debate concerning religious apparel was at a high point and had important ramifications for the visual codes identifying the clergy in England. It should not therefore surprise us to find that the plays presented on the public stages made extensive use of the apparel defined by these issues. We can state with complete confidence that in production, characters portraying Catholic, Protestant, and Puritan clergy would have been immediately identifiable to a high degree of specificity, and would have carried with them the cultural associations that defined them at the time of their presentation.

---

[27] Ibid., 103; Patrick Collinson, *The Elizabethan Puritan Movement* (London: Jonathan Cape, 1967), 70.

[28] For a list and description of the major polemics written, see Primus, *The Vestments Controversy,* 107–48.

[29] Craik, 81–2. It is important to note that *New Custom* never inveighs against Protestant religious apparel himself. Rather, at the end of the play, he makes a case for the unimportance of religious apparel altogether, finding no reason why people should be offended by the wearing of the surplice since it is meaningless (which was a common Protestant position).

[30] William Rowley, *A critical old-spelling edition of A match at midnight*, ed. Stephen Blase Young (New York: Garland, 1980), 72.

When we understand the associations intrinsic to particular articles of religious apparel, we can begin to study the very different ways in which playwrights made use of the audience's assumptions to further their dramatic aims. For instance, both Marlowe's *Doctor Faustus* (1588) and Robert Greene's *The Honorable History of Friar Bacon and Friar Bungay* (1589) feature characters costumed in the apparel of a friar, and yet each makes very different use of the associations elicited by the clothing. Marlowe's play makes straightforward use of the post-Reformation morality play convention in which friars put on the semblance of holiness but are secretly in league with the devil by having Mephistopheles appear as an old friar. The choice of a Franciscan friar is particularly poignant since they are among the most austere practitioners of Christianity, devoting themselves to lives of poverty, chastity, and obedience. Moreover, Franciscans are among the four mendicant orders, friars who live entirely on alms (the other three being Dominicans, Carmelites, and Augustinian Hermits). By having even the most ascetic Catholic be secretly a devil in disguise, *Doctor Faustus* suggests the depth of Catholic hypocrisy.

Marlowe takes this anti-Catholic argument one step further by having Faustus go to Rome and taunt the pope and his ecclesiastical court. There, before the pope, appear characters in virtually all of the religious apparel that denotes Catholicism, with cardinals, bishops, monks, and friars in attendance. In one sense, this scene would seem to offer a pro-Catholic position for it puts the pope at cross-purposes with Mephistopheles. However, the avarice of the pope as he seeks to extend his temporal authority even over emperors guarantees that he will not be seen in a favorable light. Furthermore the scene suggests that the apparel and accoutrements stipulated by the Catholic Church serve no religious or mystical purpose whatsoever; the chanting of the friars and their ceremony employing bell, book, and candle fail to have any impact on Faustus and Mephistopheles. When the chanting concludes and Faustus and Mephistopheles beat the friars (after having already struck the pope), the Catholic Church appears as an altogether secular organization whose vestments and rituals serve simply to help them consolidate political power.

Greene's *Friar Bacon and Friar Bungay* employs friar's apparel in a manner very different from *Doctor Faustus*. Rather than serve as the cunning disguise of evil, the friar's habit in Green's play becomes the clothing appropriate to the play's hero, Friar Bacon. The play achieves this new understanding of the friar's garments in two important ways. First, the habit is reinvested with the traits of poverty, chastity, and obedience that originally defined the friars who wore it. At several points in the play, it is made clear that the lives the friars lead is a simple one, devoid of the comforts of lavish dwelling or fine food. When Burden, Mason, and Clement enter Bacon's home, the friar makes it clear that he lives in a small room at a college: "Why flock you thus to Bacon's secret cell, a friar newly stall'd in Brazen-nose?" (1.2.13–14).[31] When Bacon entertains King Henry, the Emperor,

---

[31] Robert Greene, *The Honorable History of Friar Bacon and Friar Bungay. Elizabethan and Jacobean Comedy,* eds. Robert Ornstein and Hazelton Spencer (Boston: D. C. Heath, 1964).

the King of Castille, and others, he teases them with a meal consisting of pottage and broth. King Henry is outraged: "What, doest thou taunt us with thy peasants' fare . . . ?" (3.3.239). Bacon responds that "I show'd the cates to let thee see how scholars use to feed, How little meat refines our English wits" (3.3.248–50). Bacon then offers to furnish the monarchs with a feast such as they have never enjoyed before, but notes that the simple fare they just reviled is a friar's typical sustenance. Additionally, even though Edward promises Bacon £40,000 to impede Lacy's marriage to Margaret, there is no mention of the fee being paid or of the friar seeking his due.

Bacon's chastity is not mentioned in the play, but would likely have been noted by an audience raised with the notion that Catholic habits hide lascivious desire. Bacon observes the romantic plot in the play and uses his skills to forward it, but never displays any sexual motivation himself. When we consider the manner in which monks and friars appeared in post-Reformation moralities, the importance of Bacon's quiet chastity becomes clear.

Bacon's obedience takes on a particular significance in Greene's play because it proves to be primarily an English Protestant obedience to his king and not a Catholic obedience to the pope and church. He is at the command of his monarch and works to see his kingdom well ordered and distinguished on the world stage. Thus, when Bacon outperforms Jacques Vandermast, Henry responds "Bacon, thou hast honored England with thy skill, and made fair Oxford famous by thine art" (3.2.166–7). Devoted to poverty, chastity, and a distinctively English form of religious obedience, Bacon assumes an honorable identity (as the play's title promises he will), and works to reclaim his apparel from its earlier associations.

The second way in which Bacon's apparel is separated from its more negative meanings can be found in the friar's renunciation of magic at the end of the play. Having accidentally contributed to the death of two men and their sons with his mystical skills, Bacon swears to give up the use of magic. This he plans to accomplish by discarding the clothes that aid him in his conjuring. Not surprisingly, these articles of apparel are Catholic vestments. In renouncing his magic, Bacon draws a connection between Catholic vestments, magic, and devil worship:

> I tell thee, Bungay, it repents me sore
> That ever Bacon meddled in this art.
> The hours I have spent in pyromantic spells,
> The fearful tossing in the latest night
> Of papers full of necromantic charms,
> Conjuring and abjuring devils and fiends,
> With stole and alb and strange pentag[o]non . . .
> . . . With praying to the fivefold powers of [hell]
> Are instances that Bacon must be damn'd
> For using devils to countervail his God. (4.3.86–97)

This conflation of Catholicism, conjuring, and damnation was not confined to Greene's play. As Keith Thomas notes, "In the reign of Elizabeth I, therefore, the term 'conjurer' came to be a synonym for recusant priest. . . . Catholic miracles were confidently attributed to witchcraft."[32] By giving up the stole and the alb, Bacon not only renounces the Catholic faith of which they are a part, but also actually takes upon himself the character of a Reformation minister. He has already demonstrated his primary devotion to his king, and now he wishes to give up the Catholic accouterments and devote "the remnant of my life in pure devotion, praying to my God" (4.3.107–8). Bacon renounces the religious significance of his vestments and seeks heaven not through confession, but by devoting himself instead to a life of prayer. Bacon's simple friar's robe is thus divorced from Catholicism by the Protestant characteristics and honorable identity of its wearer.

Shakespeare regularly employs this newly defined and humbly appareled friar in his plays. When Romeo wishes to marry Juliet, he seeks out Friar Lawrence who presides over the ceremony. Friar Lawrence proves his good intentions by agreeing to marry the couple in order to bring peace to the divided city. In *Much Ado About Nothing*, Friar Francis will perform the marriage ceremonies for Claudio and Hero as well as Benedict and Beatrice. Further, Friar Francis contributes to the plot by suggesting the stratagem whereby Hero's innocence can be proven and the happy ending achieved. In *Measure for Measure*, Vincentio requests the assistance of Friar Thomas and assumes the guise of a friar himself so that he may observe the rule of Angelo unseen.[33] Catholic clergy are appropriate to Shakespeare's plays because nearly all of them are set in Catholic territory or in pre-Reformation England. The friars that Shakespeare presents so positively are the appropriate Catholic clergymen to preside in a Protestant theatre because they can appear in simple robes and circumnavigate the more negative associations that attend the distinctive Catholic vestments.

When the vestments do appear onstage in Shakespeare's plays, they would have been understood from the first to embody the immoral characteristics associated with them in England at the time. David Bevington has argued that, in Shakespeare, "anticlericalism is staple."[34] Certainly he is correct, but this anticlericalism was often accomplished first with the costumes that were worn. Let us consider the opening scene of *1 Henry VI* in which the Duke of Gloucester accuses the Bishop of Winchester of having prayed for Henry's death. Citing the bishop's cruel and overly ambitious monologue at the end of the scene, Jeffrey Knapp has noted that "The audience does not have long to wait before learning whether Gloucester's attack is justified."[35] However, the audience would have understood when it saw the bishop that his clothes were the literal embodiment of mendacity, cruelty, and worldly desire. It is most likely that the bishop would have appeared wearing an alb with a cope on top and donning a mitre on his head. Thus appareled, Winchester would have been the subject of Gloucester's

[32]   Keith Thomas, *Religion and the Decline of Magic* (New York: Penguin, 1971), 78.

[33]   There are exceptions. In *Twelfth Night*, Olivia and Sebastian are married by a priest.

[34]   David Bevington, *Tudor Drama and Politics: A Critical Approach to Topical Meaning* (Cambridge, MA: Harvard University Press, 1968), 201.

[35]   Knapp, "Preachers and Players in Shakespeare's England," 35.

specific attack on a corrupt prelate, but also the recipient of a general assault on the Catholic Church which is presented here as dedicated solely to accumulating political power. Knapp is on the right track when he suggests that Winchester is "like the medieval stage-vice,"[36] but would be closer to the mark if he noted that the bishop is a direct borrowing from the post-Reformation morality play which presented its vice characters in precisely this manner. The bishop is understood to be evil on first sight and secretly acknowledges his wickedness to the audience in a monologue (1.1.173–7) so as to forward the play's Protestant principles through a well-known dramatic strategy.

Shakespeare appears to take a different approach to employing ecclesiastical apparel in *Henry VIII* (1613). He begins in the typical manner by presenting Cardinal Wolsey's scarlet clothing as suitable to his avarice and impiety. Noted by Norfolk and Buckingham to be overly ambitious, fat, and devoid of noble blood, Wolsey is referred to variously as "scarlet sin" and a "piece of scarlet." This designation typifies the manner in which cardinals were regularly presented in drama. In Shakespeare's *1 Henry VI*, Cardinal Beaufort is called the "scarlet hypocrite," with his morality being understood on sight and reinforced in the dialogue. Even at the late date of 1641, James Shirley was able to assume that the title character of his play *The Cardinal* would be understood as an appropriate object of ridicule in his "reverend purples." Of course, Wolsey was a special case since he remained in English memory as a specific example of Catholic greed, and the play notes his relentless efforts to accrue wealth and even become pope. But where *Henry VIII* departs from usual practice is in presenting Archbishop Cranmer as a voice for the nascent English Protestant Church.

As the primary author of *The Book of Common Prayer* in 1549 and then again in 1552, Cranmer was largely responsible for the elimination of the vestments from church practice while Edward VI was king of England. Cranmer's death as a heretic during Mary's Catholic reign made him an ideal representative of Protestant virtue in Shakespeare's play and an appropriate foil to Wolsey's worldly ambition. Consequently, it seems likely that in the early-seventeenth-century, the actor playing Cranmer would have worn the rochet, chimere, tippet, and square cap that were appropriate to bishops in England at the time. Thus appareled, Cranmer would have appeared as a Protestant prelate when the Catholic members of the council reproached him for his "new opinions, divers and dangerous" (5.2.52–3). Further support for the likelihood that Cranmer would have worn Protestant religious clothing can be found in the extant paintings of the Archbishop, all of which portray him thus appareled. Presenting the form of a Protestant bishop and contrasting the Catholic Wolsey, Cranmer would have made a strong pro-Anglican statement when he argued "Love and meekness . . . Become a churchman better than ambition" (5.2.97–8). In this manner, the costumes in *Henry VIII* would have epitomized the contrast that can be found in the dialogue between the worldliness of the Catholic Church and the godliness of the Protestant Church.

---

[36] Ibid.

The Puritan[37] notion that Protestant religious apparel was not, in fact, godly found articulation on the stage as well, but virtually never in straightforward form. Plays from 1570 (*New Custom*) to at least 1641 (Thomas Jordan's *The Walks of Islington and Hogsden*) present the Puritan opinion that the surplices and square caps of the English clergy were remnants of the Catholic Church; however, these works almost uniformly support Protestant orthodoxy by deprecating the religious forces that opposed the government and the established church's sartorial decree.[38] This deprecation was often accomplished by presenting Puritan characters as comic zealots who foolishly and incessantly rail against the way others are dressed.

Most objectionable to stage Puritans was the surplice, which they regarded as a vestige of Catholicism. Thus, in the anonymously written *The Pilgrimage to Parnassus* (1598), Stupido gives highest praise to his uncle by noting his unwillingness to wear the clothes dictated by the English Church: "I haue a good man to my vncle, that neuer wore capp nor surples in his life, nor anie such popishe ornament" (3.1.338–40).[39] Of course, Stupido's name alone guarantees that the Puritan position he espouses will be laughed at and not genuinely considered. His opinion of religious apparel is compatible with his insipid personality, his love of insignificant theological puzzles, and his strident disdain for liberal learning and the arts. This was a common technique until the interregnum: comically ridiculous, frequently hypocritical Puritans rail against the apparel of the English clergy, thereby strengthening the Protestant cause by depicting themselves and their religious convictions as absurd. Thus, in Thomas Randolph's *Hey for Honesty, Down with Knavery* (1626–1628), Gogle, the self-proclaimed "zealous Saint of Amsterdam" condemns both Catholic and Protestant religious apparel in the same breath: "O Popery! / A profane Cope, or the Levitical smock, / I mean a Surplisse, is not more unlawful"(4.1.353–5).[40] In Shackerley Marmion's *A Fine Companion* (1633), the Puritan Chandler has "run mad with illuminations . . . he thought a man in a surplice to be the ghost of heresy." And in *The Walks of Islington and*

---

[37]   The term "puritan," Paul White explains, "was an abusive epithet for various groups of Protestant zealots both inside and outside the national church, but all so labeled privileged a personal, inward-looking religious faith centered on scripture-reading and shared dissatisfaction with the slow pace of reform within the church." Paul White, "Theater and Religious Culture," in *A New History of Early English Drama,* eds. John D. Cox and David Scott Kastan (New York: Columbia University Press, 1997), 151. The plays support the false notion that there is such a thing as a typical Puritan by indiscriminately introducing aspects of different groups into their stage characters. William P. Holden, *Anti-Puritan Satire, 1572–1642* (New Haven, CT: Yale University Press, 1954), 108.

[38]   Holden, *Anti-Puritan Satire,* 102.

[39]   Anonymous, *The Pilgrimage to Parnassus. The Three Parnassus Plays (1598–1601),* ed. J. B. Leishman (London: Ivor Nicholson & Watson, 1949).

[40]   Thomas Randolph, *Hey for Honesty, Down with Knavery* (London, 1651). It must be noted that the cope was never part of Catholic Eucharistic apparel, and as a result, it continued to be worn (although far less frequently) by English clergy after the Reformation. Mayo, *A History of Ecclesiastical Dress,* 70–71.

Hogsden, when Sir Reverence Lamard appears in a white shirt, Wildblood notes how he would appear to a Puritan: "here comes my white Knight in his Lawn sleeves, now if a Quaker saw him he would take his shirt for a Surpless, and condemn it for a Babylonish Garment, or in good sooth and verily a wicked and superstitious remnant of that foul slaps the whore of Babylon" (4.1.83–87).[41] The stage Puritan's contempt for ecclesiastical apparel in general and the surplice in particular remained constant throughout the period.

Beyond targeting religious clothing, stage Puritans similarly disparaged sumptuous apparel, railing against ostentatious display almost as often and as vociferously as they did against the surplice. This attack on rich clothing mirrors the condemnation of pride in apparel that was being issued from the pulpit and in print at the time. Scholars, starting with E. K. Chambers, have focused considerable attention on the anti-theatrical writings of the period, but those works often devote equal or even greater attention to clothing than they do to the theatre. For instance, Philip Stubbes's *Anatomie of Abuses* issues a strong condemnation of the theatres, but devotes far more space to ridiculing English "Sumptuous Attyre." At considerable length, Stubbes assaults opulent hats, ruffs, shirts, doublets, hose, stocks, shoes, coats, jerkins, cloaks, and scarves, as well as gilt swords and scabbards, the wearing of feathers or velvet visors, the use of make-up, particular hairstyles, cross-dressing, and new fashions. On stage, the most common targets of Puritan attack are large ruffs and oversized breeches. Accordingly, in *The Pilgrimage to Parnassus*, shortly after extolling his uncle for never donning Protestant religious apparel, Stupido attacks the poets who wear "such diabolical ruffs, and wicked great breeches full of sin, that it would make a zealous professors harte bleed for grife" (3.1.359–61). Similarly, in Thomas Middleton's *The Family of Love* (1603–1607), a Puritan bellows-mender preaches against crimson breeches (4.1.18).[42] And in Ben Jonson's *The Alchemist* (1610), Ananias decries costly clothing, saying "They are profane, / Lewd, superstitious, and idolatrous breeches . . . That ruff of pride / About thy neck betrays thee . . . Thou look'st like Antichrist, in that lewd hat" (4.7.46–55).[43] Puritan characters in early modern English drama were quick to condemn anything smacking of fun, and lavish apparel was a prime object of their scorn.[44]

On the early modern English stage, Puritans ultimately could more easily be identified by the clothes they refused to wear than by any uniform attire. Vehemently opposed to religious apparel and lavish clothing of any sort, stage Puritans often appeared in clothes of a markedly threadbare variety. Thus, in *The Pilgrimage to Parnassus*, Stupido appears in the "frize coate" that his uncle sent

---

[41]   Thomas Jordan, *The Walks of Islington and Hogsden* (London, 1657).

[42]   Thomas Middleton, *The Family of Love. The Works of Thomas Middleton,* Vol. 3, ed. A. H. Bullen (New York: AMS, 1964).

[43]   Ben Jonson, *The Alchemist,* in *Five Plays,* ed. G. A. Wilkes (New York: Oxford University Press, 1981).

[44]   White, "Theater and Religious Culture," 143.

him.[45] The inferior quality of this woolen cloth is made clear when Ingenioso notes how poor, unemployed schoolmasters could not afford even such simple apparel as frieze jerkins: "they coulde scarse get enoughe to apparell there heade in an vnlined hatt, there bodie in a frize Ierkin, and there feet in clouted paire of shoes" (5.1.589–91). Rather than wear such tawdry material by necessity, Stupido considers it a mark of his devoutness. In *Hey for Honesty, Down with Knavery*, Goggle similarly believes in the sanctity of his tattered apparel which consists of a worn robe and old shoes, neither of which has been changed for thirteen years: "This holy Cloak and I these thirteen years / Have freez'd together, and these upright Shoes; / Not upright once, till their ungodly soles / That always went awry, were rightly mended / By a religious conscionable Cobler" (4.1.91–5).

Thomas Heywood's *How a man May Chuse a Good Wife from a Bad* (1602) provides a fuller description of how Puritans were visually figured in drama, supporting the notion that they typically wore austere attire and introducing the importance of short hair to the stock image. Master Fuller explains how he sought to seduce a Puritan girl, but found he could only succeed by convincing her he was as devout as she. This he accomplished by doing away with his double ruff, long hair, scarf, and Spanish shoes, and furnishing himself instead in the apparel appropriate to her convictions: "My shooes were sharpe toed, and my band was plaine, / Close to my thigh my metamorphis'd breech: / My cloake was narrow Capte, my haire cut shorter."[46] The OED first dates the word *roundhead* to 1641, but clearly the association of short hair with Puritanism on the English stage began much earlier.[47] The visual expectation of short hair finds its cultural cognate in Puritan publications such as William Prynne's *The Unlovelinesse of Lovelockes* (1628), which warned that the wearing of inappropriately long hair by men or short hair by women was a damnable offense against God. Humbly attired and wearing his hair closely trimmed, Fuller quickly succeeds in his sexual conquest of the Puritan girl whose outer show of godliness hides her inner impiety.

Puritan women rail against pride of apparel as vehemently and comically as their male counterparts and are thus equally well suited to distinctively humble apparel. Jasper Mayne's *The Citye Match* (1637–1638) presents Ms. Dorcas as so devout that she will not let Madam Aurelia wear any clothes that are not specifically prescribed by scripture:

> I am never drest
> Without a sermon, but am forct to prove
> The lawfulnesse of curling irons before

---

[45]   Although frieze is understood to be a very inexpensive, unflattering fabric here, it was actually a woolen cloth that was made in several qualities and was worn by men and women in all classes of society. M. Channing Linthicum, *Costume in the Drama of Shakespeare and His Contemporaries* (New York: Russell & Russell, 1963), 76.

[46]   Thomas Heywood, *How a Man May Chuse a Good Wife from a Bad,* ed. A. E. H. Swaen (Louvain: A. Uystpruyst, 1912), 53.

[47]   Holden, *Anti-Puritan Satire,* 118.

She'l crisp me in a morning; I must show
Text for the fashions of my gownes, she'l aske
Where Jewels are commanded. (2.2.6–11)[48]

Dorcas is rendered more ridiculous by her affinity for embroidering images from the bible into Aurelia's chemise and petticoats. Aurelia says "My smock-sleeves have such holy imbroderies, / And are so learned, that I feare in time / All my apparell will be quoted by / Some pure Instructer" (2.2.33–6). Dorcas's character is defined by her fanatical religiosity which determined not just the words she spoke, but also the manner in which she appeared on the early modern stage.

Fanatical religiosity also guaranteed that stage Puritans would carry a bible to which they would invariably appeal for support for their ridiculous contentions. They did not typically quote directly from scripture, which would put the theatrical company at serious risk of breaking the 1559 royal proclamation prohibiting the treatment of religion in plays, but rather would refer to the bible for support while making wildly reductive arguments about religious minutiae. In Jonson's *Bartholomew Fair* (1614), the Puritan minister Zeal-of-the-Land Busy references an argument from Deuteronomy when he attacks the immorality of puppets for cross-dressing as women. Carrying a bible, Busy would have been prepared to issue his argument which mirrors in religious tone and substance the dialogue of Puritan characters throughout the period.

Zeal-of-the-Land Busy deserves extra comment, for instead of the austere apparel typical of stage Puritans, he wears a "scrivener's furred gown" and is taken for a schoolmaster (5.4.327–8).[49] The robe in which Busy originally appeared was probably not the long, flowing robes mandated for the Protestant clergy. Rather, Busy most likely wore a *Geneva gown*, a black preaching gown with wide sleeves and open down the front. The Geneva gown had been adopted by Calvin and was widely worn by Protestants on the continent.[50] Further evidence that Busy did not dress as a Protestant clergyman can be found in the fact that no mention is made of a square cap which was required apparel for English priests along with the robe. Numerous Puritan anti-vestment polemics attacked the priest's robes and square caps in addition to condemning the surplice. It thus seems impossible that Busy would have been identifiable as anything but a Puritan divine when he appeared in his particular clothes. Thus attired, Busy would have been a fit object of comic derision for an audience that was accustomed to seeing Puritans satirized onstage.

The apparel in which Puritans appeared on the early modern English stage, like that which was identifiably Catholic or Protestant, did not merely reflect the identity of the characters who wore it, but rather actively asserted it. Friars, cardinals, English bishops, and Puritans would all have been known on sight and

---

[48]   Jasper Mayne, *The Citye Match* (London, 1639).

[49]   Ben Jonson, *Bartholomew Fair,* in *Five Plays,* ed. G. A. Wilkes (New York: Oxford University Press, 1981).

[50]   Mayo, *A History of Ecclesiastical Dress,* 72.

understood according to the conventions of the time and the stage even before they had a chance to speak their lines. The visual language of religious apparel was thus well understood by both playwrights and audiences at the time, significantly influencing the manner in which plays were originally received.

Turks and Jews

In addition to Catholics, Protestants, and Puritans, the late sixteenth and early seventeenth century English professional theatres also staged the religious identities of non-Christian characters, providing for them distinctive apparel that served to produce specific meaning for contemporary audiences. Numerous plays from the period include Mahometans and Jews who would have been identifiable by the clothing they were wearing and understood according to the visual codes that maintained at the time.

Of the two, Muslims were the more common subject of dramatic exploration on England's professional stages. However, it is important to note that practitioners of Islam were rarely identified by their religion in English plays or other Western literature of the period. Though Muslim characters manifested their religion by frequently appealing to Mohammed (alternatively spelled "Mahomet," "Mawmet," "Mahoun," or "Mahound,"[51]) the English as well as most Europeans, preferred to refer to Muslims by ethnic names with the intent, Bernard Lewis argues, to diminish their stature and significance to something local or even tribal. Thus, Muslims are most commonly identified as Turks, Saracens, Moors, or Tatars with the various terms often indiscriminately conflated and confused. The term "Turk," specifically referring to the most powerful and important of the Muslim countries, became synonymous in European thought with Muslim and to convert to Islam was to have "turned Turk."[52]

The act of conversion actually appears in the drama of the period. In Robert Daborne's *A Christian Turned Turk* (1612), the pirate Ward converts to Islam onstage in a dumb show. This event provides the best single piece of evidence regarding the costume accorded to Turks on the English stage at the time, for it names the individual articles of apparel which, when put on in lieu of Ward's "Christian habit," served to effect his conversion and transform the wearer into a Turk, a Muslim. In this instance, the importance of clothing to establishing one's religious identity cannot be overstated, for the donning of Muslim attire literally divests Ward of his Christian identity and constitutes the act of conversion. Here is the dumb show in full:

---

[51]   Daniel J. Vitkus, Introduction, *Three Turk Plays From Early Modern England* (New York: Columbia University Press, 2000), 9.

[52]   This tendency was mirrored by Muslim writers who identified Christians by their country of origin more than by their religion. Bernard Lewis, *Islam and the West* (New York: Oxford University Press, 1993), 7.

Enter two bearing half-moons, one with a Mahomet's head following. After them, the Mufti, or chief priest, two meaner priests bearing his train. The Mufti seated, a confused noise of music, with a show. Enter two Turks, one bearing a turban with a half-moon on it, the other a robe, a sword: a third with a globe in one hand, an arrow in the other. Two knights follow. After them, Ward on an ass, in his Christian habit, bare-headed. The two knights, with low reverence, ascend, whisper the Mufti in the ear, draw their swords, and pull him off the ass. He [is] laid on his belly, the tables (by two inferior priests) offered him, he lifts his hand up, subscribes, is brought to his seat by the Mufti, who puts on his turban and robe, girds his sword, then swears him on the Mahomet's head, ungirts his sword, offers him a cup of wine by the hands of a Christian. He spurns at him and throws away the cup, is mounted on the ass, who is richly clad, and with a shout, they exit.[53]

Ward's "Christian habit" likely included a doublet, breeches, nether stocks, and perhaps a jerkin, apparel such as was common in England at the time. This ensemble would have worked well in the scene because the Turkish robe was typically worn over layers of clothing and would easily have fit on top of Ward's apparel—no time would have been wasted disrobing before putting on the new clothes. Appearing without a hat was rare for Englishmen at the time (the fact that the play bothers to note Ward's bare head supports this), but by doing so here, Ward is easily fit with the most identifiably Muslim piece of apparel, the turban. Last, a sword is gird at Ward's belt. This sword was almost certainly the distinctively curved sword of the Turks alternatively called the scimitar or falchion. The only element missing from Ward's visible transformation from Christian to Turk is a mustache. As was noted in my discussion of sex and gender, early modern Englishmen almost invariably wore facial hair, but large, sharp mustaches were a distinctive feature of the Turks and received frequent comment. In *The Spanish Tragedy*, when Hieronimo lists the articles that Balthazar will need to obtain in order to play the role of Great Soliman, the Turkish emperor, he includes "a Turkish cap, a black mustachio and a fauchion" (4.1.144–5).[54] Of course, one's true facial hair cannot be altered as quickly as one's clothes and so it seems that in *A Christian Turned Turk*, Ward

---

[53]   Scene 8, between lines 10 and 11. Robert Daborne, *A Christian Turned Turk*, in *Three Turk Plays From Early Modern England*, ed. Daniel J. Vitkus (New York: Columbia University Press, 2000).

[54]   Thomas Kyd, *The Spanish Tragedy* in *Renaissance Drama: An Anthology of Plays and Entertainments*, ed. Arthur F. Kinney (Malden, Massachusetts: Blackwell, 1999). In his notes to the play, Kinney identifies the "Turkish cap" as a fez. There are pictorial instances of very high-crowned caps worn by janissaries (Turkish infantry, many of whom were converted Christians) and perhaps it is with these in mind that Kinney makes his suggestion. However, the word "fez" did not enter the English language until the nineteenth century. Moreover, all of the extant pictures from the period showing Turkish Emperors in headdress present them wearing a turban. Consequently, it seems that "Turkish cap" here means turban.

Turcicæ Hiftoriæ,
MAHOMETHES II. EIVS NO-
MINIS, OCTAVVS TVRCORVM
IMPERATOR.

Fig. 4.3   Turkish Ruler by Amman in Phillip Lonicer, Chronicorum
             Turcicorum (1578), Vol. 1, leaf 21. By kind permission of the
             Watkinson Library at Trinity College, Hartford, Connecticut.

would not have been expected to have a distinctively Turkish mustache on the day
that he converted to Islam.

Taken together, the robe, turban, scimitar, and mustache were the visual
identifiers of Turks in the English imagination throughout the period. As early as
1510, King Henry VIII and the Earle of Essex wore these articles of clothing in
the Parliament Chamber at Westminster when they came "appareled after Turkey
fasshion" for a banquet held on Shrove-Sunday. For the occasion, they wore "long
robes of Bawdkin, powdered with gold, hattes on their heddes of Crimosyn Velvet,

with great rolles of Gold, girded with two swordes called Cimiteries."[55] Much like Ward's Muslim apparel worn on the professional stage over a century later, "Turkey fassion" in Henry VIII's court was understood to include robes, turbans, and falchions. Maskers were similarly dressed in 1555 for the "Masque of Turkish Magistrates" that Nicholas Udall designed for Shrovetide at the court of Queen Mary. For that event, the property maker was assigned to make "hedpeces of Asshen hoopewood in queynte and strange fasson"—apparently for turbans so large that some sort of framework was required to support them.[56]

The use of such large turbans suggests that size was understood to serve as a sign of the wearer's rank relative to other Turk characters. Further support for this possibility appears in the extensive historical annotations that Robert Baron included with the published version of his *Mirza, A Tragedy* in 1647. An avid follower of Ben Jonson, Baron chose to publish his play with lengthy commentary detailing the historical accuracy and academic rigor that he included in the dramatic work. Baron's discussion of the turban (which he spells "tulipant") is among the longest annotations he offers. Due to the importance of the turban in establishing a character's Muslim identity onstage and the infrequency with which Baron's annotation is referenced elsewhere, it is included here in its entirety:

> Tulipants, Turbants, & Sashes, are the head Oraments of the *Turks* and *Persians*. The *Turks* all of them wear white Shashes & Turbants, the badge of their Religion; as is the folding of the one, & size of the other of their vocations and quality. Sashes are long Towels of Calico too, & thwarted with rolles of the same, having little copped caps on the top, of green or red velvet, being onely worn by persons of rank, and he is the greatest that wears the greatest, the *Mufties* (or Prelates) excepted, which over-sized the Emperours; yet is his bigge enough according to Mr. *Sandys* who reports, that *Sultan Achmet*, wore a Turbant, in shape like to a pumpion, but thrice as great. And though many Orders have particular ornaments appointed for their heads, yet wear they these promiscuously. It is yet an especial favour to the *Turk* to suffer the *Christian* tributary Princes, and their chiefest Nobles, to wear white heads in the City. The *Persians* also wind about their heads great rolles of Calico, but some of silk and gold, somewhat higher, but not so bulkie as the Turkish Tuilipants; a little sash of gold, or fringe, hangs down behind, as do our skarfes, which ornament they lately borrowed of the *Arabian*. In Triumph they wreath about their Turbants long chaines of pearles, Rubies, Turquoise, and Emeralds of no small lustre and value. The King wears the contrary side of his Tulipant forwards, which is all the difference in habit 'twixt him and others. These Turbants they keep on continually, it being a shame with them, to be seen bare-headed: (perhaps because generally they wear no haire on the head or chin, (but on the upper lippe they have very long whiskers, and turned down-ward) some onely reserve a lock of haire upon the top of the head, as a certaine note that *Mahomet* at Doomesday, will distinguish them from

---

[55] Edward Hall, *Hall's Chronicle* (New York: AMS Press, 1965), 513.
[56] Samuel C. Chew, *The Crescent and the Rose: Islam and England During the Renaissance* (New York: Octagon Books, 1974), 456.

Christians, and by it lift them up to paradise) so that Mr. *Herbert* remembers as a singular favour, the civility of this King *Abbas*, to Sir *Dodmore Cotton*, Embassadour from our late King *Charles* to him, *Sc.* When the King drank to the Embassadour his royall Masters health, seeing the Embassadour put off his Hat, the King put off his Turbant, and bare-headed took off his cup, to the admiration of all the Court, to see so unusall a Grace from so hauthy a Prince, bestow'd upon a *Christian* Embassadour: another of his favours to him was, that whereas he thinks it honour enough to let the great *Turkes* Embassadour kiss the hem of his Garment onely, and perhaps by especiall Grace, his foot; he gave the *English* Embassadour his hand, and with it, pull'd him downe, and seated him next to himself crosse-legged, after the *Asian* mode.[57]

Baron notes the significance of the size of one's turban by stating "he is the greatest that wears the greatest." The importance of this semiotic sign to early modern drama is obvious; it provides a clear means by which English audiences would have been able to understand the social hierarchy of Muslim characters on sight. It also has direct relevance for the conversion scene in *A Christian Turned Turk*. To become a Muslim, Ward appears before the Mufti, the chief priest, who oversees the rite. But the Mufti has not previously appeared in the play, nor is he introduced in the Chorus' dialogue that precedes the scene. Rather, his position would have been understood entirely by his apparel which would have spoken his superior rank clearly to a contemporary audience that realized his larger turban (one which Baron says "over-sized the Emperours") signified the authority to rule over all of the other characters, who wore smaller turbans. With nothing else to signify the Mufti's rank, his authoritative role in the conversion scene would have been known.

In his description of turbans, Baron draws a distinction between those worn by the Turks and the slightly smaller ones that he says were typical of Persians. Perhaps this difference was staged in the apparel worn for *Mirza*, a play set in Persia (although there is no evidence the play was ever performed). However, no other plays from the period differentiate between the apparel appropriate to Persians and that of Turks. For both, the distinctive clothing included the elements listed thus far.[58]

The significance of those particular items on the English stage, however, extends further. For instance, beyond providing a means to establish rank, a Turk's turban also served as a signifier for the Muslim practice of circumcision. In *Othello*, when Othello speaks of an Ottoman, he alternatively refers to him in a single

---

[57]   Robert Baron, *Mirza, A Tragedy* in *Two Seventeenth-Century Plays*, ed. Parvin Loloi (Salzburg: University of Salzburg Press, 1998), 185–6.

[58]   *The Travailes of Three English Brothers* includes both Persians and Turks. Both almost certainly appeared in the typical apparel of a stage Mahometan, but they were also probably distinguishable from one another. However, no textual evidence suggests how their costumes might have differed. John Day, William Rowley, and George Wilkins, *The Travailes of the Three English Brothers* (London, 1607).

sentence as "a malignant and turban'd Turk" and a "circumcised dog," suggesting that the presence of the Muslim headpiece visibly asserted the absence of the foreskin (5.2.353–5). Similarly, when Ward "takes the turban," as conversion was often termed, he is required to undergo circumcision. In this manner, the turban serves as the visible sign of physical difference. The notion of circumcision, Daniel Vitkus argues, invoked considerable anxiety for Christians in early modern Europe, for it was conflated and confused with the idea of castration.[59] Thus, the danger of being captured by Turks and forced to don a turban (convert to Islam), whether onstage or in actuality, carried with it the attendant fear of forced castration.

In *Tamburlaine*, Bajazeth invokes this fear of conversion and circumcision with the words he chooses to describe the endless legions of troops he commands. He boasts:

> You know our army is invincible:
> As many circumcised Turks we have
> And warlike bands of Christians renied
> As hath the ocean or the Terrene sea
> Small drops of water when the moon begins
> To join in one her semicircled horns. (1:3.1.7–12)[60]

Bajazeth's army includes innumerable circumcised Turks and renied (converted) Christians. It is possible to read these lines as suggesting that the army consists of two groups, the one defined by circumcision and the other by conversion. To the early modern English audience, however, the notion of conversion implied circumcision. It follows that these two categories comprise a single group that is as numerous as the drops of water in the "ocean *or* the Terrene sea" (emphasis mine). If the soldiers were as numerous as the drops of water in the ocean *and* the Terrene sea, the text would argue for a division between the two categories. Instead, the "or" encourages us to view the warriors as comprised entirely of circumcised Turks, many of whom are Christian converts, and all of whom serve under the standard of the Ottoman empire. Members of the Turk army are thus presented as physically different from Christians, and would have visibly manifested that difference with their turbans, for, as N. I. Matar notes, to every writer of the Levant, the turban represented the most distinguishing characteristic of Turkish appearance.[61]

The association of turbans with circumcision offers a seemingly insurmountable challenge to the possibility of a Muslim man converting to Christianity or of a renegado (a Christian who has turned Turk) reconverting to his original religion. One cannot simply exchange a turban for an English hat if the Muslim headpiece

---

[59] Vitkus, Introduction, 5.

[60] Christopher Marlowe, *Tamburlaine*, ed. J. S. Cunningham (Manchester: Manchester University Press, 1981).

[61] N. I. Matar, "The Renegade in English Seventeenth-Century Imagination," *SEL* 33.3 (1993): 501.

signifies an irreversible physical transformation. The foreskin, removed in the ceremony of becoming a Muslim, cannot be replaced. Accordingly, in early modern society, English sailors who became renegades and then attempted to return to Christianity were often the subject of suspicion. Their willingness to trade their turbans for English headwear did not necessarily rescind the conversion that had been effected in their hearts and demonstrated in the irrevocable act of circumcision.[62] Once an Englishman had taken the Turban, it was impossible for him to entirely divest himself of it, for the circumcision it suggested could not be undone. In *A Christian Turned Turk*, Ward circumvents this trap by tricking those who are performing his circumcision into snipping the tip of an ape's tail instead of the foreskin of his penis. Sares says:

> I saw him Turk to the circumcision.
> Marry, therein I heard he played the Jew with 'em,
> Made 'em come to the cutting of an ape's tail. (9.2–4)

By skirting the irreversible act of circumcision through trickery, Ward reserves for himself the potential to convert back to Christianity. By the end of the play, Ward denounces the religion he earlier embraced. With his dying breath he curses the Turks and hopes that Christianity will join together to crush the Ottoman Empire:

> May all your seed be damned!
> The name of Ottoman be the only scorn
> And by–word to all nations; . . .
> Or may, O may, the force of Christendom
> Be reunited and all at once requite
> The lives of all that you have murdered, (16.304–10)

Through clever deception, Ward circumvents the demands of Muslim conversion and curbs the turban's ability to signify circumcision, thereby allowing him to embrace a Christian ideology later in the play.

The difficulty of reverting back to Christianity after one has taken the turban and fully embraced Islam appears in Philip Massinger's *The Renegado* (1623). At the start of the play, Antonio Grimaldi has already become a Muslim. Appearing onstage wearing a turban, Grimaldi's circumcision would have been understood by an early modern English audience, and any attempt on his part to convert back to Christianity would bring with it the possibility that he merely feigns his new religion since his body carries the mark of his Muslim allegiance.

Grimaldi begins his conversion back to Christianity through his change of apparel when he is deprived of his wealth, property, and clothing, and forced to wear rags. However, even in a different set of clothes, Grimaldi's physical transformation threatens any Christian identity he might wish to assume. To

---

[62]   Daniel Vitkus, *Turning Turk: English Theater and the Multicultural Mediterranean, 1570–1630* (New York: Palgrave, 2003), 83.

counter this risk, Grimaldi publicly embraces his new religion. He becomes so devout that he no longer bears any resemblance to the man who willingly served the Turkish Asambeg and abducted the Venetian woman Paulina. The former renegado gratefully confesses his sins to the Jesuit Francisco and welcomes the opportunity to achieve heaven through good deeds:

> What celestial balm
> I feel now poured into my wounded conscience!
> What penance is there I'll not undergo,
> Though ne'er so sharp and rugged, with more pleasure
> Than flesh and blood e'er tasted! (4.1.88–92)[63]

Grimaldi vigorously proclaims his newfound piety and makes lengthy speeches on the virtues of proper Christian living. The extent of his religious declarations makes clear the enormity of the challenge facing the renegado who would choose to convert back to Christianity after he has once taken the turban.

The turban was the most important piece of apparel denoting Muslim identity on the early modern stage, but other items also signified richly to a late sixteenth and early seventeenth century audience. The curved sword called the scimitar or falchion was widely understood throughout the period we are examining to be the weapon appropriate to Muslims. When Henry VIII and the Earl of Essex dressed as Turks in 1510, they each wore two scimitars at their sides. After Sir Robert Shirley was made the English Ambassador to Persia, he had his portrait painted by Anthony Van Dyck in 1622.[64] For the rendering, Shirley chose to appear in a lush robe and a turban, carry a bow, and wear a sword whose handle clearly shows the weapon to be a scimitar.[65] Except for this depiction of the new ambassador to Persia,[66] drawings of Englishmen throughout the first half of the seventeenth century present them wearing straight blades that had elaborate hand guards. Conversely, drawings of Muslim figures commonly included the scimitar and never present them wearing a straight sword with an elaborate hand guard. It is interesting to note that the Turkish bow, which appears in the drawing of Sir Robert Shirley and which was the famed weapon of both the Turks and the Persians, receives no mention in English drama at the time. Its military importance seems to have been elided on the public stages in favor of the distinctively curved sword.

---

[63] Philip Massinger, *The Renegado*, in *Three Turk Plays From Early Modern England*, ed. Daniel J. Vitkus (New York: Columbia University Press, 2000).

[64] This picture appears in Ann Rosalind Jones and Peter Stallybrass, *Renaissance Clothing and the Materials of Memory* (New York: Cambridge University Press, 2000), 56.

[65] A survey of the weapons that appear in other works by Anthony Van Dyck and by contemporary painters shows that the straight bladed swords that frequently adorned the hips of men in Western apparel invariably had intricate hand guards that differ markedly from the handle of the scimitar.

[66] For an insightful discussion of Sir Robert Shirley's decision to wear Persian apparel, see Jones and Stallybrass, 56–7

The English association of the scimitar with Muslims supports the likelihood that in the process of converting to Islam in *A Christian Turned Turk*, when Ward is given a sword, it is a scimitar. It is interesting to note that immediately after his conversion, the weapon is taken from him. The chorus explains:

> Now wears [Ward] the habit of a free-born Turk,
> His sword excepted, which lest they should work
> Just villainy to their seducers, is denied
> Unto all runagates, unless employed
> In wars 'gainst Christians. (8.18–22)

Ward is not permitted to retain the sword for fear he will turn it upon the Turks. At the time, the curved sword served to signify the viciousness associated with Muslims.

One story that shaped early modern English understandings of the curved sword tells of the Sultan Mahomet II (conqueror of Constantinople, not the prophet) and the Greek woman Hyerenee. Mahomet fell in love with Hyerenee and neglected his affairs of state to spend all of his time with her. When his second in command informed the Sultan of his neglect of matters of importance, Mahomet took a decisive course of action that established his priorities and his merciless authority. He made love to Hyerenee for a day and a half and then, in front of his entire court after a banquet, caught her by the hair and struck off her head with a falchion.[67] This story was so widely known in England that in Shakespeare's *2 Henry IV* (1598), Pistol is able to say "Have we not Hiren here?" (2.4.159–60) as he draws his sword, and it is clear that he threatens to decapitate Doll Tearsheet, who has been mocking him.

On the English stage, cruelty, the curved sword, and the act of decapitation became jointly associated and altogether deemed the province of the Muslim. In *The Travailes of the Three English Brothers* (1607) by John Day, William Rowley, and George Wilkins, the Sophy notes that the proper way to kill one's enemy is to decapitate him, for "then are we sure our enemy is dead, when from the body we divide the head" (ln. 51–2). So cruel are the Muslims in this play that the Sophy butchers his defeated enemies (carrying their heads aloft after victory) and admits to never having heard of honor before. The English brothers teach the Sophy about honor in the process of introducing the notion of mercy and clemency to one's prisoners.

The brutality of the Muslims, signified by the curved sword, explains why Ward in *A Christian Turned Turk* is deprived of his weapon. It is important to note that the Muslims cannot trust him even though he has converted, for English literature and the Shakespearean stage made frequent mention of the Muslim practice of parricide. The frightful acts depicted in Robert Greene's play *Selimus; Emperor of the Turks* (1594) are historically based. The Sultan Bajazet II was poisoned by his youngest son Selim who then had his elder brothers executed.

---

[67] Chew, 481.

These widely known events served to fix in the imagination of Europe the notion that the Ottomans specifically and Muslims generally were a barbarous and cruel people that would readily kill their own families, friends, advisors, and citizens to achieve power.[68] Ward cannot keep his sword even after he has joined the Turks, for the weapon symbolizes the brutality and bloodlust of those who typically wear it and threatens both Christians and Muslims alike.

Unlike the turban and the scimitar, the long robes that typically adorned the Muslim on the Shakespearean stage do not seem to have carried a great deal of ideological weight. In *A Christian Turned Turk*, Ward dons a robe in the process of becoming a Muslim and we can be fairly certain that it was the standard apparel for stage Muslims throughout the period, but it receives virtually no mention at all. One minor exception can be found in *The Renegado* in which the color of one's clothing is discussed. There, the servant Gazet warns his Venetian master Vitelli to be careful not to wear green:

> Take you heed, sir,
> What colors you wear. Not two hours since, there landed
> An English pirate's whore with a green apron,
> And as she walked the streets, one of their muftis
> (We call them priests at Venice) with a razor
> Cut it off—petticoat, smock, and all—and leaves her
> As naked as my nail; (1.1.48–54)

Daniel Vitkus explains that "green is the color sacred to Islam, traditionally worn by those who claim descent from the Prophet, and green clothing was sometimes prohibited for non-Muslims living under Islamic rule."[69] Perhaps green robes were worn to depict rank or religious importance in Massinger's play or other plays from the period, but no evidence exists to support this.

Beyond serving as a palate for color symbolism, the Muslim robe may provide a key to understanding better the most widely studied Muslim character in early modern English drama: Tamburlaine. The particular significance of the robe in Marlowe's play is its apparent absence from the costume worn by the title character. To begin, there is no mention of robes in the play. In itself, this is not unusual since robes hardly ever received comment. In Henslowe's diary, however, some of Tamburlaine's apparel is mentioned, including "Tamberlynes cotte with coper lace" as well as "Tamberlanes breches of crymson vellvet".[70] It is significant that a robe is not also listed, for if Tamburlaine did wear a robe, the specific coat

---

[68]   Chew, 490–1; Vitkus, Introduction, 21.

[69]   Daniel J. Vitkus, ed., *Three Turk Plays From Early Modern England*, (New York: Columbia University Press, 2000), 251. For further comment on the significance of the color green, see Chew, 198–9.

[70]   R. A. Foakes and R. T. Rickert, *Henslowe's Diary*, 2nd ed. (New York: Cambridge University Press, 1961), 322–3.

and breeches that warranted citation in Henslowe's diary would likely have been hidden beneath its folds.

In addition to eschewing the robe, it also seems likely that when Edward Alleyn played the part, he did not wear a turban. For evidence of this, we need to look at the pictorial representations of Tamburlaine that were disseminated in England at the time. The most widely known image is Lawrence Johnson's drawing that appears in Richard Knolles's *The Generall Historie of the Turkes* (1603).

Critics long surmised that this picture actually presents the image of Edward Alleyn in the costume he wore onstage to depict Tamburlaine.[71] If that were true, it would offer an extraordinary source of information regarding costuming practices at the time. However, John Astington has convincingly argued that the picture does not, in fact, present Edward Alleyn. And yet, the picture is included here because Astington goes too far when he suggests that we "remove Lawrence Johnson's engraving from the category of useful information about the Elizabethan stage."[72]

I do not mean to imply that the picture offers direct theatrical information, but it does suggest the manner in which Tamburlaine was understood to have appeared at the time *Tamburlaine* was popular on the English stage. In the introduction to the text that includes this print, Knolles explains that his work attempts to bring together the best work published in Europe over the previous century. It is significant that in the drawing for Tamburlaine that appears in Knolles's carefully researched text, the Scythian appears without a Turban. He is conspicuously bareheaded in a text replete with images of turbaned Muslim leaders. There are other pictorial images of Tamburlaine, and one print by Joost Amman appearing in *Türkische Chronica* by Barletius and published in Franfurt in 1577, presents Tamburlaine in a turban and wearing a robe. But Knolles had seen Amman's drawing and directed Johnson to choose a print for his work that presented Tamburlaine without the turban. Additionally, of the four extant images of Tamburlaine from the period, only Amman's presents him in a Turban. Two others (by Tobias Stimmer and André Thevet) present him in hats that could never be mistaken for Turkish headwear.[73] One final print that should be mentioned is the woodcut that appeared with the text when it was first published in 1590. This picture presents the upper half of a man wearing full plate armor, with a baldric slung across the left shoulder. He wears a mustache and beard in a western cut and is bareheaded. Although this picture may have suggested to readers how Tamburlaine was intended to appear, it likely bears no immediate connection to the play.[74]

It seems very reasonable to suggest that when Edward Alleyn played the role of Tamburlaine he never appeared as a Muslim. At the beginning of the play, he

---

[71] For a summary of this picture's critical reception see Astington, 74–5.

[72] Astington, 86.

[73] For these pictures, see Astington 79 and 82. Stimmer's drawing presents Tamburlaine in a conical fur cap. Thevet presents Tamburlaine in a medium height cap with a small brim that resembles contemporary English hats.

[74] R. A. Foakes, *Illustrations of the English Stage, 1580–1642* (Stanford: Stanford University Press, 1985), 88.

Fig. 4.4   Tamburlaine in Richard Knolles, *The Generall Historie of the Turkes* (1603), STC 15051, p. 236. By permission of the Huntington Library.

wears shepherd's apparel which he soon replaces with armor: "Lie here, ye weeds that I disdain to wear! This complete armour and this curtle-axe are adjuncts more beseeming Tamburlaine" (1.2.41–3). At a later point, we know he wore white apparel which he replaced with scarlet and then black, although the particular item that was colored is unclear. Perhaps the breeches of crimson velvet in Henslowe's list made up part of Tamburlaine's scarlet costume. Far from wearing Muslim apparel, it is possible that on the English stage, while Tamburlaine pursued his conquest of the East, he wore clothes and a hat that were indicative of the West.[75]

This spectacle lends support to recent critical commentary on *Tamburlaine* that identifies both parts of the play as supporting Western ambitions to achieve mastery over the East. Historians argue the degree to which Tamberlaine followed Islam, but uniformly agree that he was a Muslim. Jonathan Burton notes, however, that Marlowe's play distances Tamburlaine from Islam, figuring him in contrast to Bajazeth who claims Muhammad as a kinsman in *Part One* and against Callapine and the reunited forces of Islam in *Part Two*.[76] Vitkus expands this argument to identify Tamburlaine as the hero of an anti-Islamic English fantasy.

> In Marlowe's play, Tamburlaine seeks to destroy Islam, both its holy books and its holy warriors. He slaughters the Babylonians and abjures Mahomet, reducing the Ottoman powers from "millions" (2:5.2.25) to Callapine's "one host" (2:5.2.27). Then Tamburlaine and his followers wipe out that last remaining Islamic army. . . . When he accomplishes this feat, Tamburlaine fulfills a longstanding Christian-European fantasy—the complete elimination of Turkish military power.[77]

Bajazeth acknowledges the joy that Christians will have over the defeat of his army: "Now will the Christian miscreants be glad, ringing with joy their superstitious bells, and making bonfires for my overthrow" (1:3.3.235-7). Further, Tamburlaine openly admits his ambition to help Christians, saying that he will "subdue the Turk, and then enlarge those Christian captives which you keep as slaves" (1:3.3.59–60). Appearing on the early modern stage in the apparel of the West and without a turban, the historically Muslim Tamburlaine visually assumed the identity of a Christian and a European, and perhaps even an Englishman, when he defeated the forces of Islam and accomplished what the Crusades could not.

While basic rules governing the apparel appropriate to male Muslim characters in the English public theatres can be determined from the available evidence, it is much more difficult to establish what was worn by female Muslim characters. Few of the plays of the period make note of Muslim women's apparel, and when they do, there is no way to be sure that the items presented are typical of larger

---

[75]   Richmond Barbour, *Before Orientalism: London's Theatre of the East, 1576–1626* (New York: Cambridge University Press, 2003), 44.

[76]   Jonathan Burton, "Anglo-Ottoman Relations and the Image of the Turk in *Tamburlaine, Journal of Medieval and Early Modern Studies* 30 (2000): 142, 147.

[77]   Vitkus, *Turning Turk*, 51.

trends in English theatre. That stated, there are instances when costume elements are mentioned and serve an important purpose in the drama.

Massinger's *The Renegado* includes Donusa, niece to the Ottoman Emperor, and makes significant mention of her apparel. Donusa's most important costume element is her veil. She explains how the veil allows Muslim wives to be seen only by their husband:

> Our jealous Turks
> Never permit their fair wives to be seen
> But at the public bagnios or the mosques,
> And even then, veiled and guarded. (1.2.18–21)

Although Donusa is not married, she also wears a veil when she ventures outside her home, ostensibly to avoid becoming the object of men's desire. In the play, however, it is Muslim women whose desire must be held in check. Francisco explains:

> Turkish dames
> (Like English mastiffs that increase their fierceness
> By being chained up), from the restraint of freedom,
> If lust once fire their blood from a fair object,
> Will run a course the fiends themselves would shake at
> To enjoy their wanton ends. (1.3.8–13)

Hidden most of the time behind walls and veils, Muslim women apparently have no means to relieve their sexual desire. It therefore grows until its will cannot be denied. Walking abroad, Donusa's veil protects her from the male gaze but does nothing to keep her from falling in love with Vitelli at the marketplace.

The veil then serves another purpose, allowing her to signify her desire for Vitelli when she pulls it back to reveal her face. Vitelli recognizes the significance of her disclosure, for he has heard that "among the Turks for any lady to show her face bare argues love or speaks her deadly hatred" (1.3.170–2). The revealing of her visage proves the equivalent of a sexual invitation, for Donusa quickly follows it with plans to get Vitelli alone in her home.

Massinger uses the veil effectively to forward the plot of the play, but there is little reason to believe that the veil was or became a conventional costume element for Muslim women on the English stage. At every point, the play carefully explicates the meaning behind its presentation and manipulation, guaranteeing that an audience need not have any previous understanding of the article to follow the action. The only visual element endemic to virtually all Muslim women on the Shakespearean stage is their physical attractiveness, and in this they are identical to Jewish women presented in English drama of the time.

In almost every play that presents Muslim or Jewish women, reference is made to the characters' beauty. When Donusa removes her veil, she strikes Vitelli with wonder. In *The Travailes of the Three English Brothers*, Sir Robert Shirley falls in love with the Emperor's niece and braves the leader's terrible wrath to marry her. In *A Christian Turned Turk*, Ward is convinced to convert to Islam by the bewitching beauty of Voada. Similarly, in *The Jew of Malta* (1589–1590), both Mathias and Lodowick are drawn by the beauty of the Jewish Abigail, daughter to Barabas; Mathias calls her "A fair young maid, scarce fourteen years of age, the sweetest flower in Cytherea's field, cropt from the pleasures of the fruitful field" (1.2.391–3). In Shakespeare's *The Merchant of Venice* (1596–1597), Lorenzo attempts to steal Jessica, whose "fair hand [is] whiter than the paper it writ on" (2.4.12–3), from her father Shylock.

All of these women are presented as extraordinarily attractive, and yet, it is important to note that beauty is not presented in the plays as a quality appropriate to either Muslim or Jewish women. Certainly each woman listed is beautiful, but that characteristic serves primarily to mark them as appropriate subjects for conversion to Christianity. In *The Renegado*, when Asambeg learns that the Christian Vitelli has had sex with Donusa, both are threatened with death if Vitelli will not convert to Islam. He refuses to turn Turk, despite suffering "all the torments that [the Turks] could present him with to fright his constancy" (4.2.47–8), and instead convinces Donusa to become a Christian, even though it will cost her her life. Before being put to death, Donusa undergoes baptism. The rite washes clean her spirit and transforms the lusty, sinning Muslim into a stainless Christian and an appropriate bride to Vitelli:

> I am another woman—till this minute
> I never lived, nor durst think how to die.
> How long have I been blind! Yet on the sudden
> By this blest means I feel the films of error
> Ta'en from my soul's eyes. (5.3.121–5)

When the two succeed in escaping, the play invites Christian approbation for it rewards the characters who embraced their religion in the face of almost certain death. Donusa's beauty, which originally threatened Christianity by drawing a faithful subject to sin with a Muslim, ultimately reinforces Christian ideology by embracing its tenets and flouting the power of the Turks.

A similar subplot appears in *The Travailes of the Three English Brothers* in which Sir Robert Shirley marries the Sophy's niece and has a son by her. At risk of death, Sir Robert asks for and obtains permission from the Sophy to baptize his child and raise him as a Christian. Moreover, Sir Robert gets consent to build a Church as well as a house where Christian children "from their cradles, should know no other education, manners, language, nor religion, than what by Christians is deliver'd them" (2062–6). A Muslim woman's beauty thereby leads to the spreading of Christianity in the East.

Labeled a tragedy, *A Christian Turned Turk* does not end with the conversion of the beautiful Muslim woman Voada.[78] Instead, the play concludes with the

---

[78]   The title page of the plays call it: *A Christian Turned Turk or The Tragical Lives and Deaths of the Two Famous Pirates Ward and Dansiker*.

revelation that Voada's beauty serves to damn the souls of naive Christians. Ward states, "I loved that face so well, to purchase it I exchanged my heaven with hell" (16.163–4). Voada goes near to the point of conversion, listening to Ward as he begs her to embrace his love. But she responds to his entreaties with scorn and laughter. Offering a diametrical conclusion to that found in either *The Renegado* or *The Travailes of Three English Brothers*, *A Christian Turned Turk* nevertheless supports a similar argument that beauty in a Muslim is an abomination, and that it is appropriate only to Christian women.

Feminine beauty is likewise presented as appropriate only to Christian women in *The Jew of Malta* and *The Merchant of Venice*. Both plays include Jewish daughters who wish to convert to Christianity in order to be with the men they love. In Marlowe's play, Abigail's desirability is perverted by her father Barabas into a weapon and used to trick Mathias and Lodowick into killing one another. However, Abigail does not wish this and rebels against her father, choosing to become a nun. When he secretly has her poisoned, her beauty is set in opposition to her father's cruelty. In Shakespeare's work, Jessica begins the play prepared to convert to Christianity in order to marry Lorenzo. True to the comic form, she succeeds in tricking her father out of his money and escaping with her Christian fiancé. Both plays present feminine beauty in the form of daughters who embrace Christianity and work against the wishes of their Jewish fathers.

The number of female Muslim and Jewish characters who convert to Christianity is striking, surpassing the number of males who convert even though the men appear more frequently in the drama of the time. The lone Jewish male who converts to Christianity is Shylock, and it is against his will. This disparity between men and women makes sense. The act of conversion undertaken by Muslim and Jewish women is aided by the fact that they are not physically marked by their religion. Whereas Muslim and Jewish men were understood to be circumcised, the women were not. Consequently, they could more easily cross religious boundaries.[79]

The fact that circumcision is a trait shared by Muslim and Jewish men is mentioned in *The Jew of Malta*, in which Barabas tries to gain Ithamore's trust and assistance by saying, "We are villains both, / Both circumcised. We hate Christians both" (2.3.219–20). Moreover, Barabas also likely wore a turban, a visual signifier of circumcision, when he first appeared on the early modern stage. As Randall Nakayama has noted, Barabas's claim that his hat is a gift from the "Great Cham" suggests that the Jew's headpiece is, in fact, a turban.[80] Pictorial representations of Jews in travel books support the notion that Jews were known in England to wear turbans. In his *Navigations into Turkie* (1585), Nicolas De

---

[79]   James Shapiro, *Shakespeare and the Jews* (New York: Columbia University Press, 1996), 120.

[80]   Randall Nakayama, "'I know she is a courtesan by her attire': Clothing and Identity in *The Jew of Malta*," in *Marlowe's Empery: Expanding His Critical Contexts*, eds. Sara Munson Deats and Robert A. Logan (Newark: University of Delaware Press, 2002), 138.

Nicolay presents the image of a turbaned "Merchant Jew" and explains that "they weare a yealow Tulbant."[81] Similarly, Thomas Coryate, on the title page of his *Coryate's Crudities*, includes a picture of a Jew in a turban who carries a knife and chases a Christian with intent to circumcise him.[82] Although there is no further evidence to suggest that other Jewish male characters wore turbans onstage, Peter Berek notes that Barabas, more than any other contemporary or historical Jewish figure, underlies subsequent Jewish characters in English Renaissance literature.[83] It follows that aspects of Barabas's visual presentation were copied in Jewish characters appearing in later plays.

One visible aspect of Barabas that certainly was copied was his large nose. Its size is mentioned repeatedly by Ithamore who says "I worship your nose for this" (2.3.134) and who calls Barabas "bottle-nosed," (3.3.10). This physical characteristic and even the words Marlowe uses to describe it mark the Jew's nose as descended from the large, misshapen appendage traditionally worn by Satan in morality plays. In *Like Will to Like* (1568), the Devil is saluted by the vice as "bottel nosed godfather" and "bottle nosed knave." Similarly, in *Susanna* (1569), the Devil is called a "crookte nose knave."[84] Invoking the scheming malevolence of Satan, a distinctive, oversized, prosthetic nose was the most distinguishing visual identifier of a Jew on the Shakespearean stage. Nakayama has sought to complicate this argument by suggesting that in *The Jew of Malta*, Barabas's apparel speaks more powerfully than his nose. Noting that Barabas is able to assume the disguise of a French musician and fool the other characters into mistaking his identity, Nakayama concludes that "the sartorial is more powerful than the anatomical, that the dress is more important than the nose."[85] It strikes me as more likely that Barabas's nose stuck out of his new apparel so that the action of the play would depend on a successful disguise while the audience could laugh at the ridiculous nose that remained easily apparent. After all, the point of theatrical disguise is to let the audience know who the individual really is while the other characters in the play are tricked.

Bearing Satan's theatrical nose, the Jew would have been understood to be a usurer and a villain on sight. Accordingly, in *A Christian Turned Turk*, the Jewish Benwash is a greedy coward identifiable by his "fiery nose" and fit to be cuckolded.[86] *The Merchant of Venice* does not explicitly reference Shylock's

---

[81] Nicolas De Nicolay, *The Navigations into Turkie* (New York: Da Capo, 1968), 131–2. Nicolay also notes that those that dwell in the Isle of Chio wear a large yellow cap, although he does not provide a picture. An earlier picture of a Jewish Physician presents him with a tall cap on his head that is described as red scarlet in color.

[82] Thomas Coryate, *Coryats Crudities* (London, 1611).

[83] Peter Berek, "The Jew as Renaissance Man," *Renaissance Quarterly* 51 (1998): 131.

[84] Craik, 51.

[85] Nakayama, 161.

[86] Benwash has converted to Islam but he is repeatedly referred to as a Jew by others and self-identifies as a Jew during the play.

nose, but when Richard Burbage played the part, he almost certainly wore a prosthetic appendage on his face. Lines from the play suggest it. In addition to being a moneylender in the tradition of Barabas, Shylock is identified as the Devil numerous times. Launcelot says that "certainly the Jew is the very devil incarnal" (2.2.27–8), and Salanio, seeing Shylock approach, says the devil comes "in the likeness of a Jew" (3.1.20–1). The likeness of the devil in medieval drama included an oversized nose. Additionally, a ballad written by an actor in the 1630s describes Shylock's appearance and mentions his nose:

> His beard was red; his face was made
>   Not much unlike a witches.
> His habit was a Jewish gown
>   That would defend all weather;
> His chin turn'd up, his nose hung down,
>   And both ends met together. (Thomas Jordan, "The Forfeiture")[87]

Perhaps Burbage appeared differently thirty years earlier when he first personates the role, but the poem lends additional credibility to the likelihood that he wore a large prosthetic nose and suggests that an oversized nose was a staple element of Shylock's appearance at least a decade before the interregnum.

Beyond merely signifying Jewishness, the large prosthetic nose worn by stage Jews came to be associated specifically with the practice of usury, and began to appear on characters whose religion was not stated in the play. G. K. Hunter explains that in the early modern theatre, a "usurer is a Jew whether he is racially (confessionally) Judaic or not."[88] In George Chapman's *The Blind Beggar of Alexandria* (1596), the main character is a chameleon who takes on multiple personalities by changing his appearance. One of his roles is Leon, a usurer of uncertain religion, whose one definitive trait is his "great nose" (2.141).[89] William Haughton's *Englishmen for My Money* (1598) includes the Portuguese usurer Pisaro who lives in London and by all accounts is a typical merchant who appears in a ruff and a gown. His trade, however, identifies him as a Jew and his visage bears the mark, for he is referred to as "signor bottle-nose."[90] Appearing with the primary visual signifier of the Jew, Pisaro would have been marked for comic abuse from the moment he walked onto the stage to deliver the first lines of the play. Similarly, in John Marston's *Jacke Drum's Entertainment* (1600), the play list includes "Mamon the Usurer, with a great nose." In this play, "all the materials for

---

[87] Quoted in James C. Bulman, *The Merchant of Venice: Shakespeare in Performance* (Manchester: Manchester University Press, 1991), 19.

[88] G. K. Hunter, *Dramatic Identities and Cultural Tradition: Studies in Shakespeare and His Contemporaries* (Liverpool: Liverpool University Press, 1978), 28.

[89] George Chapman, *The Blind Beggar of Alexandria*, in *The Plays of George Chapman*, Vol. 1, ed. Thomas Marc Parrott (New York: Russell, 1961).

[90] William Haughton, *Englishmen for My Money, Or A Woman Will have Her Will* (London: W. White, 1616).

conventional condemnation of a monstrous Jew are present, but there is no claim that Mammon is Jewish."[91] In these plays and many more, the Jew's nose proves to be even more significant than his religion in determining the nature of his character.

The 1630's ballad discussed above also mentions Shylock's red beard and invokes the forged document "Funeral Elegy on the Death of Richard Burbadge" that John Payne Collier penned in the nineteenth century but claimed to have dated to the early seventeenth century. The poem notes that the actor played "the red hair'd Jew."[92] Just because the poem is a fake does not necessarily mean that its comments on Shylock are wrong.[93] The custom of Jews wearing red hair has antecedents in the character of Judas in Corpus Christi plays, who appeared with red hair and beard as well as with a hook nose and a usurer's bag.[94] The dramatic tradition of the Jew's sartorial ensemble, with its roots in the costumes worn by Satan and Judas, marked the wearer as the appropriate butt of jokes and threatened to seriously undercut the tragic elements of Shylock's character when he appeared on the Shakespearean stage.

The final piece of Shylock's apparel is his *gabardine*, which he mentions in the play: "You call me misbeliever, cut-throat dog, And spet upon my Jewish gaberdine" (1.3.112–3). A gaberdine was a long coat, worn loose or girdled, with long sleeves.[95] Oscar Wilde, noting the importance of costume to Shakespeare's drama, found the gaberdine of particular significance, stating that "Shylock's Jewish gaberdine is part of the stigma under which that wounded and embittered nature writhes."[96] And yet, Shylock's "wounded and embittered nature" also writhed on the early modern stage behind a large farcical nose and perhaps a comical red beard, apparel that was reminiscent of the two most obvious villains to populate the medieval stage. Additionally, the gaberdine was not a compulsory garment of the Jews and was, in fact, worn in England by Christians of varying economic classes. M. Channing Linthicum notes several instances in the sixteenth and early seventeenth century when gaberdines were worn by nobles and commoners.[97]

---

[91]   Berek, 157.

[92]   Jacob Lopes Cardozo, *The Contemporary Jew in the Elizabethan Drama* (New York: Burt Franklin, 1965), 74.

[93]   In researching the name "Shylock," Stephen Orgel has noted that it has an English origin that goes back to Saxon times and means "white-haired." The name is the same as its more common English equivalents "Whitlock" and "Whitehead." Stephen Orgel, "Shylock's Tribe" in *Shakespeare and the Mediterranean* (Newark: University of Delaware Press, 2004), 43–4. The name's original meaning does not likely have any bearing on the color of the hair worn by Burbage when he played Shakespeare's Jew.

[94]   Bulman, 19.

[95]   M. Channing Linthicum, *Costume in the Drama of Shakespeare and His Contemporaries* (New York: Russell and Russell, 1963), 201.

[96]   Oscar Wilde, "The Truth of Masks," in *The Soul of Man Under Socialism and Other Essays*, Introduction by Philip Rieff (New York: Harper Colophon Books, 1950), 4.

[97]   Linthicum, 200. Although there is a recorded instance in which a nobleman's trumpeters wore decorative gaberdines in 1623, Linthicum states that they were out of fashion for commoners by the end of the 1560s.

Furthermore, the gaberdine appears in at least one play that makes no mention of Jewish characters. In *The Pilgrimage to Parnassus*, Madido refers to an "English gaberdine" (2.26). The fact that Jews had been officially expelled from England in 1290 and few lived there before the interregnum suggests that audiences would not have known what Jewish apparel looked like. A "Jewish gaberdine" would have been unfamiliar until Burbage appeared in one and referenced it in his speech. And yet, as Berek has noted, "Marlowe and Shakespeare play a central role in creating—not imitating—the frightening yet comic Jewish figure who haunts Western culture."[98] It appears that Shakespeare appropriated the gabardine for his Jewish character, establishing a visual code that maintained and grew more significant until the late nineteenth century when Wilde's understanding of the character was prescribed by the apparel mentioned in *The Merchant of Venice* and worn on stage ever since the sixteenth century. Here, as with stage Catholics, Protestants, Puritans, and Mahometans, Shakespeare, like his contemporaries, employed costume not merely to depict religion on the early modern stage, but to fashion it to his dramatic purpose.

---

[98]   Berek, 158.

Chapter 5
"An vnder black dubblett signifying a Spanish hart": Costumes and Politics in Middleton's *A Game at Chess*

Thomas Middleton's *A Game at Chess*, has long held a place of particular importance in studies of early modern English theatre history. Performed for a record nine straight performances (a feat not accomplished again until the Restoration), Middleton's production has attracted scholarly interest by virtue of both its unparalleled contemporary success and its overt religious and political messages of anti-Catholic and anti-Spanish propaganda.[1] Performed by the King's Men at the Globe playhouse between 5 and 14 August (except for Sunday) 1624, *A Game at Chess* provides the most conspicuous instance from the period in which the stage addressed issues of immediate political significance. Certainly history plays, such as Shakespeare's series of works chronicling the Wars of the Roses, dealt with English politics, but no play dealt so directly with the politics of the moment. Even more importantly, the politics of the moment responded. John Woolley, the secretary of the English agent in Brussels, wrote "all the nues I have heard since my comming to towne is of a nue Play. It is called a game at Chess, but it may be a vox populy for by reporte it is 6 tymes worse against the Spanyard."[2] The play's politics struck such a chord and the performance was deemed so significant that it was ultimately shut down by King James himself after he received an official complaint from the Spanish Ambassador Extraordinary, Don Carlos Coloma.

Naturally, the religious and political aspects of Middleton's play have drawn scholarly attention in the past. *A Game at Chess* differs markedly from Middleton's previous plays, which are representative of the genres popular at the time. By 1623, he had written a number of city comedies for boy companies, followed by

---

[1]   Thomas Cogswell estimates that nearly thirty thousand spectators saw the performance, and Thomas Postlewait concludes that more than a tenth of London's population attended the play with more people turned away. Thomas Cogswell, "Thomas Middleton and the Court, 1624: *A Game at Chess* in Context," *Huntington Library Quarterly* 47 (1984): 273. Thomas Postlewait, "From Event to Context to Event: A Problem in the Writing of Theatre History," in *Critical Theory and Performance*, 2nd edition, eds. Janelle Reinelt and Joseph Roach (Ann Arbor: University of Michigan Press, 2007), 200.

[2]   Thomas Middleton, *A Game at Chess*, ed. T. H. Howard-Hill, Revels Edition (New York: Manchester University Press, 1993), Appendix 1, Item 2, 192.

tragicomedies, and then several tragedies that were performed by the King's Men. It is striking that Middleton followed this body of work with a play as unique as *A Game at Chess*. No previous play by Middleton, nor any other playwright of the period for that matter, addressed the politics and religion of the period so brashly, and scholars have devoted considerable attention to explicating the complex dialogue that the play entered into with the London audiences that came to see it. Still, for all of the attention that Middleton's play has received, one area of study has gone largely unconsidered: the play's visual presentation. How did the actors appear when they first performed the play and how was that visual information received by early modern London audiences? Beyond its overtly partisan dialogue, the initial performances of *A Game at Chess* also skillfully employed costumes to convey meaning and further the play's pro-Protestant, pro-English agenda. This chapter will attempt to establish what costumes were worn by the King's Men for their production of Middleton's play and demonstrate the religious and political significance this apparel had for contemporary audiences.

No inventory list exists for the apparel worn in *A Game at Chess* (or for any other early modern English play). Nevertheless, with this production, there is a great deal of historical evidence from which we can deduce what was worn. In addition to several different texts of the play, together providing considerable insight into its original composition, there is also contemporary commentary that speaks to the particulars of the production.[3] The first thing we learn from extant letters is that the actors playing the English were uniformly dressed in white and those playing the Spanish appeared in black. This color scheme served to establish the characters as pieces in a game of chess as well as to delineate clearly the diametrical moral positions of the two sides as they were presented in the play.

Several correspondences also note that the characters onstage were intended to represent well-known contemporaries from England and Spain, including royalty, which was expressly forbidden. John Holles (c. 1565–1637), then Baron Haughton, later first Earl of Clare, saw the play on 10 August 1624 and wrote to Robert Carr, Earl of Somerset, about the experience,[4] noting that it provided "a representation of all our spannishe traffike."[5] The Spanish traffic Holles mentions refers to the intense anti-Spanish feelings that were a constant in England since before the defeat of the Armada in 1588 and that grew to a fevered pitch in England in 1624. In October of the preceding year, Prince Charles and the Duke of Buckingham returned from Spain following a failed attempt to draw up a marriage contract between Charles and the Spanish Infanta. Charles's trip had been a source

---

³   T. H. Howard-Hill offers the fullest explanation of the different texts of *A Game at Chess* in the second half of his book, *Middleton's "Vulgar Pasquin": Essays on* A Game at Chess (Newark: University of Delaware Press, 1995). For a summary of the issues, see the introduction to his edition of the play, 2–10.

⁴   A. R. Braunmuller, "'To the Globe I rowed': John Holles Sees *A Game at Chess*," *English Literary Renaissance* 20:2 (1991): 341.

⁵   Middleton, *A Game at Chess*, Appendix 1, Item 7, 198.

of profound anxiety throughout England; not only did it jeopardize the life of the heir to the throne by placing him in the hands of the Spanish, it also threatened the future of the Protestant nation by allying it through marriage to a powerful and avowedly Catholic country. So great was the fear caused by Charles's trip, that his return without a Catholic wife elicited jubilation throughout England. Bonfires were lit, candles burned in windows, churches sang out in praise of the return of the prince, and the long-standing restraints against the expression of anti-Spanish and anti-Catholic viewpoints were relaxed.[6]

It is in light of these events that Holles and the rest of the English audience first saw *A Game at Chess.*[7] The foreign relations between Spain and England inform both the substance of the play and the manner in which it was received; Holles summarizes the play, saying the "descant was built uppon the popular opinion, that the Iesuits mark is to bring all the christian world vnder Rome for the spirituality, & vnder Spayn for the temporalty."[8] Holles commentary is significant to a study of the production's costumes because it indicates that he saw the apparel worn onstage as serving overwhelmingly to make the wearers distinguishable as particular players in national policy, and not merely as players on a stage. Accordingly, although Holles notes that "the whole play is a chess board, England the whyt hows, Spayn the black," and he refers briefly to black and white pieces, he primarily discusses the characters by using the names of the people they represent. He mentions "Gundomar," Count Gondomar-Don Diego Sarmiento de Acuna, the Spanish ambassador to England 1613–1618 and 1620–1622; "Ignatius Loyala," the founder of the Society of Jesus, the Jesuits, in the sixteenth century; "Bristow," John Digby, Earl of Bristol, who was a longtime ambassador to Spain, but was under house arrest at the time of the production under suspicion of supporting the Spanish cause; "Spalato," Marc Antonio de Dominis, Archbishop of Spalatro, who converted to Protestantism and was openly received by James in England but left the country and converted back to Catholicism in 1622.

Other detailed reports of the play are not first hand, but nevertheless provide insight into what was seen onstage. Don Carlos de Coloma, writing to the Conde-Duque Olivares, favorite of the Spanish King, on 20 August 1624, notes that the characters in the play are clearly meant to represent actual individuals. In addition to mentioning Saint Ignatius, the Archbishop of Spalato, and the Count of Gondomar, he states that "the king of the blacks has easily been taken for our lord the King, because of his youth, dress, and other details."[9] Sir Edward Conway,

---

[6] T. H. Howard-Hill, "Introduction," in *A Game at Chess* by Thomas Middleton, Revels Edition (New York: Manchester University Press, 1993), 16.

[7] I do not mean to suggest that all English audience members perceived the events in the same way. However, it must be acknowledged that these events were known by all who attended the production and influenced how it was experienced. For a consideration of the complex relationship between politics and *A Game at Chess*, see Postlewait's essay.

[8] Middleton, *A Game at Chess*, Appendix 1, Item 7, 198–9.

[9] Middleton, *A Game at Chess*, Appendix 1, Item 5, 194–5.

Secretary of State, wrote to the Privy Council on 12 August 1624 that King James received word from the Spanish Ambassador that a comedy was being performed wherein "they [the King's Men] take the boldnes, and presumption in a rude, and dishonorable fashion to represent on the Stage the persons of his Maiestie, the Kinge of Spaine, the Conde de Gondomar, the Bishop of Spalato, &c."[10] Taken together, contemporary reports make it clear that many of the characters onstage were immediately identifiable by virtue of the costumes they wore. To the list mentioned in the correspondences from the period, we can add the White King, the White Knight, and the White Duke who, from their roles in the play, would have been easily recognizable as King James, Prince Charles, and the Duke of Buckingham.

But the written responses to *A Game at Chess* do more than just indicate whom the costumes helped the actors impersonate. They also suggest how the apparel they wore worked to fashion the characters they played. Consider Gondomar. Contemporary report makes it clear that the role was clearly identifiable onstage. John Chamberlain notes in his commentary on the play that the actors had gone so far as to purchase one of the ambassador's old suits, or clothing made to resemble it: "they counterfeited his person to the life, with all his graces and faces, and had gotten (they say) a cast sute of his apparell for the purpose."[11] Beyond observing that Gondomar was readily identifiable, however, several contemporaries note that he appeared on the stage with his well known litter and chair. The litter was one that he frequently used while in London and the chair was specially designed with a hole in the bottom to accommodate his severe case of anal fistula. In the same sentence in which John Holles mentions Gondomar, he notes the fact that the character appeared onstage in his litter, "his open chayre for the ease of that fistulated part."[12] Don Carlos de Coloma says that Gondomar was "brought on to the stage in his little litter almost to the life, and seated on his chair with a hole in it."[13] Writing to Sir Dudley Carleton, Sir Francis Nethersole only briefly mentions *A Game at Chess*, but makes sure to note the chair: "Gondomar brought on the Stage in his chayre." Count Gondomer's particular bodily infirmity, then, was an integral part of his visible personation on the stage. A picture of Gondomar's litter and chair appear on the title page of Thomas Scott's *Vox Populi*, which was published in 1620 and served as a major source for Middleton's play.[14]

What makes Gondomar's ailment particularly important to the play is the timing with which the litter and chair are introduced—act 5. We can be certain that the actor playing the Black Knight would have been identified as Gondomar long before the fifth act. Gondomar's alleged villainies, Howard-Hill notes, were

---

[10] Middleton, *A Game at Chess*, Appendix 1, Item 8, 200.

[11] Middleton, *A Game at Chess*, Appendix 1, Item 20, 204.

[12] Middleton, *A Game at Chess*, Appendix 1, Item 7, 198.

[13] Middleton, *A Game at Chess*, Appendix 1, Item 5, 195.

[14] Howard-Hill, "Introduction," 29.

THE SECOND PART OF VOX POPVLI,
or
Gondomar appearing in the likenes of
Matchiauell in a Spanish Parliament,
wherein are discouered his treacherous & subtile Practises
To the ruine as well of England, as the Netherlandes.
Faithfully Tranflated out of the Spanish Coppie by a well-willer
to England and Holland.

Simul Complectar omnia

Gentis Hispanæ decus

Printed at Goricom by Ashuerus Jans.
1624. Stilo nouo.

Fig. 5.1   Title page of Thomas Scott's, *Second Part of Vox Populi* (1624),
STC 22103. By permission of the Folger Shakespeare Library.

Fig. 5.2   Title page of Thomas Middleton, *A Game at Chess* Q1 (1625), STC
              17882.2. By permission of the Folger Shakespeare Library.

common gossip in London before *A Game at Chess* was performed.[15] His particular physical malady was equally well known. And to make certain his audience is aware of the Black Knight's defining physical characteristic, Middleton has the Fat Bishop state "Yonder's Black Knight, the fistula of Europe"[16] at 2.2.46, long before the audience would have seen the visible representation of the Black Knight's ailment. The early modern association of physical flaw and moral infirmity, such as we see in Shakespeare's Richard III and Middleton's De Flores from *The Changeling*, informs the manner in which the Black Knight would be understood; the appearance of his specially prepared chair late in the play provides a visually operative comic stab at a character who has shown himself enormously worthy of abuse as a consequence of his admitted "20,985" schemes and machinations.

Even more than contemporary commentary, the most promising place to look for additional information regarding the costumes worn in the original production would appear to be the title page of the First Quarto. Divided into two parts, the title page presents a considerable amount of information. The top half shows a table with the left side labeled "The Black-House" and the right side "The White-House." On the one side we find the Black King, the Black Queen, the Black Duke, and the Fat Bishop. Across from them sit the White King, the White Queen, the White Duke, and the White Bishop. The bottom half of the title page shows three characters: the Black Knight, the White Knight, and, again, the Fat Bishop. Also, there are three miniature characters who appear in a bag in the back, meant to represent the chess bag that holds all of the pieces that are taken in the game.

Although the costumes presented on the page are clearly drawn and the particular articles of apparel easily distinguishable, this information is potentially misleading, for the pictures are drawn not in the form of the players who performed the roles, but in the likeness of the historical figures they were intended to represent. Thus, as John Moore has noted, the White Bishop on the title page looks distinctly like George Abbot, the Archbishop of Canterbury; the Black Duke resembles the Conde-Duque Olivares in the cut of his beard and the heavy outlines of his body; the White Duke has the strikingly triangular beard of George Villiers, the Duke of Buckingham; and the White Knight has the "same face, with the delicate profile and the large mournful eyes, which Van Dyke immortalized in portraits of [Prince] Charles."[17] In the case of the Black Knight and the Fat Bishop, scholars have gone beyond identifying the characters as representing Count Gondomar and Marc

---

[15] Howard-Hill, "Introduction," 29. Among his "villainies," Gondomar instigated the proceedings that led to the execution of Raleigh in 1619 and was a major supporter of the marriage match between Charles and the Spanish Infanta.

[16] Thomas Middleton, *A Game at Chess*, Revels edition, ed. T. H. Howard-Hill (Manchester: Manchester University Press, 1993). All quotes are from this edition.

[17] John R. Moore, "The Contemporary Significance of Middleton's *Game at Chesse*," *PMLA* 50 (1935), 763.

Antonio De Dominis and determined the actual portraits of those men that were used by the artist who made the title page.[18]

Although these images may not represent how the actors appeared in production, they signified richly to the early modern reader. For instance, the Black Queen and the White Queen appear in strikingly different apparel. Moore has addressed the appearance of the two queens, writing:

> The middle-aged White Queen, with the high forehead and prominently beaked nose of Anne, wearing the pleated ruff and high-cut bodice of an earlier style of dress, is sharply contrasted with the young Black Queen, with her more delicate features, wearing the fan-shaped ruff and the low square-cut bodice of the new style which had spread from France, the native home of Isabella of Bourbon. [19]

What Moore fails to note is that the style of dress worn by the Black Queen with its ample décolletage was most commonly worn in England by unmarried women.[20] Moreover, since this style was not commonly seen in Spain, it was specifically chosen to represent the Black Queen. Consequently, the Black Queen's apparel on the title page insinuates sexual accessibility in one who should be unavailable, and visibly mirrors her pawn's sexual forwardness with the Black Bishop's Pawn in 4.3.

More informed conclusions regarding the costumes worn in the original production can be drawn about the clergy of the White House and the Black House. It should be remembered that religious conflict pervaded the early modern period. England had broken from the Catholic Church almost a hundred years before, but had reverted to Catholicism during the reign of Queen Mary I and had feared reversion to Catholicism ever since. The recent near match of Prince Charles with the Spanish Infanta served to heighten this fear. As a result of this anxiety, the presentation of members of the English and Catholic clergy in *A Game at Chess* spoke immediately and significantly to the concerns of the people watching the performance. The play has six characters who are members of the clergy: the Black Bishop, the Black Bishop's Pawn, the White Bishop, the White Bishop's pawn, Loyola Ignatius, and the Fat Bishop.[21] The costumes they wore in performance can be ascertained from the rigid rules that defined appropriate clerical garb in Protestant England and Catholic Spain. According to these rules, the White Bishop and his pawn appeared in academic robes and a square cap, and the Black Bishop and his pawn wore Catholic vestments (Loyola Ignatius

---

[18]   T. H. Howard-Hill reproduces the pictures in his introduction to the play, 15, 25.

[19]   Moore, 762.

[20]   C. Willett Cunnington and Phillis Cunnington, *Handbook of English Costume in the Seventeenth Century* (London: Faber & Faber, 1955), 99.

[21]   Seven if, as Howard-Hill has suggested, Error is dressed as a Jesuit. He notes that Holles apparently missed his vocative "Error" and calls the character his "disciple" in T. H. Howard-Hill, "The Unique Eye-Witness Report of Middleton's *A Game at Chess*," *Review of English Studies* 42.166 (1991): 172.

and the Fat Bishop will be dealt with later).[22] It is quite possible that some of the costumes were genuine religious articles worn in the past by the clergy. Stephen Greenblatt notes that when the apparel of Catholicism was renounced in England, the church sold some of its properties to the professional players.[23] The importance of the costuming choices employed for the clergy of the Black and White houses cannot be overestimated for the clothes worn by Protestants and Catholics served to literally embody the religious ideologies of each.

The vestments worn by the Black Bishop and his pawn are vital to their roles as members of the Catholic Church, for the religious attire serves to visibly represent a priest's vow of sexual abstinence and separate him from the rest of society. Catholic religious apparel works to identify the clergy as intermediaries between God and man. The costumes worn by the Black Bishop and his pawn are identified as Catholic vestments in the White Queen's Pawn's exclamation upon first seeing the Black Bishop's Pawn: "By my penitence / a comely presentation, and the habit, to admiration reverend" (1.1.34–5). The Black Knight notes the specific articles that adorn the Black Bishop's Pawn, saying that perhaps he should wear "a three pound smock 'stead of an alb, / An epicene chasuble" (1.1.231–2). The alb and the chasuble are part of the Catholic vestments and crucial to the priest's duties.[24]

Catholic vestments visually asserted the fact that the clergy served a mystical function essential to the salvation of the congregation. Catholics maintained that it was essential to attend church regularly where they could have their sins forgiven and take part in Holy Communion. The Catholic priest or bishop's apparel consisted of a set of articles that identified and were crucial to his ability to absolve people of their sins, to sanctify water and objects, and to transubstantiate bread and wine into the body and blood of Christ during Mass.

The Protestant clergy's clothing in 1624 similarly identified the wearer's particular role in the lives of their congregations. The religion of the English Church after the Reformation advanced a very different understanding of Christianity from Catholicism, one divested of ritual, and offering a far more limited range of possibilities for the devout individual. Appropriate Protestant Christian living required that one engage the holy word directly and seek God's forgiveness on one's own.[25] In this formulation of Christianity, the church was significantly less important for it did not play any ritual role in the salvation of its adherents. The

---

[22] For a study of the development of religious apparel, see Janet Mayo's *A History of Ecclesiastical Dress* (London: B. T. Batsford, 1984), particularly chapters 5 and 6.

[23] Stephen Greenblatt, *Learning to Curse: Essays in Early Modern Culture* (New York: Routledge, 1990), 162.

[24] It is important to note that this is not the apparel in which the Fat Bishop appears on the title page. There, he wears a cassock with a *mozetta*, a short hooded cape worn over the shoulders, and a *biretta*, a stiff three-cornered hat. This was everyday-clothing for a Catholic bishop and is the apparel in which the former Archbishop of Spalatro appeared in the painting that was copied for the title page.

[25] Christopher Haigh, *English Reformations: Religion, Politics, and Society under the Tutors* (Oxford: Clarendon Press, 1993), 287.

Latin Mass was replaced with a vernacular liturgy; transubstantiation was replaced by metaphor: the bread and wine now stood for the body and blood of Christ with the taking of communion serving merely as a reassertion of one's faith and not a necessary step toward salvation. In the Protestant church, the clergy were allowed to marry and had closer contact with regular society than their Catholic counterparts. Divested of its mystical purpose, the English clergy after the reformation served the function of religious educator. The Protestant minister was a teacher to his congregation, using didactic lectures to explain the bible and eradicate ignorance and superstition. Accordingly, the attire for such a clergy was the scholar's gown that identified the wearer, both in English society and on the stage, with his role as a religious professor. It should be noted, however, that the politics surrounding the spectacular presentation of religion in England was a hotly contested issue at the time. Puritans had a long tradition of arguing vigorously against the wearing of any distinctive apparel by the clergy. Other, more moderate Protestants, sought to have the English clergy wear at least a surplice while performing the Eucharist. And some, most notably William Laud, who became Bishop of London in 1628 and Archbishop of Canterbury in 1633, sought to increase the visual spectacle of English religious practice. [26] Middleton's play works to elide the issue by openly addressing the immorality of Catholic vestments while making no comment at all on the English religious apparel worn onstage.

By presenting a contrast between the academic gowns likely worn by the Protestant minister and the vestments almost certainly worn by the Catholic priests, Middleton established the dramatic territory on which he could visually deconstruct the tenets of Catholicism through the course of his play. The preponderance of this deconstruction takes place in the actions of the Black Bishop's Pawn, which serve to systematically belie the holy functions of the Catholic priest and betray the religious purpose of his holy habit. Middleton makes little effort to proffer the White Bishop or his Pawn as significant voices for the true church. Rather, he focuses his attention on showing the Catholic clergy as mendacious, cruel, lascivious, and ungodly.

Of course, Middleton depicts the Catholic Church as thoroughly corrupt before the Black Bishop's Pawn ever enters upon the stage. At the start of the play, Ignatius Loyola presents himself in no uncertain terms as an evil, power-hungry schemer:

> Hah! Where? What angle of the world is this,
> That I can neither see the politic face
> Nor with my refined nostrils taste the footsteps
> Of any of my disciples, sons and heirs
> As well of my designs as institutions?

---

[26] For a thorough discussion of the vestment controversy in the sixteenth and early seventeenth centuries, see J. H. Primus, *The Vestments Controversy* (Kampen: J. H. Kok, 1960) and Zachary Lesser, *Renaissance Drama and the Politics of Publication* (New York: Cambridge University Press, 2004), 81–114.

I thought they'd spread over the world by this time,
Covered the earth's face and made dark the land
Like the Egyptian grasshoppers.
Here's too much light appears shot from the eyes
Of truth and goodness never yet deflowered. (1.1.1–9)

The image of Jesuits that Ignatius presents is an extreme one, but it is not dissimilar to how Catholics were widely depicted in Protestant writing (not merely Puritan). As historian Roger Lockyer has noted, "the history of England in the seventeenth century is incomprehensible without taking into account the hysterical anti-Catholicism that coloured popular attitudes: to call a man a papist was to accuse him of the vilest perfidy and treachery."[27] Middleton depicts Ignatius as a caricature of evil, but it was likely the way he was understood by his audience. In England's collective memory, the Gunpowder Plot of 1605, when Catholics led by Guy Fawkes attempted to blow up the houses of Parliament with all the royal family, was still fresh, its foiling the cause for annual celebration (which continues to this day). In 1619, the continent was riddled with conflict as Catholic Spain pursued open war with the Protestants in the German states, most notably Frederick V, Elector of the Palatinate of the Rhine, who was married to the English Princess Elizabeth.[28] The Spanish-born Ignatius embodied the fear and anger the English had toward Spain, the most powerful Catholic country in Europe.

What distinguishes the actions of the Black Bishop's Pawn from the words of Ignatius, however, is that the Pawn primarily pursues the religious functions promised by his apparel. He has political significance as well, but only in the form of metaphor: the perfidious Catholic cleric unsuccessfully attempts to corrupt and seduce the innocent, virginal English maiden (the White Queen's Pawn). The actions that the Black Bishop's Pawn pursues relate specifically to his profession as a representative of the Catholic Church. Significantly, his apparel is frequently mentioned and serves an important function in his designs.

When he has decided to pursue the White Queen's Pawn, the Black Bishop's Pawn's opening thought is to win her through the visible display of his religious power: "Let me contemplate, / With holy wonder season my access, / And by degrees approach the sanctuary / Of unmatched beauty set in grace and goodness" (1.1.70–3). The Catholic vestments were, in and of themselves, an affront to Protestant thought. As Robin Clifton explains, "Catholicism's elaborate cycle of observances, its complex ritual and dramatic ceremonial, drew biting criticism

---

[27]   Roger Lockyer, *Tudor and Stuart Britain: 1471–1714* (London: Longmans, 1964), 231.

[28]   In 1618, Frederick misguidedly accepted the throne in Bohemia when it was offered to him by the Protestant Bohemian nobles upon the death of the Emperor Mathias. This went counter to the long custom whereby the Catholic Habsburg emperors were also the kings of Bohemia. The two results were (1) that Frederick became a hero in England for championing the Protestant cause on the continent and (2) open war ensued which ravaged Europe and left Frederick and Elizabeth exiled in the Netherlands. Lockyer, 236.

from most Protestant writers. . . . This complex ceremonial resulted in part from the laity's weak preference for a spectacular and visible religion, but equally relevant was the clergy's desire for power."[29] By appealing to his "holy wonder," the Black Bishop's Pawn highlights what the English considered to be the hypocrisy of Catholicism: its reliance on literally spectacular deceit at the expense of true religiosity.

Continuing to pursue his religious function, the Black Bishop's Pawn entices the White Queen's Pawn to become a Catholic. She readily accedes to his wishes, taking his pious figure to represent an equally pious heart. The White Queen's Pawn's first undertaking as a newly converted Catholic is confession. The Black Bishop's Pawn promises that the practice will "make your merit, which through erring ignorance / Appears but spotted righteousness to me, / Far clearer than the innocence of infants" (1.1.87–9). However, in an aside he marks the true purpose of taking confession:

> Now to the work indeed, which is to catch
> Her inclination; that's the special use
> We make of all our practice in all kingdoms,
> For by disclosing their most secret frailties,
> Things, which once ours, they must not hide from us,
> (That's the first article in the creed we teach'em)
> Finding to what point their blood most inclines,
> Know best to apt [adapt] them then to our designs. (1.1.108–15)

The confessional is not a Protestant practice. The implication in *A Game at Chess* is that the Catholic clergy acknowledges the ungodliness of its practices and purposefully uses its holy office to further its impious designs. Accordingly, in the next act, the Black Bishop's Pawn instructs the White Queen's Pawn that obedience is a fundamental principal of Catholicism, and then demands that she have sex with him, reprimanding her for breaking her religious duty when she has the audacity to demur. The White King notes that although the deeds of the Black Bishop's Pawn are vile in and of themselves, they take on a far more pernicious aspect as a result of his religious clothing:

> When we find desperate sins in ill men's companies
> We place a charitable sorrow there,
> But custom and their leprous inclination
> Quits us of wonder, for our expectation
> Is answered in their lives; but to find sin,
> Ay, and a masterpiece of darkness, sheltered
> Under a robe of sanctity, is able
> To draw all wonder to that monster only. (2.2.127–34)

---

[29] Robin Clifton, "Fear of Popery," in *The Origins of the English Civil War*, ed. Conrad Russel (New York: Macmillan, 1973), 147.

The clear argument in *A Game at Chess* is that the "masterpiece of darkness" is endemic to the "robe of sanctity" worn by the Catholic clergy; the vestments signify darkness where they should signify light.

According to the logic of *A Game at Chess*, the Catholic religion is, itself, little more than a masquerade. Costume serves a function for the clergy who employ it to bewilder people into believing in their holiness and accepting the tenets of their religion, which serve merely to extend the reach of their power. This view of Catholicism is further supported by the Black Bishop's Pawn's willingness to take off his religious vestments and put on a different costume when he believes it will help him more effectively to pursue his designs. In 3.3, the Black Bishop's Pawn appears, according to the text, in "rich attire" or "richly accoutred" as part of the Black Queen's Pawn's plan to snare the White Queen's Pawn and trick her into having sex with the Black Bishop's Pawn. Because priests are bound to a life of poverty,[30] the Black Bishop's Pawn's change of clothing into expensive apparel is a double offense.

The White Queen's Pawn falls for the Black Queen's Pawn's ruse. She believes in the power of the Black Queen's Pawn's magical glass and accepts that the costumed Black Bishop's Pawn is her future husband. However, the White Queen's Pawn's inherent innocence demands that she be married before she go to bed. This request gives the Black Bishop's Pawn pause, for his holy vows will not permit him to take a wife. Swapan Chakravorty has suggested that the Black Bishop's Pawn's last-minute qualms derive from his vow of celibacy,[31] but his earlier attempt to rape the White Bishop's Pawn and the Black Queen's Pawn's accusation that he has fathered bastards suggests that the vow to which he refers is the public vow of matrimony and serves merely as a last minute reminder of the private religious hypocrisy in which he is about to take part. He has taken off his clothing and just as easily removed any semblance of morality.

Throughout *A Game at Chess*, Middleton stresses the notion that one's clothes should represent one's identity and that the ability to change apparel demonstrates the vilest deceitfulness. This understanding of clothing has antecedents in morality plays and interludes in which only Vice characters disguised themselves. As Jean MacIntyre and Garrett Epp note, most costume changes in early English drama have negative implications—a visible rendering of the doctrine that, because God is unchanging, changeability is itself a sign of ungodliness.[32] The Black Bishop's

---

[30] The Black Knight's Pawn notes that "This' a strange habit for a holy father, A president of poverty especially" (4.1.6–7).

[31] Swapan Chakravorty, *Society and Politics in the Plays of Thomas Middleton* (Oxford: Clarendon Press, 1996), 178.

[32] Jean MacIntyre and Garrett P. J. Epp, "'Cloathes Worth All the Rest': Costumes and Properties," *A New History of Early English Drama*, eds. John D. Cox and David Scott Kastan (New York: Columbia University Press, 1997), 275. T. W. Craik notes that "the pretence of vices to be virtues is a theme almost universal in the interludes, and in allegorical literature in general," *The Tudor Interlude: Stage, Costume, Acting* (Leicester: Leicester University Press, 1967), 87.

Pawn provides an example of this, but not the most pernicious one. The clearest example of the perfidy attached to the changing of one's apparel can be found in the actions of the White King's Pawn who changes sides onstage through the removing of his white upper garment to show black underneath. Holles mentions it in his letter:

> one of the white pawns, wth an vnder black dubblett, signifying a Spanish
> hart, betrays his party to their avuantage, auanceth Gundomars propositions,
> works vnder hand the Princes cumming into Spayn: which pawn so discouered,
> the whyt King reuyles him, objects his raising him in wealth, in honor, from
> mean[d]e condition, next classis to a lab[r]ouring man: this by the character is
> supposed Bristow.[33]

It is likely that the character wore a white jerkin or jacket on top of his black doublet earlier in the play and simply took it off to show his "Spanish hart."

The White King's Pawn presents a special problem. He is identified by Holles as the Earl of Bristol but is understood by most modern critics to represent Lionel Cranfield, Earl of Middlesex and Lord Treasurer. Cranfield would have fit the character of the White King's Pawn as well as Bristol in August of 1624: he was impeached by the House of Commons in May 1624, the month before Sir Henry Herbert licensed *A Game at Chess* for performance. Indeed, the White King's Pawn also has some characteristics of Sir Toby Matthew, an English Catholic who was pro-Spanish.[34] Looking at the various historical individuals, A. R. Braunmuller has concluded that "we may never know—reading Holles's letter and other seventeenth- and twentieth-century accounts suggests it is self-defeatingly arbitrary to ask —whether some, or most, of the spectators at the Globe understood the White King's Pawn to represent the Earl of Middlesex or the Earl of Bristol, or some other contemporary figure, or an amalgam of several figures, or none."[35] What is certain is that seemingly loyal English subjects may have inner identities that belie their outward appearance and that true subjects of the crown must be vigilant against those who might change their apparel and reveal a Catholic or Spanish allegiance.

The anxiety surrounding one's ability to change clothes and alter one's loyalty was keen in early modern English society. The nature of this fear comes into focus when we recognize that apparel did not merely work as a system of signs denoting one's religion and allegiances. Rather, the clothes themselves constituted one's religion and allegiances. As Ann Rosalind Jones and Peter Stallybrass have noted, "the materials we wear work as inscriptions upon us," particularly in pre- or

---

[33]   Middleton, *A Game at Chess*, Appendix 1, Item 7, 199.

[34]   Postlewait.

[35]   Braunmuller, 353. Jane Sherman suggests that "the White King's Pawn is not so much Cranfield as a composite of Northampton, Carr, Suffolk, Secretary Lake, and Secretary Calvert" in "The Pawns' Allegory in Middleton's *A Game at Chesse*," *Review of English Studies*, n.s. 29.114 (1978): 156.

protocapitalist societies.[36] In the decision to put on a set of apparel, one asserted his or her particular place in the body politic. In *Hamlet,* Polonius says "apparel oft proclaims the man" (1.3.72).[37] If Polonius is right, society must work to make sure that people wear the clothes appropriate to their particular gender, class, country, and religion, and do not change their apparel. Numerous cultural forces were in place to guarantee that one could not readily change the type of clothes one wore. The most conspicuous example of this is the numerous sumptuary decrees that were passed during the reign of Queen Elizabeth to keep people from dressing in apparel inappropriate to their social station.[38] The pulpit similarly decried sartorial excess as well as cross-dressing and the practice of wearing foreign fashions.[39] Writers and playwrights also took part in deriding individuals that wore the wrong clothes, asserting the notion that one's apparel must accurately depict one's identity.[40]

The fear that attended the changing of one's clothes influenced how the Fat Bishop was received. Clearly representative of Marc Antonio De Dominis, the Fat Bishop's actions are based on historical fact. Beginning the play as a member of the White House, the Fat Bishop represents De Dominis after he left his Archbishopric of Spalatro and converted to Protestantism. His conversion in the play to the Black House represents De Dominis's decision in 1622 to leave England and convert back to Catholicism. With a character whose actions mirror historical events this closely, it may seem that the character's costume served no greater purpose than to identify him as the turncoat the audience understood him to be. However, the manner in which the character was dressed likely had a large impact on how he was perceived onstage. Still, it is difficult to determine the specific apparel he wore. We can say with some certainty how he was costumed once he converted to the Black House. When he revealed his new allegiance, the Fat Bishop probably wore the vestments appropriate to his renewed Catholicism. His visible transformation can be noted in the first lines he speaks after changing sides. Shortly after the White King's Pawn reveals his black apparel and shows his loyalty to the Black House, the Fat Bishop enters:

---

[36]   Ann Rosalind Jones and Peter Stallybrass, *Renaissance Clothing and the Materials of Memory* (New York: Cambridge University Press, 2000), 184.

[37]   My edition of Shakespeare is *The Riverside Shakespeare,* 2nd edition, ed. G. Blakemore Evans (Boston: Houghton Mifflin, 1997).

[38]   See Frances Elizabeth Baldwin, *Sumptuary Legislation and Personal Regulation in England* (Baltimore: The Johns Hopkins University Press, 1926). Sumptuary legislation was discontinued by King James in 1604, but its prescriptions were widely known in 1624 and beyond the Interregnum.

[39]   See Roze Hentschell, "A Question of Nation: Foreign Clothes on the English Subject" in *Clothing Culture, 1350–1650,* ed. Catherine Richardson (Burlington, VT: Ashgate, 2004), 49–62. Also see Stephen Orgel, *Impersonations: The Performance of Gender in Shakespeare's England* (New York: Cambridge University Press, 1996), particularly chapter 2.

[40]   Hentschell, 50–3.

> FAT BISHOP: Is there so much amazement spent on him
> That's but half black? There might be hope of that man;
> But how will this House wonder if I stand forth
> And show a whole one, instantly discover
> One that's all black where there's no hope at all?
> WHITE KING: I'll say thy heart then justifies thy books;
> I long for that discovery
> FAT BISHOP: Look no farther then:
> Bear witness all the House I am the man
> And turn myself into the Black House freely;
> I am of this side now. (3.1.281–90)

The Fat Bishop previously wore white to identify himself as a member of the White House, but now chooses to don the black color that demonstrates his new allegiance.

Before he changes sides, however, it is difficult to determine if the Fat Bishop wore the academic robes of the Protestant clergy or white Catholic vestments. To fit with the Protestant ideology that he had ostensibly embraced before the start of the play, the Fat Bishop would have needed an academic gown. And yet, the audience would have known who he was and how he had switched allegiances from Catholicism to Protestantism, and then back to Catholicism only two years before. He was widely known as a turncoat and would have been a target of the audience's derision wearing the clothes of a Catholic while basking in the protection of the White house. This hypocrisy informs the Fat Bishop's first lines, which suggest that despite his membership in the Protestant White House, he wears clothes that identify him with Catholicism:

> FAT BISHOP: Pawn!
> FAT BISHOP'S PAWN: I attend at your great holiness's service.
> FAT BISHOP: For great I grant you, but for greatly holy,
> There the soil alters. Fat cathedral bodies
> Have very often but lean little souls. (2.2.1–5)

His "fat cathedral body" would seem to imply that the actor was corpulent and draped in visibly Catholic apparel.[41] Nevertheless, it is possible that the Fat Bishop is merely drawing attention to his former Catholicism so as to make certain the audience recognizes whom he represents underneath Protestant clerical robes.

The Fat Bishop's opening lines convince me that he wore white Catholic vestments when he first entered upon the stage, but the evidence is not definitive. What is certain is that in either configuration, the Fat Bishop is marked for our scorn by his decision to alter his apparel and change sides. The Black Knight drives home the very real danger inherent in the Fat Bishop's proclivity to change

---

[41]   In *A Critical Study of the Work of William Rowley*, Gillian A. Sanderman argues that William Rowley, who had the reputation of playing fat clown parts, performed the role of the Fat Bishop, Ph.D. diss. University of London, 1974.

apparel when he notes how many in England currently wear English clothes that hide their true loyalty to Spain and their desire to spread Catholicism.

> For venting hallowed oil, beads, medals, pardons,
> Pictures, Veronica's heads in private presses,
> That's done by one i'th'habit of a pedlar;
> Letters conveyed in rolls, tobacco-balls.
> When a restraint comes, by my politic counsel
> Some of our Jesuits turn gentlemen-ushers,
> Some falconers, some park-keepers, and some huntsmen;
> One took the shape of an old lady's crook once
> And despatched two chores in a Sunday morning,
> The altar and the dresser! (4.2.48–57)

This danger is contained in *A Game at Chess* when, at the end of the play, all those who would betray their apparel are safely put away in the bag, the chess game's symbolic representation of either death or hell. Moreover, the literal turncoats are bested by the White Knight and the White Duke who visit the Black House and suggest that they are willing to negotiate a marriage, but never take off the white clothes that signify their true, English, Protestant hearts.

Thus far, I have devoted little attention to the White King and the Black King. The practice of overlooking these characters is not uncommon in studies of Middleton's play since the two have very small roles. And yet, in light of the significance of the characters they represent (the monarchs of England and Spain respectively) and the importance of the King to the game of chess, these two characters should be considered more closely. As noted above, Don Carlos de Coloma stated that the Black King was identifiable as the King of Spain "because of his youth, dress, and other details." Costuming a character in *A Game at Chess* so that he would be identifiable as the King of Spain would not have been difficult (although very few of the people in the audience had likely ever seen Philip IV). However, the suggestion that the character was young carried with it particular associations at the time.

The most obvious way in early modern England by which youthfulness could be depicted onstage was through the use of an actor who had no facial hair. While this has small significance today, it would have been offensive to the Spanish at the time. As Will Fisher has stated, "facial hair often conferred masculinity: the beard made the man."[42] Fisher takes this argument further, suggesting that boys (males without facial hair) were literally a different gender from men during the early modern period. He cites Beatrice in *Much Ado About Nothing* who questions the usefulness of a beardless youth, saying "What should I do with him? Dress him in my apparel and make him my waiting-gentle-woman?" (2.1.34–5). A man without facial hair, Fisher suggests, was considered fit for no greater duties.

---

[42] Fisher, Will. "The Renaissance Beard: Masculinity in Early Modern England." *Renaissance Quarterly* 54 (2001): 156.

The fact that the title page of *A Game at Chess* represents the Black King's young age by presenting him without facial hair corroborates the likelihood that the character's youthfulness was depicted onstage through the absence of a mustache or beard. The visual representation of Philip's unmanliness is particularly significant to *A Game at Chess* because of the Black King's relative unimportance to the development of the drama. His actions do not motivate the plot, but his fall is understood, by the rules of chess, to signify the end of the game. By entering upon the stage without a beard, the character serves the performance much more fully than he does the written script. Without uttering a word, he suggests that England's Catholic rival is led by an unmanly whelp. In direct opposition, Moore notes, the character depicting James I appears on the title page as a rather elderly man bearded like the royal head on the gold sovereigns called "jacobuses."[43] There is little to suggest what was worn by the character playing the White King in production, but it seems safe to assume that a play with the political biases of *A Game at Chess* would present him with the reverend and respectable countenance owed to the monarch who both ruled the country and was the royal sponsor of the acting company.

Taken in total, costumes and clothing informed the substance, the staging, the politics, the publication, and the reception of Middleton's *A Game at Chess*. Moreover, all evidence suggests that the importance of theatrical apparel to Middleton's play is not exceptional for the period, but representative of typical practices.[44] Costumes provided one of the primary means by which information was transmitted in performance at the time. On the largely bare stage of the Globe, the actors' costumes provided virtually the entire visual experience of the play. As *A Game at Chess* demonstrates, the visual presentation of one's apparel could establish, modify, or transform the wearer's sex, social station, country of origin, and religion. Before an actor spoke a line of dialogue, his costume would have asserted or changed his identity, to a high degree of specificity, for an audience that was attuned to the visual semiotics of the time. It is crucial, therefore, that we consider the complex ways that theatrical apparel signified in the early modern period and, indeed, throughout theatre history.

---

[43]   Moore, 761–2.

[44]   Jean MacIntyre examines how the theatrical companies' accumulation of costumes affected dramatic scripts in late sixteenth and early seventeenth century drama in *Costumes and Scripts in the Elizabethan Theatres* (Edmonton, Albert: University of Alberta Press, 1992).

Works Cited

Astington, John H. "The 'Unrecorded Portrait' of Edward Alleyn." *Shakespeare Quarterly* 44 (1993): 73–86.

Bailey, Amanda. *Flaunting: Style and the Subversive Male Body in Renaissance England*. Toronto: University of Toronto Press, 2007.

———. "Livery and its Discontents: 'Braving it' in *the Taming of the Shrew*." *Renaissance Drama* 33 (2004): 87–137.

———. "'Monstrous Manner': Style and the Early Modern Theater." *Criticism* 43, no. 3 (2001): 249–84.

Baker, J. H. "A History of English Judges' Robes." *Costume: The Journal of the Costume Society* 12 (1978): 27–39.

Baldwin, Frances Elizabeth. *Sumptuary Legislation and Personal Regulation in England*. Baltimore: The Johns Hopkins University Press, 1926.

Balsam, M. S. and Edward Sagarin. *Cosmetics, Science, and Technology*. Vol. 3. New York: Wiley-Interscience, 1974.

Barbour, Richmond. *Before Orientalism: London's Theatre of the East, 1576–1626*. New York: Cambridge University Press, 2003.

Barnes, Barnabe. *The Devil's Charter*, edited by Ronald Brunless MacKerrow. Louvain: Uystpruyst, 1904.

Baron, Robert. "Mizra, A Tragedy." In *Two Seventeenth-Century Plays*, edited by Parvin Loloi. Vol. 1. Salzburg: University of Salzburg Press, 1998.

Bartels, Emily C. "*Othello* and Africa: Postcolonialism Reconsidered." *William and Mary Quarterly, 3d Ser.* 54, no. 1 (1997): 45–64.

Bartley, J. O. *Teague, Shenkin and Sawney: An Historical Study of the Earliest Irish, Welsh and Scottish Characters in English Plays*. Cork: Cork University Press, 1954.

Beaumont, Francis and John Fletcher. "Loves Cure, Or, the Martial Maid." In *The Works of Francis Beaumont and John Fletcher, Vol. 7*, edited by A. R. Waller. Cambridge: Cambridge University Press, 1909.

———. *The Works of Beaumont and Fletcher; the Text Formed from a New Collation of the Early Editions*, edited by Alexander Dyce. Boston: Phillips, Sampson, and Co., 1854.

Beier, Lee. "Social Discourse and the Changing Economy." In *A Companion to Renaissance Drama*, edited by Arthur F. Kinney, 50–67. Malden, MA: Blackwell, 2002.

Bellany, Alastair and Andrew McRae, eds. *Early Stuart Libels: An Edition of Poetry from Manuscript Sources. Early Modern Literary Studies* Text Series I. 2005, http://www.earlystuartlibels.net/htdocs/early_jacobean_section/B3.html (accessed September 22, 2009).

Benhamou, Reed. "The Restraint of Excessive Apparel: England 1337–1604." *Dress* 15 (1989): 27–37.

Bentley, Gerald Eades. *The Profession of Player in Shakespeare's Time, 1590–1642*. Princeton, NJ: Princeton University Press, 1984.

Berek, Peter. "Cross-Dressing, Gender, and Absolutism in the Beaumont and Fletcher Plays." *Studies in English Literature, 1500–1900* 44, no. 2 (2004): 359–77.

———. "The Jew as Renaissance Man." *Renaissance Quarterly* 51 (1998): 128–62.

Berry, Ralph. *Shakespeare and Social Class*. Atlantic Highlands, NJ: Humanities Press International, 1988.

Bevington, David. *Tudor Drama and Politics: A Critical Approach to Topical Meaning*. Cambridge, MA: Harvard University Press, 1968.

Book of Common Prayer. Society for Archbishop Justus. http://justus.anglican.org/resources/bcp/ (accessed November 11, 2009).

Braunmuller, A. R. "'to the Globe I Rowed': John Holles Sees *A Game at Chess*." *English Literary Renaissance* 20, no. 2 (1991): 340–56.

Brome, Richard. *A Critical Edition of Brome's the Northern Lass*, edited by Harvey Fried. New York: Garland, 1980.

———. "*The Damoiselle, Or the New Ordinary*." In *Five New Playes*. London: 1658.

Brooks, Cleanth. *The Well Wrought Urn: Studies in the Structure of Poetry*. New York: Harcourt, Brace, 1947.

Bulman, James C. *The Merchant of Venice: Shakespeare in Performance*. Manchester: Manchester University Press, 1991.

Burnett, Mark Thornton. *Masters and Servants in English Renaissance Drama and Culture*. London: Macmillan, 1997.

Burton, Jonathan. "Anglo-Ottoman Relations and the Image of the Turk in *Tamburlaine*." *Journal of Medieval and Early Modern Studies* 30 (2000): 125–56.

Callaghan, Dyampna. *Shakespeare without Women: Representing Gender and Race on the Renaissance Stage*. New York: Routledge, 2000.

Cardozo, Jacob Lopes. *The Contemporary Jew in the Elizabethan Drama*. New York: Burt Franklin, 1965.

Carrol, William C. *Fat King, Lean Beggar: Representations of Poverty in the Age of Shakespeare*. Ithaca, NY: Cornell University Press, 1996.

———. *Macbeth: Texts and Contexts*. Boston: Bedford/St. Martin's, 1999.

Carson, Neil. *A Companion to Henslowe's Diary*. New York: Cambridge University Press, 1988.

Cerasano, S. P. "'Borrowed Robes,' Costume Prices, and the Drawing of *Titus Andronicus*." *Shakespeare Studies* 22 (1994): 45–57.

Certain Sermons Or Homilies Appointed to be Read in Churches in the Time of Queen Elizabeth and Reprinted by Authority from King James. Philadelphia: Edward C. Biddle, 1844.

Chakravorty, Swapan. *Society and Politics in the Plays of Thomas Middleton*. Oxford: Clarendon Press, 1996.

Chambers, E. K. *The Elizabethan Stage*. 4 vols. Oxford: Clarendon Press, 1923.

Chapman, George. *The Blind Beggar of Alexandria*. In *The Plays of George Chapman*, edited by Thomas Marc Parrott. Vol. 1. New York: Russell, 1961.

———. *The Conspiracie and Tragedie of Charles Duke of Byron*. London: G. Eld, 1608.

Chapman, George, Ben Jonson, and John Marston. *Eastward Ho!* edited by R. W. Van Fossen. Manchester: Manchester University Press, 1979.

Chew, Samuel C. *The Crescent and the Rose: Islam and England during the Renaissance*. New York: Octagon Books, 1974.

Clifton, Robin. "Fear of Popery." In *The Origins of the English Civil War*, edited by Conrad Russel, 144–67. New York: Macmillan, 1973.

Cogswell, Thomas. "Thomas Middleton and the Court, 1624: *A Game at Chess* in Context." *Huntington Library Quarterly* 47 (1984): 273–88.

Collinson, Patrick. *The Elizabethan Puritan Movement*. London: Jonathan Cape, 1967.

Cooke, J. *Greene's Tu Quoque Or, the Cittie Gallant*, edited by Alan J. Berman. New York: Garland, 1984.

Corbin, Peter and Douglas Sedge, eds. *Thomas of Woodstock Or Richard the Second, Part One*. Manchester: Manchester University Press, 2002.

———. *The Oldcastle Controversy: Sir John Oldcastle, Part I and the Famous Victories of Henry V*. Manchester: Manchester University Press, 1991.

Coryate, Thomas. *Coryats Crudities*. 2 vols. London: 1611.

Craik, T. W. *The Tudor Interlude: Stage, Costume, and Acting*. Leicester: Leicester University Press, 1967.

Cressy, David. "Gender Trouble and Cross-Dressing in Early Modern England." *Journal of British Studies* 35, no. 4 (1996): 438–65.

Cunnington, C. Willett and Phillis Cunnington. *Handbook of English Costume in the Seventeenth Century*. London: Faber and Faber, 1955.

Cunnington, Phillis and Catherine Lucas. *Occupational Costume in England from the Eleventh Century to 1914*. New York: Barnes and Noble, 1967.

Daborne, Robert. *A Christian Turned Turk*. In *Three Turk Plays from Early Modern England*, edited by Daniel J. Vitkus, 149–240. New York: Columbia University Press, 2000.

Davidson, Clifford. *Technology, Guilds and Early English Drama*. Kalamazoo, MI: Medieval Institute, 1996.

Day, John, William Rowley, and George Wilkins. *The Travailes of the Three English Brothers*. London: 1607.

De Nicolay, Nicolas. *The Navigations into Turkie*. New York: Da Capo, 1968.

Dekker, Thomas. *The Shoemaker's Holiday*, edited by Anthony Parr. London: A & C Black, 1990.

———. *The Dramatic Works of Thomas Dekker*, edited by Fredson Bowers. Vol. 1. Cambridge: Cambridge University Press, 1962.

———. *"Lust's Dominion."* In *The Dramatic Works of Thomas Dekker*, edited by Fredson Bowers. Vol. 4. Cambridge: Cambridge University Press, 1961.

————. "The Honest Whore, Part II." In *The Chief Elizabethan Dramatists, Excluding Shakespeare*, ed. William Allan Neilson, 425–55. Boston and New York: Houghton Mifflin, 1911.

————. *The Guls Horne-Booke*. London: 1609.

Doebler, John. *Shakespeare's Speaking Pictures: Studies in Iconic Imagery*. Albuquerque: University of New Mexico Press, 1974.

Dollerup, Cay. "Danish Costume on the Elizabethan Stage." *The Review of English Studies* 25, no. 97 (1974): 53–8.

Downer, Alan S. "The Life of our Design: The Function of Imagery in the Poetic Drama." *Hudson Review* 2 (1949): 242–63.

Drew-Bear, Annette. "Face-Painting in Renaissance Tragedy." *Renaissance Drama* 12 (1981): 71–93.

Duffy, Michael. *The Englishman and the Foreigner*. Cambridge: Chadwyck-Healey, 1986.

Dusinberre, Juliet. "Women and Boys Playing Shakespeare." In *A Feminist Companion to Shakespeare*, edited by Dyampna Callaghan, 251–62. Malden, MA: Blackwell, 2000.

Elam, Keir. "English Bodies in Italian Habits." In *Shakespeare, Italy, and Intertextuality*, edited by Michele Marrapodi, 26–44. Manchester: Manchester University Press, 2004.

Everett, Barbara. "'Spanish' Othello: The Making of Shakespeare's Moor." In *Shakespeare and Race*, edited by Catherine M. S. Alexander and Stanley Wells, 64–81. New York: Cambridge University Press, 2000.

Feuillerat, Albert, ed. *Documents Relating to the Revels at Court in the Time of Queen Elizabeth*. Louvain: 1914.

Findlay, Alison. "Gendering the Stage." In *A Companion to Renaissance Drama*, edited by Arthur F. Kinney, 399–415. Malden, MA: Blackwell, 2002.

Fisher, Will. *Materializing Gender in Early Modern English Literature and Culture*. New York: Cambridge University Press, 2006.

————. "The Renaissance Beard: Masculinity in Early Modern England." *Renaissance Quarterly* 54, no. 1 (2001): 155–87.

Foakes, R. A. *Henslowe's Diary*. 2nd ed. New York: Cambridge University Press, 2002.

————. *Illustrations of the English Stage, 1580–1642*. London: Scolar Press, 1985.

Ford, John. *The Chronicle History of Perkin Warbeck, A Strange Truth*, edited by Peter Ure. London: Methuen, 1968.

Forse, James H. *Art Imitates Business: Commercial and Political Influences in Elizabethan Theatre*. Bowling Green, OH: Bowling Green State University Popular Press, 1993.

Garner, Shirley Nelson. "'Let Her Paint an Inch Thick': Painted Ladies in Renaissance Drama and Society." *Renaissance Drama* 20 (1989): 121–38.

Gillies, John. *Shakespeare and the Geography of Difference*. Cambridge: Cambridge University Press, 1994.

Goodman, Ellen. *The Origins of the Western Legal Tradition: From Thales to the Tudors* Annandale, NSW: Federation Press, 1995.

Greene, Robert. *A Quip for an Upstart Courtier*, edited by Charles Hindley. London: Reeves and Turner, 1871.

Greenblatt, Stephen. "Fiction and Friction." In *Reconstructing Individualism: Autonomy, Individuality, and the Self in Western Thought*, edited by Thomas C. Heller, Morton Sosna, and David E. Wellbery. Stanford: Stanford University Press, 1986. 30–52.

———. *Learning to Curse: Essays in Early Modern Culture*. New York: Routledge, 1990.

———. *Shakespearean Negotiations: The Circulation of Social Energy in Renaissance England*. Berkeley: University of California Press, 1988.

Greene, Robert. *Robert Greene's the Scottish History of James IV: A Critical, Old-Spelling Edition*, edited by Charles H. Stein. Salzburg: Inst. f. Engl. Sprache u. Literatur, Univ. Salzburg, 1977.

———. *The Honorable History of Friar Bacon and Friar Bungay. Elizabethan and Jacobean Comedy*, edited by Robert Ornstein, Hazelton Spencer. Boston: D. C. Heath, 1964.

Griffiths, Paul. *Youth and Authority: Formative Experiences in England 1560–1640*. New York: Oxford University Press, 1996.

Gurr, Andrew. *The Shakespearian Playing Companies*. Oxford: Clarendon, 1996.

———. *The Shakespearean Stage*. 3rd ed. New York: Cambridge University Press, 1992.

———. *Playgoing in Shakespeare's London*. Cambridge: Cambridge University Press, 1987.

Haigh, Christopher. *English Reformations: Religion, Politics, and Society under the Tudors*. Oxford: Clarendon Press, 1993.

Hall, Edward. *Hall's Chronicle*. New York: AMS Press, 1965.

Harding, Samuel. *Sicily and Naples, Or the Fatall Union: A Tragedy*. Oxford: 1640.

Harrison, William. *Description of England*, edited by L. Whitington. Vol. 2. London: Walter Scott, 1899.

———. *Harrison's Description of England in Shakespeare's Youth*, edited by Frederick J. Furnivall. London: N. Trübner & Co., 1877.

Haughton, William. *Englishmen for My Money, Or A Woman Will have Her Will*. London: W. White, 1616.

Hazlitt, W. Carew, ed. *A Select Collection of Old English Plays*. Vol. 9. London: Reeves and Turner, 1874.

Heal, Felicity. "Reciprocity and Exchange in the Late Medieval Household." In *Bodies and Disciplines: Intersections of Literature and History in Fifteenth-Century England*, edited by Barbara A. Hanawalt and David Wallace, 179–98. Minneapolis: University of Minnesota Press, 1993.

Healy, Thomas. "Drama, Ireland and the Question of Civility." In *Early Modern Civil Discourses*, edited by Jennifer Richards. New York: Palgrave, 2003.

Henderson, Katherine Usher and Barbara F. McManus, eds. *Hic Mulier; Or, the Man Woman in Half Humankind: Contexts and Texts of the Controversy about Women in England, 1540–1640*. Urbana: University of Illinois Press, 1985.

Hentschell, Roze. *The Culture of Cloth in Early Modern England: Textual Constructions of a National Identity*. Burlington, VT: Ashgate, 2008.

———. "Luxury and Lechery: Hunting the French Pox in Early Modern England" in *Sins of the Flesh: Responding to Sexual Disease in Early Modern Europe*, edited by Kevin Siena, 133–57. Toronto: Centre for Reformation and Renaissance Studies, 2005.

Heywood, Thomas. *How a Man may Chuse a Good Wife from a Bad*, edited by A. E. Swaen. Louvain: A. Uystpruyst, 1912.

———. *The Dramatic Works of Thomas Heywood Now First Collected with Illustrative Notes and a Memoir of the Author*. London: G. Pearson, 1874.

Highley, Christopher. *Shakespeare, Spenser, and the Crisis in Ireland*. New York: Cambridge University Press, 1997.

Hinds, Allen B., ed. *Calendar of Papers, Venetian*. Vol. 15. London: HMSO, 1909.

Hoak, Dale. "The Iconography of the Crown Imperial." In *Tudor Political Culture*, edited by Dale Hoak, 54–103. New York: Cambridge University Press, 1995.

Hoenselaars, A. J. *Images of Englishmen and Foreigners in the Drama of Shakespeare and His Contemporaries*. London and Toronto: Associated University Presses, 1992.

Holden, William P. *Anti-Puritan Satire, 1572–1642*. New Haven, CT: Yale University Press, 1954.

Holmes, Martin R. *Shakespeare and His Players*. London: J. Murray, 1972.

Hornback, Robert. "Emblems of Folly in the First *Othello*: Renaissance Blackface, Moor's Coat, and 'Muckender'." *Comparative Drama* 35 (2001): 72–6.

Howard, Jean E. "Shakespeare, Geography, and the Work of Genre on the Early Modern Stage." *MLQ: Modern Language Quarterly* 64, no. 3 (2003): 299–322.

———. "Crossdressing, the Theatre, and Gender Struggle in Early Modern England." *Shakespeare Quarterly* 39, no. 4 (1988): 418–440.

Howard-Hill, T. H. *Middleton's "Vulgar Pasquin": Essays on A Game at Chess*. Newark: University of Delaware Press, 1995.

———. "The Unique Eye-Witness Report of Middleton's *A Game at Chess*." *Review of English Studies* 42, no. 166 (1991): 168–78.

Hughes, Paul L. and James F. Larkin. *Tudor Royal Proclamations*. Vol. 3. New Haven, CT: Yale University Press, 1969.

Hughes, Thomas. *The Misfortunes of Arthur*, edited by Harvey Carson Grumbine, Francis Flower and William Fulbeck. Berlin: E. Felber, 1900.

Hunter, G. K. "Flatcaps and Bluecoats: Visual Signals on the Elizabethan Stage." *Essays and Studies* 33 (1980): 16–47.

———. *Dramatic Identities and Cultural Tradition*. Liverpool: Liverpool University Press, 1978.

Iyengar, Sujata. *Shades of Difference: Mythologies of Skin Color in Early Modern England*. Philadelphia: University of Pennsylvania Press, 2005.

J. W. *The Valiant Scot by J. W.: A Critical Edition*, edited by George F. Byers. New York: Garland, 1980.

Jardine, Lisa. *Still Harping on Daughters*. Sussex: Harvester Press, 1983.

Jones, Ann Rosalind and Peter Stallybrass. *Renaissance Clothing and the Materials of Memory*. New York: Cambridge University Press, 2000.

Jones, Eldred D. "The Physical Representation of African Characters on the English Stage during the 16th and 17th Centuries." *Theatre Notebook* 17 (1962): 17–21.

Jonson, Ben. *The Alchemist*. In *Five Plays*, edited by G. A. Wilkes. New York: Oxford Univerity Press, 1981.

———. *Bartholomew Fair*. In *Five Plays*, edited by G. A. Wilkes. New York: Oxford University Press, 1981.

———. *The Complete Plays of Ben Jonson*, edited by G. A. Wilkes. Vol. 2. Oxford: Clarendon Press, 1981.

———. *Epicoene Or the Silent Woman*, edited by R. V. Holdsworth. New York: W. W. Norton, 1990.

———. *Three Comedies*, edited by Michael Jamieson. London: Penguin, 1966.

Jordan, Thomas. *The Walks of Islington and Hogsden*. London: 1657.

Kastan, David Scott. *Shakespeare After Theory*. London: Routledge, 1999.

Kelly, Francis M. *Shakespearian Costume*. Revised by Alan Mansfield, ed. New York: Theatre Arts Books, 1970.

Killigrew, Thomas. *The Parson's Wedding*. In *Six Caroline Plays*, edited by A. S. Knowland, 433–553. London: Oxford University Press, 1962.

Knolles, Richard. *The Generall Historie of the Turkes, from the First Beginning of that Nation to the Rising of the Ottoman Familie: With all the Notable Expeditions of the Christian Princes Against them . . .* London: Adam Islip, 1603.

Kyd, Thomas. "The Spanish Tragedy." In *Renaissance Drama: An Anthology of Plays and Entertainments*, edited by Arthur F. Kinney, 45–94. Malden, MA: Blackwell, 1999.

Laquer, Thomas. *Making Sex: Body and Gender from the Greeks to Freud*. Cambridge, MA: Harvard University Press, 1990.

Laver, James. *The Concise History of Costume and Fashion*. New York: Harry N. Abrams, 1969.

———. *Costume of the Western World: Fashions of the Renaissance*. New York: Harper and Brothers, 1951.

Levin, Richard. "The Longleat Manuscript and *Titus Andronicus*." *Shakespeare Quarterly* 53, no. 3 (2002): 323–40.

Laura Levine. "Men in Women's Clothing: Anti-Theatricality and Effeminization from 1579 to 1642." *Criticism* 28, no. 2 (1986): 121–43.

Lewis, Bernard. *Islam and the West*. New York: Oxford University Press, 1993.

Lily, John. *Mother Bombie*. London: William Stansby, 1632.

Linthicum, M. Channing. *Costume in the Drama of Shakespeare and His Contemporaries*. New York: Russell & Russell, 1963 [Oxford: Clarendon Press, 1936].

Lockyer, Roger. *Tudor and Stuart Britain, 1471–1714*. London: Longmans, 1964.

Macalister, R. A. S. *Ecclesiastical Vestments: Their Development and History.* London: Elliot Stack, 1896.

MacIntyre, Jean. *Costumes and Scripts in the Elizabethan Theatres.* Edmonton: University of Alberta Press, 1992.

MacIntyre, Jean and Garrett P. J. Epp. "'Cloathes Worth all the Rest': Costumes and Properties." In *A New History of Early English Drama*, edited by John D. Cox and David Scott Kastan, 267–85. New York: Columbia University Press, 1997.

Mahler, Andreas. "Italian Vices: Cross-Cultural Constructions of Temptation and Desire in English Renaissance Drama." In *Shakespeares's Italy: Functions of Italian Locations in Renaissance Drama*, edited by Michele Marrapodi, A. J. Hoenselaars, Marcello Cappuzzo and F. Falzon Santucci, 49–68. Manchester: Manchester University Press, 1997.

Mann, David. *Shakespeare's Women: Performance and Conception.* New York: Cambridge University Press, 2008.

Marlowe, Christopher. *The Complete Plays*, edited by J. B. Steane. New York: Penguin, 1969.

———. *Dr. Faustus.* In *Christopher Marlowe: The Complete Plays*, edited by J. B. Steane. New York: Penguin, 1969.

———. *Edward II.* In *Christopher Marlowe: The Complete Plays*, edited by J. B. Steane. New York: Penguin, 1969.

———. *Tamburlaine*, edited by J. S. Cunningham. The Revels Edition. New York: Manchester University Press, 1981.

Marston, John. *The Malcontent*, edited by George K. Hunter. Manchester: Manchester University Press, 1999.

Massinger, Philip. *The City-Madam*, edited by T. W. Craik. London: Ernest Benn, 1964.

———. *The Renegado.* In *Three Turk Plays from Early Modern England*, edited by Daniel J. Vitkus. New York: Columbia University Press, 2000.

Matar, N. I. "The Renegade in English Seventeenth-Century Imagination." *Studies in English Literature* 33, no. 3 (1993): 489–505.

Mayne, Jasper. *The Citye Match.* London: 1639.

Mayo, Janet. *A History of Ecclesiastical Dress.* London: B. T. Batsford, 1984.

McLuskie, Kathleen. "The Act, the Role, and the Actor: Boy Actresses on the Elizabethan Stage." *New Theatre Quarterly* 3, (1987): 120–30.

Melchiori, Giorgio. *Shakespeare's Garter Plays: Edward III to Merry Wives of Windsor.* Newark: University of Delaware Press, 1994.

Middleton, Thomas. *The Family of Love.* In *The Works of Thomas Middleton*, edited by A. H. Bullen. Vol. 3. New York: AMS Press, 1964.

———. *A Game at Chess*, edited by T. H. Howard-Hill. Revels Edition. New York: Manchester University Press, 1993.

———. *A Mad World, My Masters*, edited by Standish Henning. Lincoln: University of Nebraska Press, 1965.

———. *No Wit, no Help Like a Woman's.* Regents Renaissance Drama Series, edited by Lowell E. Johnson. Lincoln: University of Nebraska Press, 1976.

————. *Thomas Middleton: The Collected Works*, edited by Gary Taylor, John Lavagnino. Oxford: Clarendon, 2007.

Middleton, Thomas and Thomas Dekker. *The Roaring Girl*, edited by Paul Mulholland. Revels Edition. Manchester: Manchester University Press, 1987.

Mohl, Ruth. *The Three Estates in Medieval and Renaissance Literature*. New York: Columbia University Press, 1933.

Moore, John R. "The Contemporary Significance of Middleton's *Game at Chesse*." *PMLA* 50 (1935): 761–8.

Nagler, A. M. *A Source Book in Theatrical History*. New York: Dover, 1952.

Nakayama, Randall. "'I Know She is a Courtesan by Her Attire': Clothing and Identity in *the Jew of Malta*." In *Marlowe's Empery: Expanding His Critical Contexts*, edited by Sara Munson Deats and Robert A. Logan, 150–63. Newark: University of Delaware Press, 2002.

Nashe, Thomas. *Pierce Penilesse, His Supplication to the Divell*, edited by G. B. Harrison. London: 1924.

Neill, Michael. "'Mulattos,' 'Blacks,' and 'Indian Moors': *Othello* and Early Modern Constructions of Human Difference." *Shakespeare Quarterly* 49, no. 4 (1998): 361–74.

A New Enterlude of Godly Queene Hester: Edited from the Quarto of 1561. Ed. W. W. Greg. London: David Nutt, 1904.

Nichols, John. *The Progresses and Public Processions of Queen Elizabeth*. 3 vols. London: Printers to the Society of Antiquaries, 1823.

O'Day, Rosemary. *The Professions in Early Modern England, 1450–1800: Servants of the Commonweal*. Essex: Pearson Education Limited, 2000.

————. "The Anatomy of a Profession: The Clergy of the Church of England." In *The Professions in Early Modern England*, edited by Wilfrid Prest, 25–63. New York: Croom Helm, 1987.

Ogden, Dunbar. *The Staging of Drama in the Medieval Church*. Newark: University of Delaware Press, 2002.

Orgel, Stephen. *The Illusion of Power: Political Theater in the English Renaissance*. Berkeley: University of California Press, 1975.

————. *Impersonations: The Performance of Gender in Shakespeare's England*. New York: Cambridge University Press, 1996.

————. "Nobody's Perfect: Or, Why did the English Stage Take Boys for Women?" *South Atlantic Quarterly* 88, no. 1 (1989): 7–29.

————. *Shakespeare and the Mediterranean*. Newark: University of Delaware Press, 2004.

Orgel, Stephen and Roy Strong. *Indigo Jones: The Theatre of the Stuart Court*. 2 vols. Berkeley: University of California Press, 1973.

Peele, George. *The Battle of Alcazar*. In *The Dramatic Works of George Peele*, edited by John Yoklavich. Vol. 2. New Haven, CT: Yale University Press, 1961.

Peele, George. *Edward I*, edited by Frank S. Hook. In *The Life and Works of George Peele*, edited by Charles Tyler Prouty. Vol. 2. New Haven, CT: Yale University Press, 1961.

The Pilgrimage to Parnassus. The Three Parnassus Plays (1598–1601), edited by J. B. Leishman. London: Ivor Nicholson & Watson, 1949.

Pineas, Rainer. "The English Morality Play as a Weapon of Religious Controversy." *Studies in English Literature* 2, no. 2 (1962): 157–80.

Platter, Thomas. *Thomas Platter's Travels in England*. Translated by Clare Williams. London: Jonathan Cape, 1959.

Postlewait, Thomas. "From Event to Context to Event: A Problem in the Writing of Theatre History." In *Critical Theory and Performance*, edited by Janelle Reinelt and Joseph Roach. Revised edition. 198–222. Ann Arbor: University of Michigan Press, 2007.

———. "Theatricality and Antitheatricality in Renaissance London." In *Theatricality*, edited by Tracy C. Davis and Thomas Postlewait, 90–126. New York: Cambridge University Press, 2003.

Potter, Robert. "The Cardinal's New Clothes: Politics and Morality in the 1520s." *Research Opportunities in Renaissance Drama* 31 (1992): 61–3.

Primus, J. H. *The Vestments Controversy*. Kampen: J. H. Kok, 1960.

Prynne, William. *Histrio-Mastix*. London: 1633.

Rackin, Phyllis. *Shakespeare and Women*. New York: Oxford University Press, 2005.

———. "Shakespeare's Crossdressing Comedies." In *A Companion to Shakespeare's Works: The Comedies*, edited by Richard Dutton and Jean E. Howard, 114–36. Malden, MA: Blackwell, 2003.

———. "Androgyny, Mimesis, and the Marriage of the Boy Heroine on the English Renaissance Stage." *PMLA* 102, no. 1 (1987): 29–41.

Rainoldes, J. *Th' Overthrow of Stage-Playes*. Middleburgh, 1599.

Randolph, Thomas. *Hey for Honesty, Down with Knavery*. London: 1651.

Reynolds, Graham. "Elizabethan and Jacobean: 1558–1625." In *Costume of the Western World: Fashions of the Renaissance*, edited by James Laver, 127–88. New York: Harper & Bros., 1951.

Ribeiro, Aileen. *Fashion and Fiction: Dress in Art and Literature in Stuart England*. New Haven, CT: Yale University Press, 2006.

Rose, Mary Beth. "Women in Men's Clothing: Apparel and Social Stability in *the Roaring Girl*." *English Literary Renaissance* 14.3 (1984): 367–91.

Rowley, Samuel. *When You See Me You Know Me*. London: 1605.

Rowley, William. *A Critical Old-Spelling Edition of A Match at Midnight*, edited by Stephen Blase Young. New York: Garland, 1980.

Sanderman, Gillian A. "A Critical Study of the Work of William Rowley." Ph.D. diss., University of London, 1974.

Scarisbrick, J. J. *Henry VIII*. Berkeley: University of California Press, 1968.

Schlueter, June. "Rereading the Peacham Drawing." *Shakespeare Quarterly* 50, no. 2 (1999): 171–84.

Shakespeare, William. *The Norton Shakespeare*, edited by Stephen Greenblatt, Walter Cohen, Jean E. Howard and Katharine Eisaman Maus. 2nd ed. New York: W. W. Norton, 2008.

————. *The Riverside Shakespeare*, edited by G. Blakemore Evans. 2nd ed. Boston: Houghton Mifflin, 1997.

Shapiro, James. *Shakespeare and the Jews*. New York: Columbia University Press, 1996.

Shapiro, Michael. *Gender in Play on the Shakespearean Stage: Boy Heroines & Female Pages*. Ann Arbor: University of Michigan Press, 1996.

Sharpham, Edward. *The Fleire*. London: 1607.

Sherman, Jane. "The Pawns' Allegory in Middleton's *A Game at Chesse*." *Review of English Studies* n.s., 29, no. 114 (1978): 147–59.

Shirley, James. *The Ball: A Comedy; as it was Presented by Her Majesties Servants at the Private House in Drury Lane. Written by George Chapman and James Shirley*. London: 1639.

Smuts, R. Malcolm. "Art and the Material Culture of Majesty in Early Stuart England." In *The Stuart Court and Europe: Essays in Politics and Political Culture*, edited by R. Malcolm Smuts, 86–112. New York: Cambridge University Press, 1996.

Speed, John. *Theatre of the Empire of Great Britaine*. London: 1612.

Spencer, Edmund. *A View of the State of Ireland*, edited by Andrew Hadfield, Willy Maley. Oxford: Basil Blackwell, 1997.

Stallybrass, Peter. "Worn Worlds: Clothes, Mourning, and the Life of Things." In *Cultural Memory and the Construction of Identity*, edited by Dan Ben-Amas and Liliane Weissberg, 27–44. Detroit, MI: Wayne State University, 1999.

————. "Worn Worlds: Clothes and Identity on the Renaissance Stage." In *Subject and Object in Renaissance Culture*, edited by Margreta de Grazia, Maureen Quilligan and Peter Stallybrass, 289–320. New York: Cambridge University Press, 1996.

Stone, Lawrence. *Crisis of the Aristocracy*. Abridged Edition. Oxford: Oxford University Press, 1967.

Stubbes, Phillip. *Phillip Stubbes's Anatomy of the Abuses in England in Shakespeare's Youth, A.D. 1583, Part 1*, edited by Frederick J. Furnivall. London: The New Shakespeare Society, 1877–1879.

Suzuki, Mihoko. "Gender, Class, and the Social Order in Late Elizabethan Drama." *Theatre Journal* 44, no. 1 (1992): 31–45.

Thomas, Keith. *Religion and the Decline of Magic*. New York: Penguin, 1971.

The Tragedy of Master Arden of Faversham, edited by Martin White. London: A & C Black, 1990.

Vaughan, Virginia Mason. *Performing Blackness on English Stages, 1500–1800*. New York: Cambridge University Press, 2005.

Vitkus, Daniel. *Turning Turk: English Theater and the Multicultural Mediterranean, 1570–1630*. New York: Palgrave, 2003.

Vitkus, Daniel J. "Introduction." In *Three Turk Plays from Early Modern England*. New York: Columbia University Press, 2000.

————. *Three Turk Plays from Early Modern England*. New York: Columbia University Press, 2000.

————. "Turning Turk in *Othello:* the Conversion and Damnation of the Moor." *Shakespeare Quarterly* 48, no. 2 (1997): 170–76.

Webster, John. *The Duchess of Malfi*, edited by Elizabeth M. Brennan. New York: W. W. Norton, 1993.

Weiss, Adrian. "Father Hubburd's Tale." In *Thomas Middleton: The Collected Works*, edited by Gary Taylor and John Lavagnino, 149–82. New York: Oxford University Press, 2007.

Whigham, Frank. *Ambition and Privilege: The Social Tropes of Elizabethan Courtesy Theory*. Berkeley: University of California Press, 1984.

————. *Seizures of the Will in Early Modern English Drama*. New York: Cambridge University Press, 1996.

————. "Sexual and Social Mobility in *the Duchess of Malfi*." *PMLA* 100, no. 2 (1985): 167–86.

White, Paul Whitfield. "Theater and Religious Culture." In *A New History of Early English Drama*, edited by John D. Cox and David Scott Kastan, 133–52. New York: Columbia University Press, 1997.

Wickham, Glynne. *The Medieval Theatre*. 3rd ed. New York: Cambridge University Press, 1987.

Wilde, Oscar. *The Truth of Masks*. In *The Soul of Man Under Socialism and Other Essays*. New York: Harper Colophon Books, 1950.

Williams, Deanne. *The French Fetish from Chaucer to Shakespeare*. New York: Cambridge University Press, 2004.

Winwood, Ralph (Sir). *Memorials of Affairs of State*. Vol. 2. London: 1725.

Wrightson, Keith. *English Society, 1580–1680*. New Brunswick, NJ: Rutgers University Press, 1982.

————. "Estates, Degrees, and Sorts." *History Today* 37, no. 1 (1987): 17–22.

Wroath, Lady Mary. *The Countesse of Mountgomeries Urania*. London: 1621.

Wyther, George. *Abvses Stript and Whipt, Or Satirical Essayes*. London: 1613.

Index

"Abuses Stript and Wipt: or Satyricall Essays" (Wither), 89
academicians, 74–5
Act of Supremacy (1534), 48, 125
Act of Uniformity, 132
Adelman, Janet, 35n70
Admiral's Men, 50, 79, 80, 82
albs, 128, 132, 171
Alchemist, The (Jonson) 14, 104, 105, 106, 139
alcohol, 89–92
Alleyn, Edward, 50, 75, 152–4
Anatomie of Abuses (Stubbes), 139
androgyny, 36–8
apprentices, 67–9
archbishops, 128–9
Arden of Faversham (Anonymous), 57–60
armor, 55
As You Like It (Shakespeare), 5, 25, 26, 32, 33–4, 38, 39
Astington, John, 152

Bacon, Edmund, 51
Bailey, Amanda, 4, 43, 56, 62n55
Ball, The (Shirley), 107–8
Balsam, M. S., 29
bands (apparel), 10–11, 15, 17–18
Baron, Robert, 145–6
Bartels, Emily, 97
Bartholomew Fair (Jonson), 141
Bartley, J. O., 114–15
basque, 14
Battle of Alcazar, The (Peele), 95, 96, 99
beards, 24–6, 31, 180
beggars, 74
Berek, Peter, 158, 161
Berry, Ralph, 65
Bevington, David, 136
biretta (hat), 171n24
bishops
    Anglican, 129, *131*, 137, 141

Catholic, 124, 128–30, 136–7
blackface, 93–6
blackness, 93–6
Blind Beggar of Alexandria, The (Chapman), 159
bombast, 12
bonnets, 15, 113–14
boots, 15
Book of Common Prayer, 6, 128, 129, 132, 137
brats (clothing), 111–12, 113
breasts, prosthetic, 28
breeches; *see also* canions; galligaskins; pludderhoser; slops; trunk hose; Venetians
    as apparel for male characters, 10, 12, 31
    baggy, as symbol of drunkenness, 89–92
    English, 117
    Irish, 111
    Italian, 117
    Puritan ridicule of, 139
    Spanish, 104, 106
brógs (shoe), 111
Brooks, Cleanth, 53
bum rolls, 17, *18*, 66
Burbage, Richard, 24, 93, 95, 97, 159, 160n93, 161

Callaghan, Dympna, 29, 96
canions, *11, 12*
canvas, 67
capes, 10, 14; *see also* mozetta
Cardinal, The (Shirley), 137
cardinals, 124–5, 127–8, 137, 141
Carleton, Sir Dudley, 94
Carol, William, 74
Carson, Neil, 82
cassocks, 124
Catholics, 6–7, 123–30, 132, 134–7, 170–75, 178–9; *see also* clergy

Celts, 111
chains, gold, 92n34
Challenge for Beauty (Heywood), 101, 119
Chamberlain, John, 166
Chambers, E. K., 139
Changeling, The (Middleton and Rowley),
    73, 169
Charles I, King of England, 45
chasuble, 128, 132, 171
chemises, 10, 15
chimere (gown), 129, 137
chopines (shoe), 100, 101
Christian Turned Turk, A (Daborne), 109,
    142–5, 146, 148, 150–51, 156–7, 158
Christians, 124–42; *see also* Catholics;
    clergy; Protestants
circumcision, 146–8, 157
City Madam, The (Massinger), 69
City Ordinance of 1582 (London), 68
Citye Match, The (Mayne), 140–41
clergy
    Catholic, 6, 124–30, 132, 134–8, 170–75
    Protestant, 6, 131–2, 138, 141,
        170–72, 178
Clifton, Robin, 173–4
Cloaks; *see also* copes
    as apparel for female characters, 17
    as apparel for male characters, *11*, 14, 84
    Dutch, 92
    Italian, 100
    Puritan ridicule of, 139
coats, 51, 68, 72, 97n56, 110
codpieces, 24, 26–7
Cogswell, Thomas, 163n1
coifs, 18, 19
commoners, 67–73
companies, playing: and investment in
    costumes, 3, 7, 50
Conflict of Conscience, The (Woodes),
    131–2
conversion, religious, 142, 146–50, 157
copes (cloak), 128, 132, 138n40
Coriolanus (Shakespeare), 25–6, 31
Coryate, Thomas, 100–102, 107, 158
Coryats Crudities (Coryate), 101–*2*, 107,
    110, 158
Cosmetics; *see* make-up
Countess of Montgomery's Urania, The
    (Wroth), 22

Coxcomb (Beaumont and Fletcher), 111–12
Craik, T. W., 127–8
Cranmer, Archbishop Thomas, 124, 137
cross-dressing, 3–5, 19–23, 28, 31–9, 139
crowns, 45, 48–9, 55–7; *see also* tiaras
croziers, 128–9
Cymbeline (Shakespeare), 34

damask, 57, 117
Damoiselle, The (Brome), 110
Danish, 88–9, 91–2
decapitation, 150
Dekker, Thomas; *see individual plays*
Devil's Charter, The (Barnes), 30
disease, venereal, 109n91
Doctor Faustus (Marlowe), 75–7, 126–7, 134
Doebler, John, 125
Dollerup, Cay, 92
doublets
    as apparel for Christians, 143
    as apparel for male characters, 10–12,
        24, 31, 84
    French, 110
    Italian, 100
    Puritan ridicule of, 139
Downer, Alan
    on crowns, 55
dresses, 10, 15–16, 24, 101, 103
drunkenness, 89–92
Duchess of Malfi, The (Webster), 73, 101, 103
Dusinberre, Juliet, 4–5
Dutch, 79, 89–91
Dyck, Anthony Van, 149

Eastward Ho! (Chapman et al.), 60–63, 65,
    69, 110
Edward I (Peele), 104, 115
Edward II (Marlowe), 26, 100
Edward III, King of England, 51, 57
Edward VI, King of England, 137
Elam, Keir, 103
Elizabeth I, Queen of England
    crown of, 49
    and Protestantism, 132
    in *Richard III*, 53
    and religion in plays, 123
    and "Sermon Against Excess of
        Apparel," 119
    sumptuary laws of, 43, 45–7, 59n51, 177

English, 116–21, 164–5, 170
Englishmen for My Money (Haughton), 79, 89, 92, 103, 159
Enterlude of Welth and Helth, An, 90
Epicoene (Jonson), 5, 30, 34–5, 63–4, 77
Epp, Garrett, 79–80

facial hair, 179–80; *see also* beards; mustaches
falchions, 145, 149
Family of Love, The (Middleton), 139
Famous Victories of Henry V, The (Anonymous), 49
farthingales, 10, 16–18, 19, 66–7, 110
Father Hubburd's Tales (Middleton), 21
feathers, 108, 139
femininity, 27–9, 31–3, 36–8
fez (hat), 143n54
Fine Companion, A (Marmion), 138
Fisher, Will, 4, 25, 27, 31
flat caps, 15, 68
Fleire, The (Sharpham), 101, 119–20
Flemish, 89–90
Foakes, R. A., 85, 106
footwear, 10, 15, 19, 68; *see also* boots; brógs; chopines
foreigners, 79–122; *see also individual nationalities*
foreparts, *16–17*
Four Prentices of London, The (Heywood), 34, 69, *70*
French, 79–81, 82, 106–111
friars, 125–8, 134–6, 141
frieze (fabric), 115, 140
fustian (fabric), 67

gabardines (coat), 160–61
gallants, 64–5
galligaskins, 12, *13,* 81
Game at Chess, A (Middleton), 7, 163–80
garters, *11,* 12, 50–53
gender, 1, 5, 9–39 ; *see also* androgyny; cross-dressing; femininity; masculinity; women
Germans, 89
Gillies, John, 99
Godly Queene Hester, 44
gorgets, 55
gowns; *see also* chimere; night-gowns; robes; togas

academic, 74–5, 77, 172
as apparel for female characters, 10, 17
as apparel for male characters, 10, 14, 64
judges', 75, 77
Greene's Tu Quoque, 60, 61, 72
Greenblatt, Stephen, 2, 3, 7, 34, 171
Gull's Hornbook, The (Dekker), 50
Gurr, Andrew, 15

hair
    red, 159–60
    short, 140
    styles worn by female characters, 19, 27–8
Hamlet (Shakespeare)
    foreign apparel in, 87–8, 91–2, 101, 106–7
    hats in, 15
    and identity, 177
    makeup in, 29
    and masculinity of costumes, 24–5
handkerchiefs, 24
Harrison, William, 42, 51, 65, 103, 119
Hats; *see also* bonnets; fez; flat caps; headdresses; monmouth caps
    academic, 75
    as apparel for female characters, 18–19
    as apparel for foreigners, 84
    as apparel for male characters, 10, 15
    Danish, 92
    fur, 92
    square, 133, 137, 138, 141
    Turkish, 143
    wide-brimmed, as worn by Spaniards, 104, 105, 106
headdresses, 10, 18–19; *see also* coifs; hoods; wreaths, laurel
Henry IV, Part 1 (Shakespeare), 60, 110–11, 114
Henry IV, Part 2 (Shakespeare), 48, 60, 150
Henry IV, King of England, 48
Henry V (Shakespeare), 48, 82, 108–9, 110, 114, 116
Henry V, King of England, 48
Henry VI, Part 1 (Shakepeare), 51–2, 110n92, 136–7
Henry VI, Part 2 (Shakepeare), 67
Henry VIII (Shakespeare), 51, 108, 109, 137
Henry VIII, King of England, 45, 124, 144–5, 149

Henslowe, Philip: diary of, 6, 45, 49, 50,
         57, 80–82, 85, 86, 94, 97, 127,
         151–2, 154
Hentschell, Roze, 119
herald's coat, 110
Hey for Honesty, Down with Knavery
         (Randolph), 114, 138, 140
Heywood, Thomas; *see individual plays*
Hic Mulier (Anonymous), 27–8, 45
Hierarchy; *see* social rank
Highley, Christopher, 111
Holles, John, 164–6
homoerotic desire, 20–23
homosexuality, 20–21
Honest Whore, The (Dekker), 15
*Honorable History of Friar Bacon and
         Friar Bungay* (Greene), 134–5
hoods, *16,* 18, 19, 67, 110
hooks, Welsh, 115
hose, 24, 80–82, 108–9, 139
*How a man May Chuse a Good Wife from
         a Bad* (Heywood), 140
Howard, Jean, 3, 37
Howard-Hill, T. H., 170n18, 170n21
Hunter, G. K., 43, 92n33, 97, 159

ionar, 111
Irish, 111–13
Italians, 80–81, 83, 99–103; *see also*
         Romans; Venetians (people)

Jacke Drum's Entertainment (Marston),
         159–60
James I, King of England 45, 62, 63, 165–6
Jardine, Lisa, 3, 21
jerkins
   as apparel for Christians, 143
   as apparel for male characters, 10–13, 63
   frieze, 140
   Puritan ridicule of, 139
Jesuits, 172–3
Jew of Malta, The (Marlowe), 108, 156–8
Jews, 6–7, 157–61
Johnson, Lawrence, 152
Jones, Ann, 3, 43, 50, 82, 120, 176
Jonson, Ben, 21, 63; *see also individual
         plays*
judges, 74–5, 77
Julius Caesar (Shakespeare), 6, 67, 83–4

Kelly, Francis, 87
kersey (cloth), 118
King Johan (Bale), 129
King Lear (Shakespeare), 74
King's Men, 79, 163–4
Kinney, Arthur, 143
kirtles, 10, 15, 17
knights, 43, 57, 58, 62–3, 169
Knights of the Garter, 49, 50–52
Knolles, Richard, 152

lace, 50
Laud, William, 172
Laver, James, 14
lawyers, 74–5, 77
leather, 67
leeks, 114–15
leine, 111
Levin, Richard, 85
Levine, Laura, 3
Lewis, Bernard, 142
Life of Caesar (Plutarch), 83
Lingua: Or The Combat of the Tongue
         (Tomkins), 100
Linthicum, M. Channing, 160
Lockyer, Roger, 173
Lord Mayor's Day, 105
Love's Cure, or the Martial Maid (Ford),
         35–6
Love's Labour's Lost (Shakespeare),
         117–18
Lust's Dominion, or the Lascivious Queen
         (Dekker et al.), 94, 95, 96–7

MacIntyre, Jean, 55, 79–80, 180n44
McLuskie, Kathleen, 23
Mad World, My Masters, A (Middleton),
         71–2
Magnificence (Skelton), 124–5
Mahler, Andreas, 101
make-up 24, 28–30, 139
Malcontent, The, 90, 103, 108
maniple, 128
Mann, David, 28
Mary I, Queen of England, 48, 132, 170
masculinity, 24–7, 31–3, 36–8, 58
masks, 1
Masque of Blackness, The, 94
masques, 1–2, 80n5, 93–4, 145

Match at Midnight, A (Rowley), 133
Mayor, Lord, 64, 104
Merchant of Venice, The (Shakespeare)
    cross-dressing in, 34
    drunkenness in, 89
    foreign apparel in, 119
    Italian apparel in, 100
    Jews in, 158–9, 160–61
    women in, 156, 157
Merry Wives of Windsor, The
    (Shakespeare), 60, 79, 115
Michaelmas Term (Middleton), 118
Middleton, Thomas, 7, 21, 163–4, 175; *see*
    also individual plays
Midsummer Night's Dream, A
    (Shakespeare), 24, 29
Mirza, A Tragedy (Baron), 145–6
Misfortunes of Arthur, The (Hughes), 112
mitre, 128
monasteries, 125–6
monks, 125–6, 127–8
monmouth caps, 115
Moore, John, 169, 170, 180
Moors, 92–9, 142
Morson, Fynes, 114
mozetta (cape), 171n24
Much Ado About Nothing (Shakespeare),
    25, 31, 89, 120, 136, 179
Muslims, 6–7, 142–57; *see also* Turks
mustaches, 143–4

Nashe, Thomas, 22, 88
nether hose/stocks, 10–12, 109, 143
New Criticism, 53
New Custom, 127, 133, 138
New Historicism, 3
night-gowns, 17, 84
No Wit, No Help Like a Woman's
    (Middleton), 89, 90
nobility, 45–65
North, Thomas, 83
noses, 158–9
nuns, 125–6

Old Fortunatus (Dekker), 113
Orgel, Stephen, 1–2, 3, 9, 28, 160n93
Othello (Shakespeare)
    Danish in, 88–9
    Italians in, 99
    Moors in, 93–4, 95, 97–8
    as set in Venice, 79
    Turks in, 146–7

paint, 94–5
pallium (scarf), 129n19
panes, 12
Parker, Archbishop Matthew, 132–3
Parson's Wedding, The (Killigrew), 66–7
Peacham, Henry, 84–5, *86*
peascod bellies, *11*–12
peplum, 14
Perkin Warbeck (Ford), 112–13
Persians, 146n58, 149
petticoats, 17, 37, 63, 141, 151
physicians, 74–5, 77
picadils, *11, 16*
Pierce Penilesse his Supplication of the
    Divell (Nashe), 22, 88, 89
Pilgrimage to Parnassus (Anonymous),
    138, 139–40, 161
placards, 15–*16*
Platter, Thomas, 50
pludderhoser, 88, 91–2
Poetaster (Jonson), 21, 66
popes, 124–5, 127–8
Postlewait, Thomas, 21, 163n1
priests
    Anglican, *131*
    Catholic, 124, 128, *130,* 171
Professors; *see* academicians
prostitutes, 101
Protestants, 6, 123, 131–3, 141, 170–74;
    see also clergy
Prynne, William, 21, 140
Puritans, 7, 133, 138–42, 172

Quip for an Upstart Courtier, A (Greene), 117

Rackin, Phyllis , 3, 20, 26, 37, 38–9
Rainoldes, John, 20–21
religion, 6, 123–61; *see also* Catholics;
    Jews; Muslims; Protestants;
    Puritans
Renegado, The (Massinger), 101, 148–9,
    151, 155–6, 157
Reynolds, Graham, 19
Richard II (Shakespeare), 49, 55, 100
Richard II or Thomas of Woodstock, 120

Richard III (Shakespeare), 6, 48, 53, 54, 169
Roaring Girl, The (Middleton and Dekker),
    37–8
robes
    academic, 74–5, 77, 170, 178
    as apparel for male characters, 10, 14, 84
    judges', 75, 77
    Muslim, 143–5, 151–2
rochet, 129, 132, 133, 137
Romans, 83–6
Romeo and Juliet (Shakespeare), 1–2,
    109, 136
Roo, John (Rouse), 125
rosettes, 15
ruffs, 10, 14–*16*, 17–18, 104–6, 139

Sagarin, Edward, 29
Saracens, 142
sarcenet (fabric), 57
satin, 57, 59, 61
Satyre of the Thrie Estaitis, Ane, 127–8
scabbards, 139
scapula (fabric), 126
Schlueter, June, 84–5
scian (dagger), 111
scimitars (sword), 144, 149
Scottish, 111, 113–14
Selimus (Greene), 150
"Sermon Against Excess of Apparel," 119
servants, 71–3
Shakespeare, William; *see also individual*
        plays
    and clergy, 136–7
    and crowns, 48–9
Shapiro, Michael, 23, 32, 33
Shirley, Sir Robert, 149
shirts, 10–12
Shoemaker's Holiday, The (Dekker), 6,
    63–7, 90–91, 110
Shoes; *see* footwear
Sicily and Naples, 95–6
silk, 49–50, 54, 58–60, 62, 63, 64–6, 71,
    75. *See also* damask
Sir John Oldcastle, 112
skirts, *16*–17
slashing, *11*–12, 15
slops (breeches), 12, *13,* 89, 90, 92
social rank
    costumes by, 1–2, 5–6, 10–11, 41–78

in early modern period, 41–2
in medieval period, 41–2
hairstyle differences by, 19
and sumptuary laws, 5, 43–7, 50, 54,
    57, 58–60
Spaniards, 103–6, 164–5, 170
Spanish Tragedy, The (Kyd), 106, *107,* 143
Speed, John, 112
Stallybrass, Peter, 3, 4, 28n46, 43, 50, 82,
    120, 176
stoles, 128
stomachers, 15–16
Stone, Lawrence, 62
stones, 15
Stubbes, Philip, 139
sumptuary laws, 5, 43–7, 50, 54, 57, 58–60
supportasse, 18
surplices, 129, 132, 133, 138, 139
Swiss, 89
swords
    as apparel of Turks, 143, 149–51
    as part of costumes, 24, 26, 31, 57–8,
        60, 62, 66
    Puritan ridicule of, 139

tabards, 110–11
taffeta, 57, 59, 77n94
Tamburlaine (Marlowe), 33, 53–6, 147,
    151–55
Taming of the Shrew, The (Shakespeare),
    72–3
Tatars, 142
Thankful Remembrancer of God's Mercie,
    A (Carleton), 105
Thomas, Keith, 136
tiaras, 124
tippet (scarf), 129, 137
Titus Andronicus (Shakespeare), 6, 84–5,
    95, 96–8
togas, 83–4, 85
Travailes of the Three English Brothers,
    The (Day et al.), 150, 156, 157
Troilus and Cressida (Shakespeare), 42–3
trunk hose, *11,* 12, *13*
tunics, 84, 85, 111, 124, 126–7, 128
turbans, 143–9, 152, 154, 157–8
Turks, 98–9, 142–51
Twelfth Night (Shakespeare), 12, 26, 31,
    34, 58, 71

Two Gentlemen of Verona, The
(Shakespeare), 27, 28, 38–9

Unlovelinesse of Lovelockes, The
(Prynne), 140

vagabonds, 74
Valiant Scot, The, 114
veils, 126, 155
velvet, 57, 59, 71, 75, 117, 139
Venetians (breeches), 12, *13,* 80–82
Venetians (people), 79–80, 100
Very Lamentable Tragedy, A, 85
Vitkus, Daniel, 98, 99, 147, 151, 154
Volpone (Jonson), 75, 79
Vox Populi (Scott), 166, *167*

Walks of Islington and Hogsden, The
(Jordan), 138–9
Welsh, 111, 114–15
Welsh Embassador, The (Dekker), 115
Westward Ho! (Dekker and Webster), 90
whalebone, 15, 17, 66
When You See Me You Know Me
(Rowley), 51

Whigham, Frank, 57, 73
whinyard (sword), 113, 114
whiteface, 29
Wilde, Oscar, 160
Wiley Beguiled (Anonymous), 26–7
wimples, 126
wings, 11, *16*
wire, 17
Wolsey, Cardinal Thomas, 124–5, 137
Women; *see also* femininity
Christian, 157
and exclusion from performance, 4
French, 110
Italian, 101, 103
Muslim and Jewish, 154–7
and social rank, 63, 66
unmarried, 170
wood, 15, 17
wool, 67, 116–18, 126, 140
Woolley, John, 163
wreaths, laurel, 85–6
Wrightson, Keith, 41–2
Wroth, Lady Mary, 22